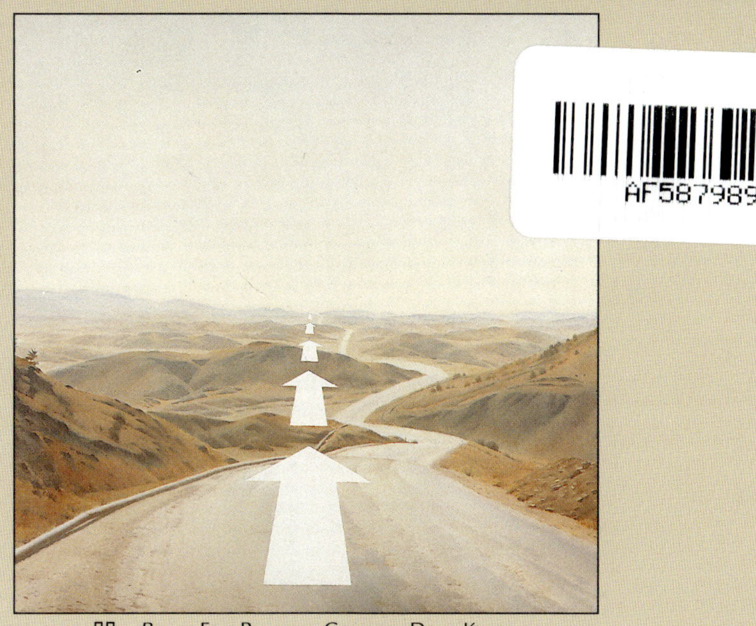

AF587989

□□ *Road*. Eric Bulatov. Courtesy Dany Keller. Galerie München.

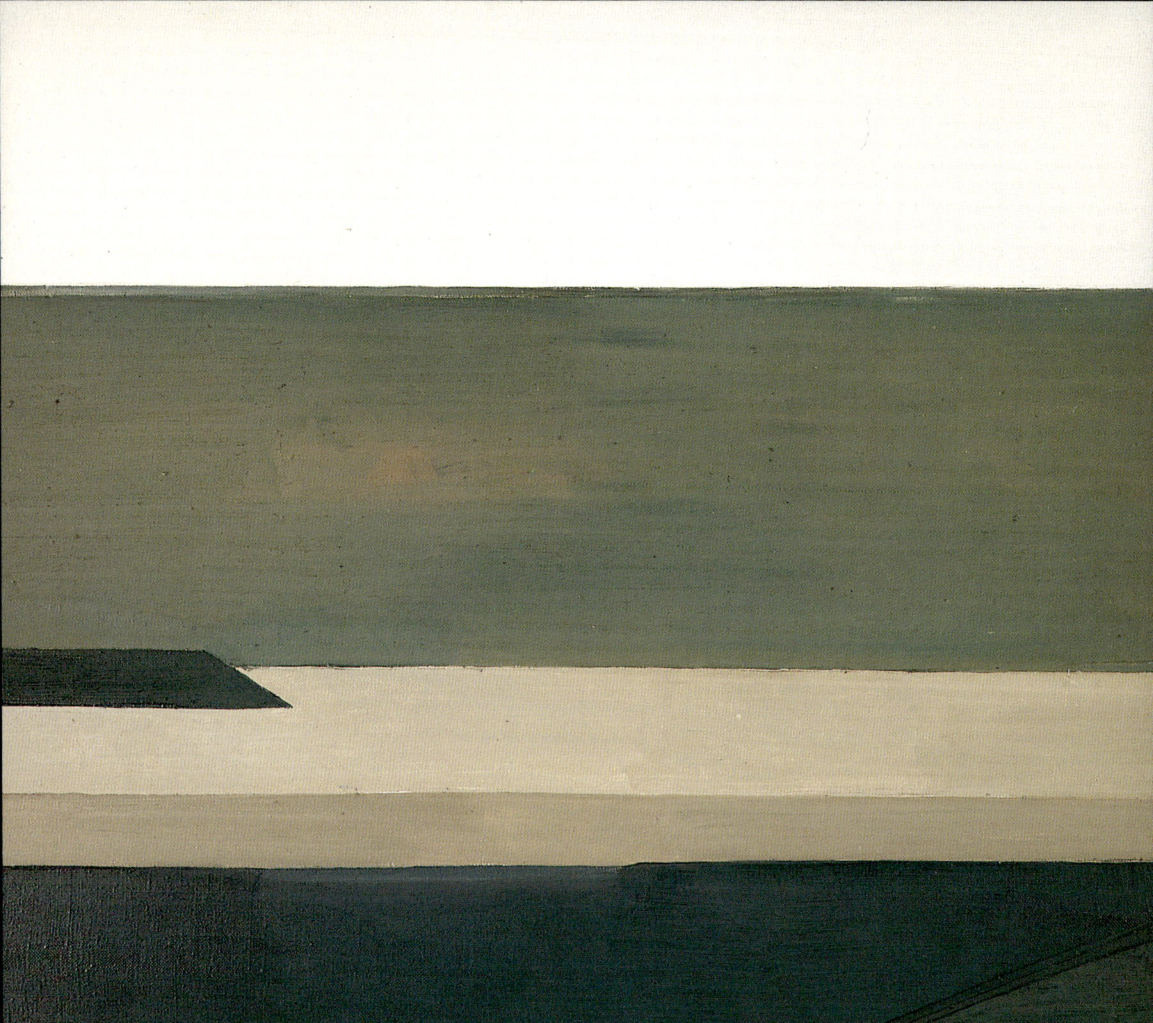

editorial/ alexei v. novikov / editor-in-chief

The structure of the visible image of the world is extremely conservative. To change one's habitual perception of its shapes and outlines is as difficult as changing one's political beliefs. Our stereotypes of the eye may be attributed to the burden of gravity and the upright way we walk. In other words, our visual perception of the world bears the imprint of both the cosmic structure and the Earth's organic nature. Say "rain" and you will find yourself in the vertical dimension; say "road" and you are lost in the vastness of horizontal expanses. One need only shift one's viewpoint, and the picture of the world — indeed the world itself — becomes transfigured.

When one regards and appreciates a map as a picture, the chaos of continental outlines reveals a fair amount of orderliness. The way that leads one out of the chaos of terrestrial folds to the harmony of global space winds through a system of cartographic projections. Envisage a real road, which strings up landscapes and sights, rather than an uninspiring video track, and the urge to apply the theory of film production and composition to one's travel plans becomes irresistible.

Territory and its entire visible space turn out to be a text or an ornament which is broken down into elementary components — circles, squares, triangles, crosses, points, and lines — only to be reassembled as a rational construction of the cultural landscape. Territory can even be perceived as a stage where the motionless still figures and symbols in towns' coats of arms come to life, enacting a historical play in the country's geographical theater.

Space alternates between being reality itself and being a projection of reality — perceived reality: this is the main contention of this first issue of geoGraffity.

the harmony of global space / victor n. sholpo

The polar axis of the Earth, in addition to being a rotation axis, emerges as an axis of symmetry as well. // Looking from either pole at the projection of the planet's relief and imagining that you are turning any half (say, northern) of the globe against the other, you will see that major global relief forms coincide on the equator at every 90 degrees.// And not only on the equator.

With the development of space flight our image of the Earth has changed dramatically. Now that photographs of the Earth from space give an outside view of the globe that is duplicated by the thousands and broadcast on television to millions, the model of our planet is starting to lose its age-old connotations of vast expanses and undiscovered countries. Rather, it makes us think now how tiny the Earth is, it being so easy to take in any part of its surface in a glance. Indeed, it takes a satellite only an hour and a half to travel around the world, and there is no problem whatever in getting a detailed photograph of any spot on the surface.

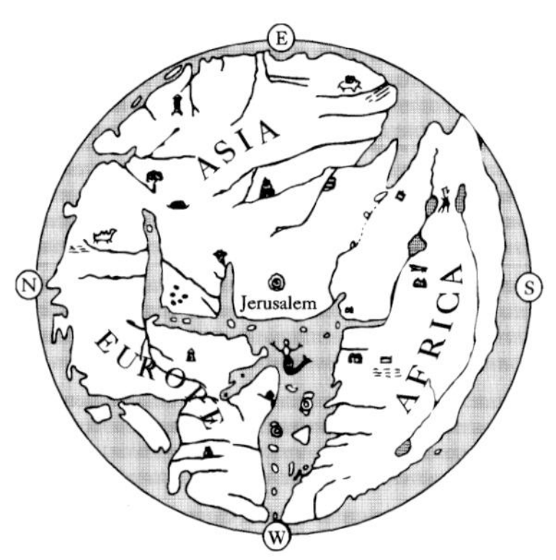

▯▯ The Hereford map of the world (planisphere), by Abbot Richards Heldingham (1260), is kept in the Hereford city cathedral on the Wye River. This map, as well as others of its kind, was a source of geographical knowledge in its days. The contours of the Mediterranean sea and the Aegean Sea can be recognized. There is a hint of the outline of the Black Sea, Arabia, the Red Sea, and the Persian Gulf. The center of the map is taken by Jerusalem, and in the eastern part, on the margins, beyond the Earth's circle, is situated the biblical Eden. (After A. B. Ditmar, *From Ptolemy to Columbus*, 1989)

▯▯ Opposite page. The world view of contemporary man is strongly influenced by cosmic photographs presenting a new image of the Earth's surface.

And there is still more to it. It has been common knowledge since the time of the ancient astronomers that the Earth belongs to a family of planets, but it is only now that this knowledge has become specific and, one might say, tangible. The planets are no longer just balls or points of light, traveling according to their own laws, different from those of the stars. In the family of planets we have come to know near and distant relatives; we have learned a lot about their surfaces — enough to make models of the Moon, Venus, and Mars. It is now possible to study the atmospheres of the planets, their surface temperatures and atmospheric pressures, as well as the composition of their rocks and dust. The Earth is, so to speak, no longer alone in the expanse of the solar system, but it still remains a unique home for mankind, the only reservoir of intelligent life in the vast expanses of near outer space.

But do we have a really adequate idea of this home of ours? Do we have a good understanding of how it is organized? Sure, the continental contours look familiar to us; we recognize distinctive coast lines of the seas, the windings of major rivers, and mountain ranges. These features are recognizable even in schematic drawings that appear with newspaper articles or TV news programs. Graphic representations of the Earth in maps, atlases and globes strike us as being something we have known since birth. There is hardly anyone who wonders about the implications of this very pattern of water and land arrangement, of the graphics of continents and ocean beds. Is this pattern determined or regulated by anything? Does it belong to the intrinsic nature of the Earth, or is it just chance or an adventitious inlay of uplifts, folds, joints, faults, and cleavages that make up Earth's relief? The questions are worth considering because the answers can greatly affect our understanding of the planet, of its current life and future development, and, consequently, of the laws regulating it.

Almost everybody would believe intuitively that chance plays hardly any role here, that there must be some essential laws behind the structure of the surface of the Earth. This perception is only natural for us, because from our experience we have learned that everything in nature is regulated by some law and held together by stable cause and effect relationships. Indeed, the three-dimensional space of the world is symmetrically organized and, even subconsciously, is perceived as harmonious. The horizontal line and the dome of the celestial hemisphere, the rhythm of hills and mountain ridges, the monotonous dynamics of the

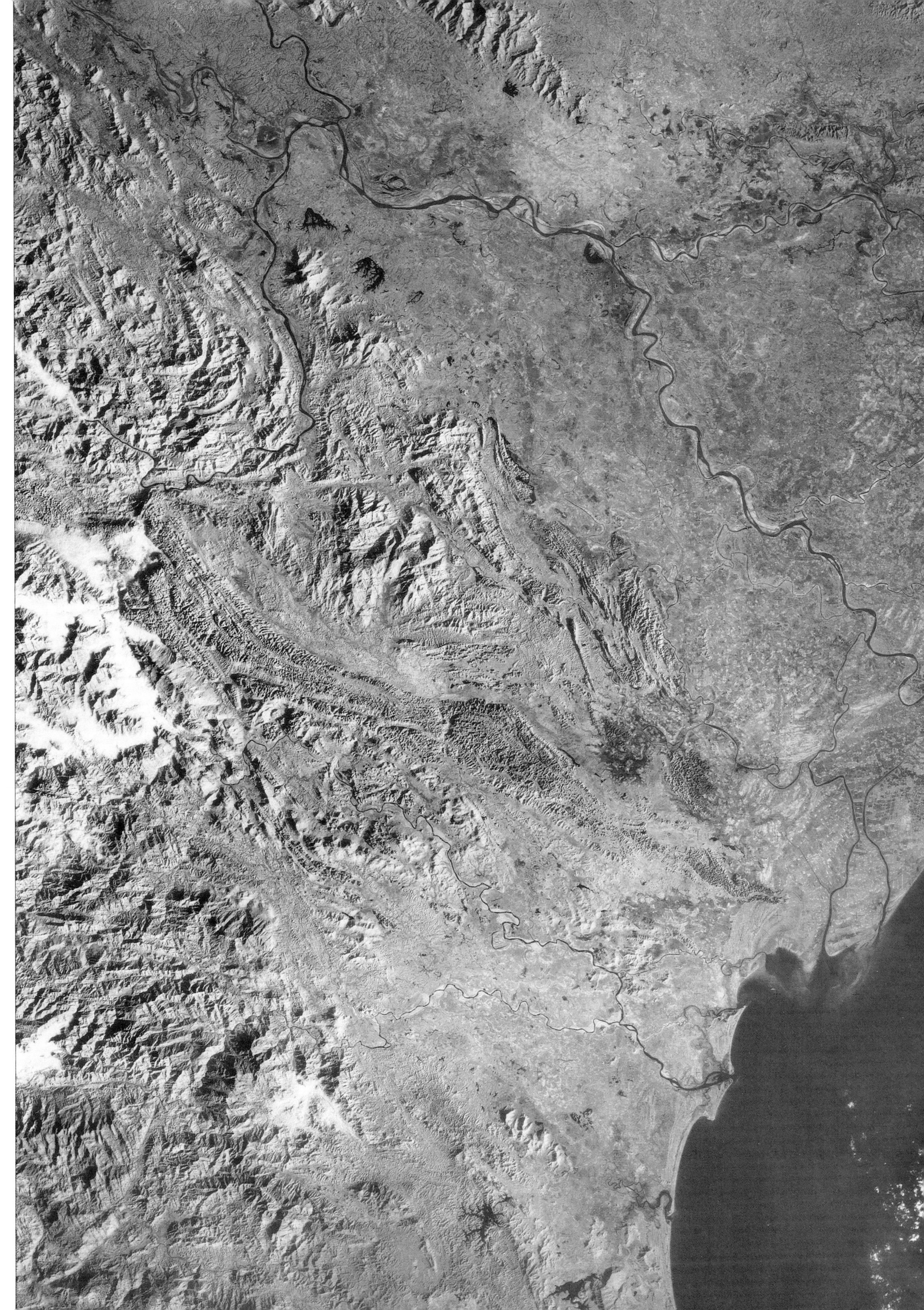

tide, the pendulum of day and night, and the eternal circle of the seasons of the year — everything seems to exist and develop within certain rhythms and recurrences. In organic nature as well we frequently run into symmetries and similarities. In the vegetable kingdom various kinds of radial symmetry prevail, while bilateral symmetry is characteristic of the animal kingdom. In a word, the regular organization of the world has become for us, subconsciously, one of the fundamental principles of its structure, a principle that we feel rather than infer.

This probably explains why ancient civilized peoples, when trying to get an idea of the surface of the known world, would always end up producing schemes ruled by some laws of symmetry. It was the case even when these schemes had to be hypothetical. Ancient thinking was dominated by the idea of a symmetrical world. Aristotle's scheme of the *oikoumene* which, as might be expected, had the Balkans and the Aegean Sea in the center, was balanced along the West-East axis. Alexander the Great, during his campaigns, put a lot of time and effort into verifying and proving the symmetry of the world. And when some corrections had to be made in the South — to indicate the sea route from the mouth of the Indus River to the Red Sea — this necessarily entailed some respective changes in the North to preserve the symmetry of the world.

One might find instructive the idea of the structure of the Earth held by geographers from the early Middle Ages until the time of the great geographic discoveries. Numerous conceptions of the inhabited part of the Earth were reflected in circle-bounded maps, called planispheres, which presented pictures of the sphere of the Earth. This does not mean that in those days the Earth was seen as a flat disk (after Ptolemy, the general belief was that the Earth was spherical) — this was just a way to represent the sphere on a plane. In most cases these planispheres carried proportionate and commensurate patches of land, symmetrically arranged within the space of the map.

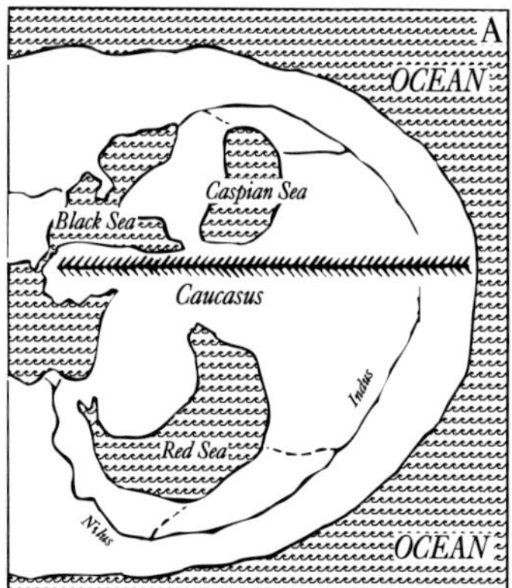

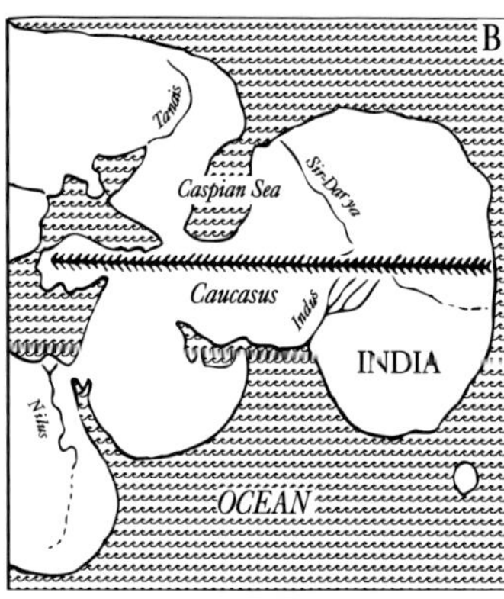

GREEK BELIEFS AT THE TIME OF ARISTOTLE AND THE CAMPAIGNS OF ALEXANDER THE GREAT ABOUT THE CONFORMATION OF THE EASTERN PART OF THE *OIKOUMENE*: A) HYPOTHESIS OF THE UNITY OF THE NILE AND INDUS RIVERS; B) RECONSIDERATION OF GEOGRAPHIC CONCEPTIONS AFTER ALEXANDER'S CAMPAIGNS (AFTER F. SHACHERMEYR, *ALEXANDER DER GROSSE. DAS PROBLEM SEINER PERSONALICHKEIT UND SEINE WIRKENS*, WIEN, 1972.)

Modern earth science began with the introduction of the globe, which gives a realistic reflection of the current view of the Earth.

As early as the 17th century, the English natural scientist and philosopher Francis Bacon pointed to the physical similarities found on the surface of the Earth. In *Novum Organum*, in the second book of aphorisms, Bacon wrote:

> nor do they [similar or proportionate instances] immediately establish any axiom, but merely indicate and observe a certain relation of bodies to each other. But although they be not of much assistance in discovering forms, yet they are of great advantage in disclosing the frame of parts of the universe, upon whose members they practise a species of anatomy, and thence occasionally lead us gently on to sublime and noble axioms, especially such as relate to the construction of the world, rather than to simple natures and forms.
>
> . . . But leaving such to themselves, similar instances are not to be neglected, in the greater portion of the world's conformation; such as Africa and the Peruvian continent, which reaches to the Straits of Magellan; both of which possess a similar isthmus and similar capes, a circumstance not to be attributed to mere accident.
>
> Again the new and old world are both of them broad and expanded towards the north, and narrow and pointed towards the south. (F. Bacon, *Advancement of Learning and Novum Organum*, 1899, New York: The Colonial Press, pp. 402, 404).

An urge to bring out and comprehend the general laws of the conformation of the Earth's surface is a theme that runs through many volumes by geographers and geologists of the 19th century, including some of the most prominent scholars of the time. Charles Lyell,[1] who asserted the idea of evolutionary development and the principle of actualism in geology, was the first to notice irregularity in water and land arrangement on the surface of the planet. He introduced the notion of antisymmetry of the Earth, which later was called the antipodal phenomenon. In the first edition of his most important book, *The Principles of Geology* (1830-1833), one can find a projection of the hemispheres shifted so as to place London in the center of one of them. This trick makes it evident to the viewer that the hemisphere containing London is for the most part continental and that the opposite is all taken up by the ocean.

As early as 1829, Elie de Beaumont,[2] the author of the contractional hypothesis[3] which captured the attention of geologists of the world for several decades, suggested that the Earth is changing its shape in the course of cooling down. He described it as the process of molding a sphere into a giant crystal (not to be confused with the usual image used to describe the idea of contraction — an apple being baked). According to Elie de Beaumont, parallel mountain ridges correspond with the great circles of the spheroid and present the edges of a pentagonal dodecahedron inscribed in a sphere.

[1] Charles Lyell — 1797-1875, English geologist.

[2] Jean Batiste Arman Louis Leon Elie de Beaumont —1798-1874, French geologist, author of the contractional hypothesis (1829, published in Guill in 1852).

[3] Contractional hypothesis — a concept which says that rock folds result from contraction caused by the Earth's cooling, which reduced its volume, diameter, and surface area.

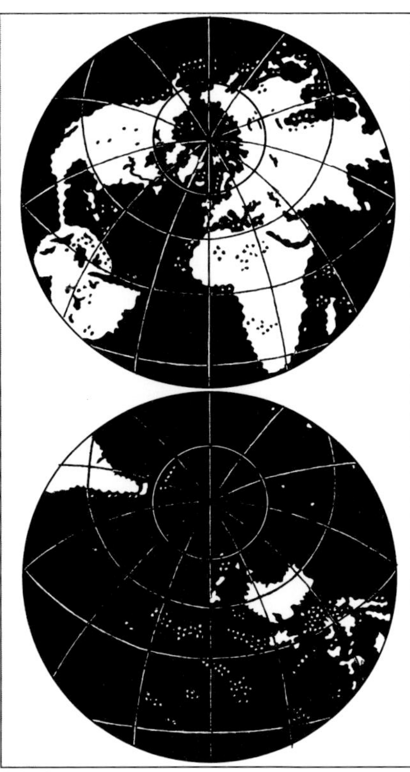

Lyell's projection of the hemispheres, illustrating their antipodal character. London is placed in the center of the continental hemisphere, while New Zealand occupies a place in the center of the ocean hemisphere. Antarctica is missing in Lyell's scheme.

Their points of intersection coincide with the corners of this regular polyhedron. According to this theory, parallel mountain systems come into being simultaneously. Thus the number of great circles reflects the number of catastrophes the Earth has gone through. But in the long run this theory was abandoned, because ultimately Elie de Beaumont counted in all eighty-five mountain systems of different extension, which excluded the exact and precise symmetry he professed.

Yet the high authority of Elie de Beaumont, who contributed much to the theory of ore deposits and the petrology of igneous rocks, made the contractional theory rather attractive, and the theory had its adherents.

The drive that urged natural scientists of the last century to find some general regularities in the conformation of the globe was primarily rooted in their firm belief that such regularities must exist. The fact that such a renowned scholar, explorer, and natural scientist as Alexander von Humboldt took interest in the problem of the organized structure of the Earth enhanced the enthusiasm. Humboldt believed that mountain systems of the globe could be attributed either to latitudes or to longitudes, and he singled out a set of important parallels and meridians. The same idea was favored by the well known French geologist Marcel Bertran,[4] who in 1892 advanced a hypothesis of orthogonal lines of deformation. He argued that the Earth was consistently changing its shape, warping with regard to the net of orthogonal folds or flexures, with the former encircling the pole, being undulatory and roughly parallel to the

[4] Marcel Bertran — 1847-1907, French geologist. Produced the concept that tectonic movements are periodic as well as products of orogenic epochs. Bertran studied general tendencies in geological processes.

equator, and the latter being almost perpendicular to the former and meeting at one point in the direction of the polar lands. Later he developed the idea that it was this very double grid of orthogonal lines that determined the direction of the globe's deformations and lines of gradual construction of the continents.

English geologist W. L. Green in the late 19th century came up with the idea of comparing the organization of the Earth's surface with the structure of a tetrahedron. Green proposed to sort out the infinite number of axes of symmetry in the sphere and to untangle some significant axes which corresponded to the existing symmetrical structures of the global surface, particularly of the continents and oceans. This approach actually allows one to discern the symmetry of a tetrahedron in the organization of the global surface: if one of its faces looks upwards and we agree to consider it the north, then that face will correspond to the Arctic Ocean. In this case the remaining faces will correspond to the other oceans — the Indian, the Atlantic and the Pacific. Continents will correspond to the edges and corners of the tetrahedron. This hypothesis — or as it used to be called, the tetrahedron theory — found numerous supporters and followers at the turn of the century. It was developed and substantiated by Lapparent,[5] Levi,[6] Peschel,[7] Sacco,[8] and many others. Most followers of the tetrahedron theory were trying to develop this idea within the contraction hypothesis, holding that the contraction of the globe is determined by some geometrical laws and that the globe, in the process of cooling, loses its spherical form, approaching the form of a regular crystal — a tetrahedron. The rotation of the planet counteracts this tendency to crystallize and pulls the earth back to the spherical form, but each new stage of contraction causes the faces and ridges of a tetrahedron to reappear on the planet's surface.

The tetrahedron hypothesis leaned heavily upon the so called geographical homologies — similarities and congruities of relief forms. The most important contribution to the identification of geographical homologies was made by Reclus, French scholar, writer, and tireless explorer, whose life was full of adventure and dramatic experience. Reclus wrote a 19-volume world physical geography, *The Earth — Description of Global Life*, and also a six-volume work, *The Earth and Man*.

The geographic homologies identified by Reclus are as follows: 1) the overwhelming "continentality" of the northern hemisphere and the "rule of the ocean" in the southern hemisphere; 2) the shape of triangles discerned in the form of all the continents that narrow towards the South and the form of the oceans narrowing towards the North being a rough mirror reflection of these triangles; and 3) a ring of land around the deep-sea trench near the North Pole and a ring of oceans around the patch of land at the South Pole. Early in the 20th century the English geologist Gregory, in his

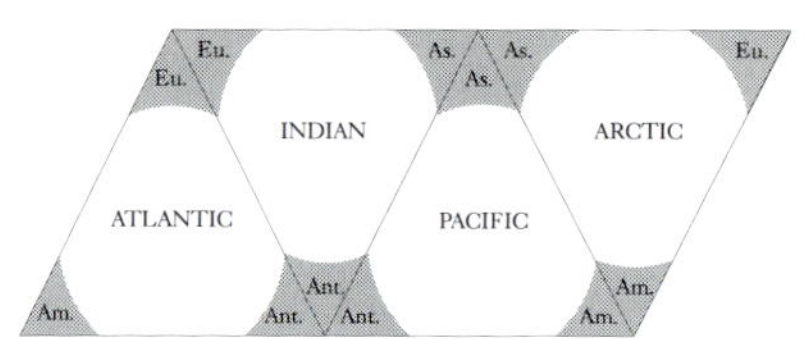

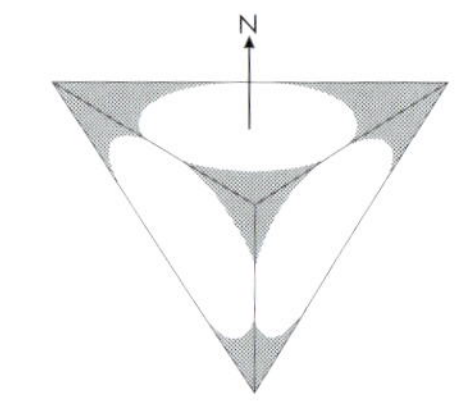

□□ Development of axonometric projection, illustrating the tetrahedron theory of W. L. Green. The faces of the tetrahedron represent the oceans, and the edges and corners correspond to the continents. It should be borne in mind, however, that this is a very rough correspondence.

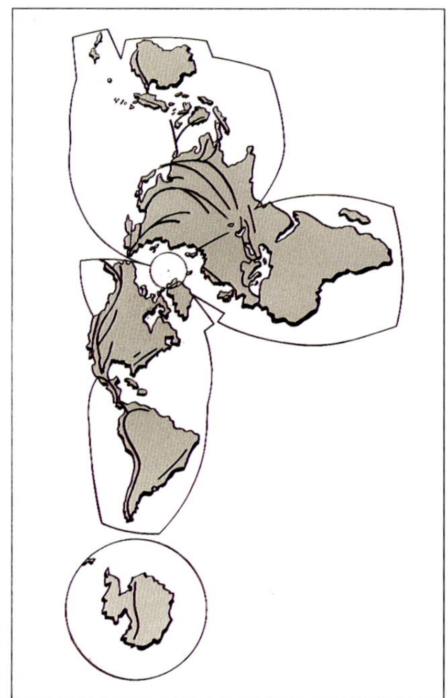

□□ A. P. Karpinsky's development of the continents that brings out geographical and geological homologies — similarities in the configuration of the continents — South and North America and Eurasia, including Australia, but excluding Africa. Mountainous folded areas make up a common trunk with branches springing out in places of similarity and conformity.

[5] Albert August Lapparent — 1839-1908, French geologist, who published works on geology and minerology. Author of manuals.

[6] Augusto Michel-Levy — 1844-1911, French geologist, minerologist, petrologist. Major works were devoted to conditions of rock crystallization.

[7] Oskar Peschel — 1826-1875, German geographer. Major works were on general geography and the theory of land cultivation. His works in relief analysis promoted geomorphology as a science.

[8] Federico Sacco — 19th-20th century Italian geologist, professor of Geology at Turin University.

book *The Origin of Earth* made them four, formulating one more homology — the antipode phenomenon, which can be reduced to the following: the contours of the continents, outlined by one end of a rigid diameter of the global sphere, will be mirrored by its second end and will be found almost entirely in the ocean. He made this "almost" reservation because 18 percent of the land area will coincide with other land areas. This "almost" is quite illustrative in the sense that all the similarities, symmetries, and regularities formulated in homologies are not quite precise. The approximate nature of the regularities will be further discussed in this article.

Many prominent geologists took into consideration and tried to develop the idea of geographical homologies. Suess[9] was the first to establish a fundamental difference in the geological structure of the Atlantic and Pacific shores. He attributed great importance to this difference in connection with the geographical homologies, which featured the Pacific hemisphere as a specific area of the planet, antisymmetric to the opposite hemisphere.

An interesting and illustrative attempt to compare major landforms of the Earth with the corresponding geological structures was undertaken by Karpinsky.[10] He described his idea in the short article "On Regularities in Outlines, Arrangement and Structures of the Continents" which was published in 1888. Using uncommon polar projections which left the continents of the Western Hemisphere in their usual relationship to each other while positioning Eurasia, Africa and Australia to form a slightly curving line, Karpinsky revealed a similarity in the shape of all the continents: South America similar to North America, and each of them similar to Eurasia united with Australia. Viewed from this perspective, young folded areas appear to be a common trunk running along the left edge of the continents. There are branches springing off this trunk which occupy a regular and similar place on each continent. Besides folded areas, larger ancient platforms and major depressions occupy quite specific positions in such continental outlines. Karpinsky called this similarity in the structure of different continents by the name of geological homologies. He noted, however, that any mathematical regularity either in the arrangement of the continents or their outlines, or in similar geological structures, cannot be expected. Refusing to look into reasons for this similarity in continental structures, Karpinsky explained that he would hardly be able to undertake a profound analysis of this problem, but he thought it important to draw attention to it.

In the 20th century, studies of regularities of geological structures were advanced and stimulated by such prominent scholars as Stille[11] and Fourmarier,[12] who established certain symmetries and similarities in the global distribution of structures and active tectonic areas on the Earth. And in our times Belousov and Milanovsky[13] paid their tribute to the problem.

An important part of the enormous scientific heritage of Stille, who addressed tectonic problems of various areas of the Earth, is inquiry into the problem of the orientation of differently aged structures, as well as of the combination of different such orientations and of structural similarity of different areas, sometimes very remote from one another. He also pointed to global regularities in the symmetrical arrangement of structures with regard to the conventional geological equator, which runs around the globe, but in the Eastern Hemisphere shifts from the geographical equator to the North, and in the Western, slightly to the South.

Fourmarier, discussing the regularities in the arrangement of continents and oceans, emphasized the symmetry of geological structures against the S-shaped curved line — the "great circle" crossing the Pacific Hemispere: "starting from the Bering Strait, it runs alongside Hawaii, to the West of Easter Island, and ends at the South Pole in the center of Antarctica." Another line of the same sort, according to Fourmarier, runs across the continental hemisphere through Africa, the Alpine belt in Eurasia, and the Baltic shield. It reaches the North Pole, where it meets the Pacific axis. Symmetrical to this axis are the S-shaped axis lines of continents and oceans, and the major continental features. "Certainly, symmetry in the architecture of the earth-crust is far from being perfect," Fourmarier wrote, "but this phenomenon should

[9] Edward Suess — 1831-1914, Austrian geologist. His major publication, *The Face of the Earth* (3 volumes, 1883-1909), summed up the concepts of the structure and development of the Earth's crust, based on the contraction hypothesis.

[10] A. P. Karpinsky — 1846-1936, Russian geologist, founder of the Russian scientific school of geology.

[11] Hans Stille— 1876-1966, German geologist, a classicist of modern geology. He conducted studies in regional and global tectonics, and introduced the concept of global orogenic phases — periods of global tectonic movements known as Stille's Phases.

[12] Paul Frederick Joseph Fourmarier — 1877-1967, Belgian geologist who studied the tectonics of folded areas. Fourmarier developed the concept that the Earth's structure was stable and tried to prove the rotational symmetry of the Earth's crust.

[13] V. V. Belousov, E. E. Milanovsky — modern Russian geologists.

not be neglected, even though its causes are oblique. In any case, it appears to testify to the fact that the arrangement of continents on the Earth's surface is not accidental." (P. Fourmarier, *Le probleme de la derive des continents*. Bruxelles,1967.)

From this brief digression into the history of geology we can see that the problem of the Earth's surface conformation and the regular geological structure of the earth-crust was a problem of interest and concern for many scholars, including celebrities. Surprisingly their names are inscribed in the history of geology and the history of science not because they studied this global problem, but generally because their names are associated with quite different ideas, questions, and challenges. The problem of the regular organization of global geological structure has never been central to earth science; it has always remained marginal in geology. We remember the great disputes in geology between the Neptunians and Plutonians, between catastrophists and evolutionists. Opposing the uplift theory, the idea of contraction affirmed itself, but in due time was ousted by other theories such as pulsation hypothesis, expansion theory, undulation hypothesis, and continental drift. There were no open discussions specifically devoted to the regularities in the general structure of the Earth, to the order in chaos. This seems strange, because global generalizations have been suggested for a very long time and many of them are still valid as empirical generalizations of well-known facts.

A question naturally arises: why has this problem of global importance always remained in the background? There seem to be two main reasons that account for this. The first and foremost, it seems, arises from the fact that for a long time geology developed as an applied science, practically oriented. Geology originated from the ore-connoisseur and thus was guided by the necessity to provide developing civilization with the required mineral resources. The challenge to understand the conditions of ore-rock formation (sedimentary, igneous, metamorphic) gave rise to plutonism and neptunism. The tasks of understanding the processes of mountain formation and the structure of folded areas, because they contained the main deposits of accessible mineral resources, generated the theories of uplift and, thereafter, of contraction. Theoretical conceptions and generalizations followed the requirements of exploration for mineral resources. Only now, when we cannot expect to find any more big mineral deposits close to the surface, and when geologists dig into the depths of the continents and oceans for mineral wealth, the necessity to comprehend the global evolutionary processes, the regularities in the structure and the development of the whole lithosphere becomes a top priority. Another stimulus comes from the fundamental challenge of ecology — the task of preserving the biosphere.

The second reason lies in the fact that any research into the regularities of surface conformation could be reduced to empirical, very approximate generalizations of the phenomena and facts available for observation. Moreover, these generalizations, as we have seen earlier, were usually far from being either specific or accurate. The authors themselves would often stress the absence of mathematical accuracy. Importantly, these generalizations were practically never backed by any genetic hypotheses — no physical explanation was ever suggested. Even more importantly, no inferences were drawn from these regularities, to say nothing of practical applications. Under these conditions the generalizations were nothing more than interesting observations, ingenious constructions that so far implied nothing either for the theory or for the practice of geology.

Yet it should be noted that through the 20th century interest in the problem of the spatial organization of the Earth's conformation was steady, although the problem itself remained in the background of the development of science and was never featured in important discussions. In the late part of the 1950s and early part of the 1960s there appeared a trend that acquired the semiofficial name of astrogeology. This trend was built around the idea that the whole structure of both the relief and the geological composition of the Earth's crust is formed and determined by irregularities in the various movements of the planet. The most important of these movements — rotation on its axis, revolving in its orbit around the sun, and tidal motions — build up a complex irregular field of tensions which is responsible for the whole variety of tectonic movements and deformations, molding the shape of our planet. Lichkov,[14] the founder and leader of this trend, wrote: "Earth tectonics, which shifts continents and raises new mountains, was conceived in the interior of the planet as a result of confrontation between the gravitational forces of the planet and the forces of rock cohesion happening in the context of the planet's rotation. This confrontation stimulates any further development of tectonics as well as its restructuring" (B. L. Lichkov, *Principles of Modern Earth Theory*, 1965, p. 70).

Yet these ideas failed to get wide recognition, primarily because they were too straightforward and unequivocal in asserting the role of external forces influ-

[14] B. L. Lichkov — 1888-1966, Russian geologist, founder of the concept that the hydrosphere plays the decisive role in the Earth's geological history.

encing the Earth. The energy of these influences is too insignificant to be an immediate cause of tectonic changes in the Earth's crust.

There followed numerous attempts to comprehend the regularities in the Earth's surface and to interpret them as a combination of annular, spiral, and vortical structures. It should be noted that this trend was largely brought about by the space age, when numerous and various photographs of the Earth's surface from space became available to geologists and geographers. These images brought out some general physiographic features especially clearly. Common topographical maps also carry these features, but there they are obscured by a host of minute details. Vortical and spiral structures had been known long before the space age. For example, the famous Chinese geologist J. S. Lee[15] long ago wrote about such structures in the Chinese Platform. But still many geologists are quite skeptical and cautious about such interpretations because all of these circles, spirals, and vortexes can be identified only roughly.

There remains one other attempt to grasp the regularities in the Earth's figures that calls for our attention. This attempt seems to be the least sophisticated, and thus it might prove the most promising and fruitful. It belongs to Alexei Shulga, a researcher, a power engineering specialist, and a prospector from Moscow, who was infatuated with cartography and spent many years searching for general regularities behind the structure of the Earth's relief. The story of this quest could make a novel, full of drama, disappointments, and revelations. In this article, however, we have to restrict ourselves to the results of his many years of work.

Starting in the last century, many of Shulga's predecessors were driven by a desire to compare the spheroid of the Earth with this or that regular polyhedron, or even with a combination of polyhedrons. Practically all of Plato's bodies were tried: Elie de Beaumont attempted to approximate the sphere with a dodecahedron; there were attempts to combine a dodecahedron with an icosahedron; and the tetrahedron went as far as to generate a whole theory. However, for some obscure reason, the cube was left out, probably because it seemed so elementary, so transparent. But it appears that among all the other polyhedrons it has the greatest number of elements of symmetry. This is the inference Shulga drew from his research. He held to the conclusion that the organization of the Earth's spheroid is closest to the symmetry of the cube. The geographical homologies, formulated by Gregory, fit into this symmetry.

The symmetries and similarities established by Shulga can be checked on a globe or on hemispheric maps, or on a Mercator projection of the Earth. Let us undertake this test of symmetries. On the equator, a physically relevant line, we find major global relief forms repeat themselves every 90 degrees. The equator runs through three continental massifs (South America, Africa and Oceania, which bridges Asia and Australia and where continental crust prevails), and each of these massifs extends 30 degrees along the equator. Western shores of neighboring continents are separated from each other by 90 degrees; the same is true for eastern shores. The system of mid-oceanic ridges, which constitutes the major relief element within the oceans, also seems to conform to the pattern. The axis of the East Pacific uplift crosses the equator at 110 degrees longitude west; the axis of the Mid-Atlantic Ridge at 20 degrees longitude west. The ridge in the middle of the Indian Ocean meets the equator at 70 degrees longitude east, while the fourth boundary to divide the equator into four equal sections appears to be a deep trench off the Solomon Islands at 160 degrees longitude east, this belonging to the system of trenches of the western margin of the Pacific Ocean and thus forming a major global relief feature. This organized system was also emphasized by E. E. Milanovsky, who asserted that its characteristics of similarity and accordance with the fourth-order symmetry were not restricted to the equator but were true for the entire length of these linear structures.

The polar axis of the Earth, in addition to being a rotation axis, emerges as a symmetry axis as well. Looking from either pole at a projection of the planet's relief and imagining that you are turning any half (say, northern) of the globe against the other, you shall see that major global relief forms coincide on the equator every 90 degrees. And not only on the equator. As you remember, the antipodal character of the polar areas was established in the last century.

Thus we have identified one among the three axes of cubic symmetry which connect the centers of the opposite faces and coincide with the rotational axis of the Earth. There remain the other two. If we agree to take as the center of the faces of the cube circumscribing the sphere the center of the continental masses on the equator, and then go 45 degrees of longitude east and west, then from Africa to the west and from South America to the east, we shall find ourselves at the Mid-Atlantic Ridge; to the east of Africa at the mid-oceanic ridge of the Indian Ocean; and to the east of Indonesia at the deep trench that separates the ocean bed from a transitional zone taken up by a system of island arches and marginal seas. Now we see that the middle part of the surface of the Earth's spheroid breaks down into

[15] J. S. Lee — 1889-1971, Chinese geologist.

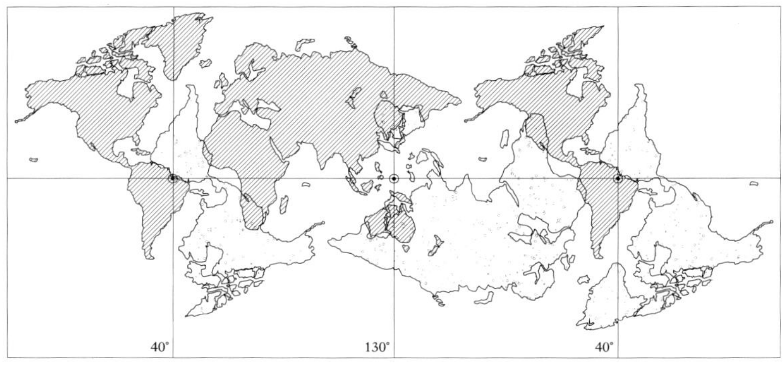

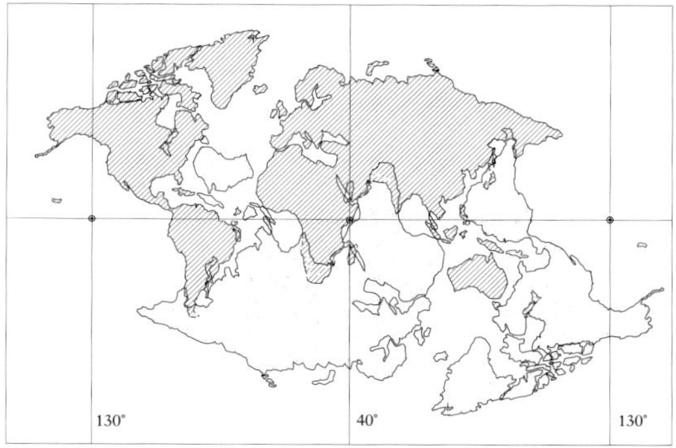

TESTING THE SYMMETRY OF THE CHIEF RELIEF FORMS OF THE EARTH ACCORDING TO THE METHOD SUGGESTED BY SHULGA. THE CONTINENTAL CONTOURS ON THE FIXED JACKET ARE HATCHED AND THEY ARE SHOWN IN THEIR USUAL POSITION ON THE MERCATOR PROJECTION. ON THE MOVABLE JACKET THE CONTINENTS ARE DOTTED. THE MOVABLE JACKET IS ROTATED BY 180 DEGREES. COORDINATES OF THE ROTATION AXIS OF THE MOVABLE JACKET ARE ON THE EQUATOR AT 40 DEGREES LONGITUDE EAST AND 140 DEGREES LONGITUDE WEST. THE SAME, SHIFTED BY 90 DEGREES: 130 DEGREES OF LONGITUDE EAST AND 40 DEGREES LONGITUDE WEST. IN BOTH CASES THE CONTINENTAL CONTOURS ON THE FIXED AND MOVABLE JACKETS COINCIDE.

the four faces of the circumscribing cube. The face with South America in the center is congruous and symmetrical with the center of its face in Indonesia, while the African face is an antipode of and symmetrical with the Pacific. But it is rather antisymmetrical, as Africa is, geologically, the most uplifted continent, and the Pacific Ocean is the deepest and most vast of all the oceans. Keep in mind that antisymmetry does not mean absence of symmetry (i.e., asymmetry), but a kind of opposite symmetry, inside-out or topsy-turvy symmetry. The same is true for the northern face, with the gap of the Arctic Ocean being an antipode to and symmetrical with the southern face of the uplift of Antarctica.

The two horizontal axes of the Earth's symmetry — if we consider, as usual, the polar axis to be vertical — stand out at the equator. One of them runs from 130 degrees longitude east to 50 degrees longitude west, the other from 40 degrees longitude east to 140 degrees longitude west. They are, as should be expected, perpendicular to each other in the equatorial plane; taken together with the third axis — the polar one — they constitute a system of orthogonal Cartesian coordinates, familiar for us in our three-dimensional world. One can check to see how these axes work and if the similarities and conformities, that is, laws of symmetry, are observed in the conditions of rotation around them. To do this you must imagine that the common globe is wearing a transparent, movable jacket on which are the outlines of the continents. If you turn this coat 180 degrees around either horizontal axis of symmetry, you shall see how closely continents from the movable cover coincide with those on the fixed one. The degree of conformity in this case is higher than in the Gregory experiment. In the latter, as you recall, 18 percent of land coincided with other land, but in the former, such overlappings are practically non-existent. Thus Shulga's axes fulfill the role of axes of antisymmetry.

The movable and transparent jacket we have put on the globe model is handy for further experimentation. For example, you can turn the movable coat 180 degrees around the polar axis, bringing together the Eastern and Western hemispheres. Only now you have to supplement the continental outlines with the basic orographic network — river valleys and chief watersheds. This process brings out a host of conformities of various lines and forms of relief. For instance, the Aleutian arc of islands coincides precisely with the continental watersheds of Europe, separating the rivers of the northern sea basins from the Mediterranean basin. It is not only 180 degree rotations that will produce such wonderful congruities and conformities among different relief structures, but also 90-, 60-, and 30-degree turns. Any rotation which is a multiple of 30 degrees and an integer divisor of 180 degrees will yield a variety of conformities and similarities of different relief forms. This looks like a trick or an amusing game, but in actual fact this trial of the Earth's figure with symmetry testifies to the fact that not only the global relief of the Earth is ruled by the symmetry and antisymmetry of the cube on the global scale, but also that the internal organization of the faces turns out to conform to the laws of periodicity and similarity with a spacing of 30 degrees.

Within each face there can be found a hierarchic sequence of relief forms, from major down to minor, that reveal the similarities on one level of hierarchy and down through the levels. "Relief forms on the Earth repeat each other with almost the same monotony and consistence as a wallpaper pattern," Shulga would repeatedly say. "The point is in making out this pattern, untangling it from a maze of complicating detail."

It should be remembered, however, that despite having a whole set of the cube's axes of symmetry, the planet remains a spheroid, and all the straight lines on the faces of the cube become curvilinear. In this case circular, spiral, or vortical structures, which have become so much favored by some geologists lately, can enter the hierarchy of structures that fill in the faces of the cube or appropriate cells of the spheroid.

Shulga's discovery (we hold we can rightfully call the global system of symmetry and antisymmetry a scientific discovery on the level of observed phenomena, that is on the phenomenological level), opens up new venues and possibilities for research in studies about the Earth. Even though the nature and causes of this phenomenon still remain unclear, we can test whether the geological build-up and deeper structures of the Earth's interior agree or disagree with the cells of symmetrically organized and hierarchically graduated relief on the Earth's surface.

We should remember V. I. Vernadsky's idea about the role and relations of empirical generalizations and hypotheses in scientific research: "In the history of natural science and related studies most significant are not scientific theories and hypotheses that are usually highlighted in surveys of the history of science and that tend to see more connection between the development of philosophical thought and advance in science than really exists. What is really significant are empirical generalizations, which are frequently erratically identified with scientific hypotheses." And, further on: "An empirical generalization can exist and be used as a foundation of a scientific study even if it is unclear and in contradiction to current theories and hypotheses" (*Reflections of a Natural Scientist*, pp. 20-21, 71). And, certainly, it should be admitted now that it is impossible to provide any exhaustive and well-grounded explanation of the disclosed phenomenon of the regular organization of the Earth's structure. Cause-and-effect relationships are too sophisticated. However, a reasonable hypothesis based on the latest achievements in thermodynamics of complex systems can be suggested. Yet it is such a broad and complicated topic that it cannot possibly be discussed here.

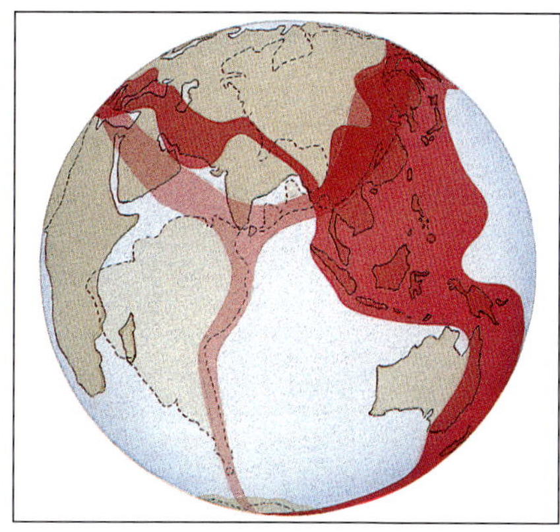

▯▯ THE CURRENT DISTRIBUTION OF THE TECTONIC ACTIVITY BELTS ON THE EARTH'S SURFACE (SHOWN IN BRIGHT CRIMSON ON THE SURFACE THE VIEWER FACES, IN SUBDUED CRIMSON ON THE OPPOSITE SURFACE). THE PACIFIC BELT FORMS A WHOLE CIRCLE, ALMOST COINCIDING WITH A GREAT CIRCLE; THE MEDITERRANEAN-ATLANTIC BELT FORMS A SEMI-CIRCLE, WHICH JOINS THE PACIFIC BELT IN THE CARIBBEAN AND IN INDONESIA.

Summing up, let us once again emphasize the approximate character of the regularities under discussion. Even the method suggested by Shulga to check symmetries and antisymmetries characteristic of the Earth will reveal not only conformities of various outlines and figures but also deviations from them. Though Shulga's approximation is the most accurate ever suggested, even here there remains a considerable amount of "almost," "almost conforms with," "almost precisely." For instance, such an important feature of the contemporary structure of the Earth as the distribution on its surface of the belts of tectonic activity — where the endogenous processes of today and of the recent past of the planet's geological history, that is earthquakes, vulcanism, abrupt and contrasting movements in the Earth's crust — are most intensive. This activity is known to be concentrated in two global belts on the Earth — the circum-Pacific and Mediterranean-Himalaya belts. The Pacific belt goes along the edge of all the continents, surrounding the ocean, and forms almost precisely the great circle of the planet's spheroid, though slightly lopsided and a bit shifted. As to the Mediterranean-Himalaya belt, it extends latitudinally through the south of Europe and through the Middle East as far as the Pamirs, then swerves to the south and in Indonesia joins the Pacific belt. There is a lot of evidence that to the west of Europe it can be continued through the Atlantic as far as the Caribbean, where it again catches up with the Pacific belt. And this Mediterranean-Himalaya-Atlantic belt, which amounts to a semi-circle, almost corresponds with a great circle as well. It does not look accidental. Not only the location of the belts of tectonic activity seems regular, but also their deviation from the mathematically accurate geometrical position seems regular. If the figure of the Earth and its internal structure were an absolutely regular and geometrically perfect body, it would just mean that Earth had reached some final stable stage in its evolution and was not evolving further. But this is not the case. The Earth is almost perfect; it is nearing stability, but has not actually reached it. And this fact argues that it is still an evolving system. One can only guess about the causes, the forces involved in this evolution, and about the sophisticated interaction of internal and external forces which affect the evolution. But these must form the subject of another discussion. ▮▮

the geometric alphabet of cultural landscapes /andrei v. bokov

MAN'S ACQUISITION OF THE CIRCLE WAS JUST AS DIFFICULT, JUST AS LONG A PROCESS, AND JUST AS DRAMATIC AS THE "STRAIGHT AND RECTANGULAR" REVOLUTION WHICH FOLLOWED.

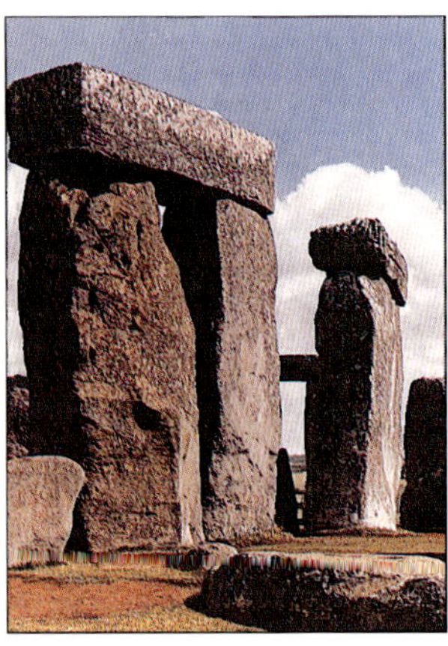

When our hands outline the shapes of squares, circles, or spirals, it is as if they are following programs forever ingrained in the subconscious. It is possible that these programs are preserved in a hereditary memory; maybe a single education is not enough for man to be able to recall the Universal of every shape. Polygons, crosses, periodic lines, circles, stars, waves, and more are favorite subjects of the first and most simple designs that can be found in children's drawings and in the "graffiti" of adults.

Such images and reflexes are indisputably tinged with human affirmation and approval. Our respect for the circle, the cross, and the square hardly wavers. Our relation to these shapes is intimately linked to the geometric character of the letters of the alphabet, to numerals, coats of arms, signs, badges, decorations, logos, and, in addition, to the symbols on the map of a town like the star-shaped Theater of the Red Army,[1] which had to be camouflaged during World War II.

The eye becomes accustomed to the most intricate, most complicated, and even the most scandalous designs — such as those in "free" compositions or those in the paintings of Jackson Pollock.[2] We begin to guess at echoes and signs of order — at first only dimly, but later more clearly. We liken art of a landscape to a geometric figure — a "circular" lake or a "triangular" peninsula. Or we cover it with a network of coordinates. Our own Earth was inconceivable before we threw the net of longitudes and latitudes onto it and had marked out the equator and the poles. No less characteristic in this respect was our understanding of the heavens.

[1] The Theater of the Red Army is located in Moscow.

[2] Jackson Pollock — 1912 - 1956, American painter, abstract expressionist.

Such a procedure is really just the way we acclimatize ourselves to the natural world, culturalize it, and thus recreate and reconstruct it in human form. This reconstruction concerns, above all, those objects which are not directly presented to us — whether they be abstract or concrete. Among abstract objects are included such familiar images as the sky as a circle, or the earth as a square; or of the circular form of Moscow and the square form of St. Petersburg. Few cosmological representations and few pictures of the world such as globes, or even the very latest maps of geodesics, can be tested without the use of those figures with which we organize and structure so many of our more complicated and unusual activities.

However, these figures do not directly exist. That is to say, they do not exist in the same way as the molds which children use to make castles in the sand. They exist instead in our vast numbers of tools; in

the numerous ways of producing "circles" and "squares;" in the technology and techniques which are created by civilizations and forced on us by sheer inertia — inertia which is a destructive force in relation to the non-circular and the non-quadratic. Beginning with the simplest ruler, set-square, and pair of compasses, we can grasp the entire system of production of objects and space, without having to undergo the painful transition to some empty or "other" form.

It seems paradoxical that the epithet "irregular," which is so often applied to the towns or town planning of whole epochs, is never completely applicable to the very architecture, buildings, and constructions which belong to the same time.

In the course of time, circles and squares, straight lines, and corners all acquired the huge dimensions of Roman camps, or the towns of Peking, Versailles and Chicago. The sphere of influence of these shapes gradually extended from those objects which go to make up man's immediate surroundings to phenomena which exist on a world scale.

Man's increasing control over the world, realized with a rarely seen persistency, tends in the final analysis to call forth both an unconscious and a conscious reaction of resistance to the imposition of regularity. Such are outbursts of "counter-geometric" intuition so characteristic of artists with temperaments like Arp's[3] or Pollock's; or, too, those objectively acting mechanisms which will deform any geometric scheme.

MODELS OF SPACE AND FORM

Geometric universals are internal, hidden forms; they are forms of concepts, or generalizations. As a rule they are not directly presented to perception. It is only on very rare occasions that conception and form coincide — for example, with the Egyptian pyramids, a brick, or a straight stretch of road. In the vast majority of cases we come up against universals which are already transformed and modified.

Geometric material which is laid down in the foundations of a future house, be it consciously or unconsciously, has no authorship. And accordingly, however independent our modern creators of form — our designers, architects, or town planners — consider themselves to be, they essentially remain, above all else, interpreters who are in fact creating authorship out of the whole of humanity. The isomorphism of geometric abstraction is made to appear natural and fully understandable to man by the common morphologies of the architecture, furniture and implements of a given historical style. So too is it made clear to us by the fact that most artists (for example, Aalto[4] or Le Corbusier[5]) are attached to the same motifs — motifs which at times lead to the creation of buildings, at times to crockery designs, to tapestries, or even towns.

The similarities between the plan of an ideal renaissance town and a piece of jewelry, or between a Marshall's star and the plan of a fortress — these are certainly not evidence of some essential affinity. Rather, they are an indication of general sources and roots. Such roots enable us to speak of a unity at all levels of the man-made world, an entirety of all culture — and an entirety which is, moreover, fundamentally powerful, energetic, and active.

At the same time, if we look at the world without preconceptions, the absence of any strict link between universals and objects at different levels is confirmed. In particular, if we increase the size of an object, we are not left with something which has a different basis. The totality of basic universals always remains a guarantee of the one-ness and the stability of the world.

Two-dimensionality is the most fundamental condition of geometric universals in their capacity as elements of both space and form. Nearly all the "objectless" art of the twentieth century — for example, the works of Kandinsky,[6] Picasso,[7] Mondrian,[8] and Delaunay[8]— hardly touches the third dimension at all and exists only on the level of the plane.

[3] Jean Arp — 1887 - 1966, Alsatian sculptor, a pioneer in abstract art.

[4] Alvar Henric Aalto — 1898 - 1976, Finnish architect; one of the most influential proponents of functional design.

[5] Le Corbusier, pseudonym of Charles Edouard Jeanneret — 1887 - 1965, Swiss-born, French architect, city planner, painter; one of the founders of modern architecture.

[6] Wassily W. Kandinsky — 1866 - 1944, Russian-born painter; a founder of abstract art. Left Russia in 1925, spent years in Germany and France; died in Neuilly-Sur-Seine, a suburb of Paris.

[7] Pablo Picasso — 1891 - 1973, Spanish painter; key figure in the art of twentieth century.

[8] Piet Mondrian — 1872 - 1944, Dutch abstract painter. Known for straight-line compositions.

[9] Robert Delaunay — 1885 - 1941, French painter who first introduced vibrant color into cubism and thereby originated the Orphic style of cubism; one of the first completely nonrepresentational painters.

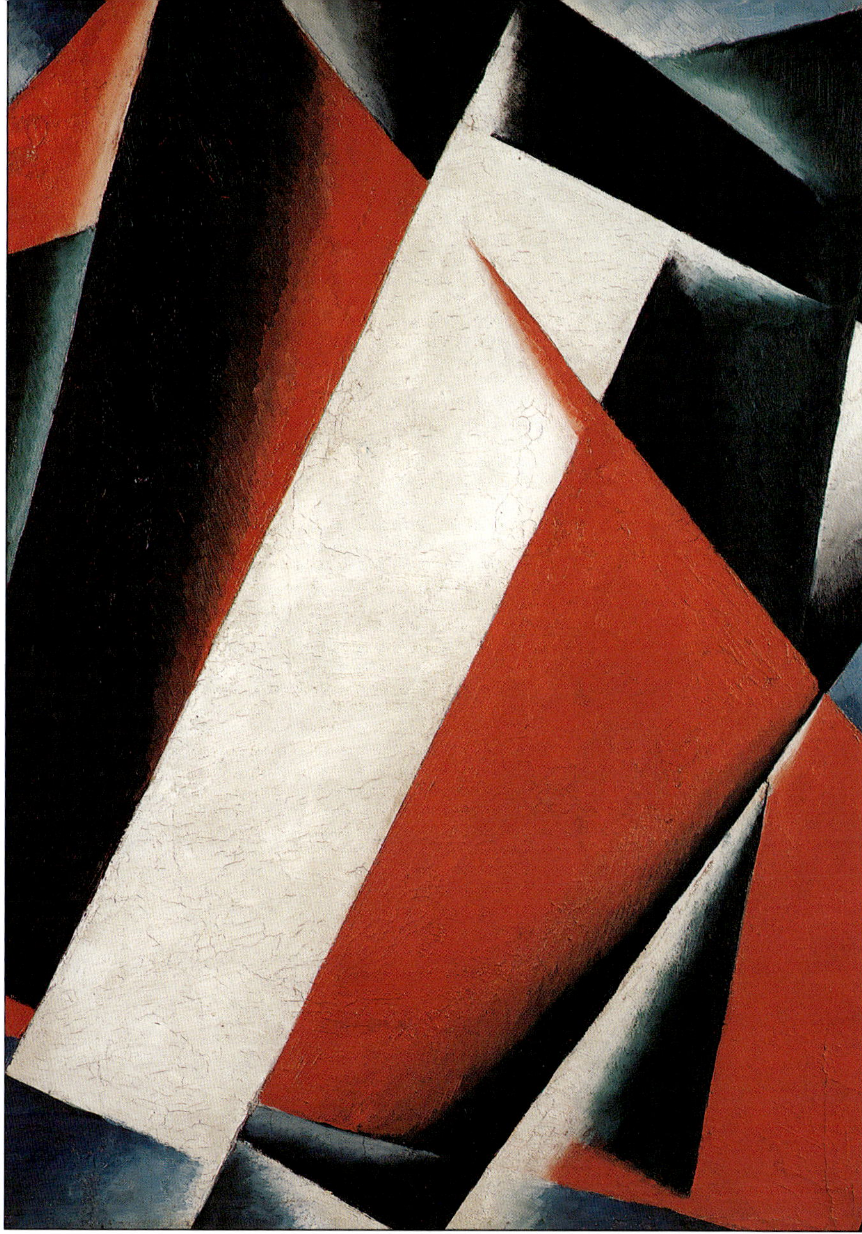

□□ *Painting architectonics.* L. Popova. An ode to a square. A square as an element in the poetic construction of the world.

The world appeared two-dimensional both in the childhood of individual man and in the childhood of mankind as a whole. As evidence of this, we need only look at the drawings of young children and at all the graphic arts of our most distant ancestors. Both children's drawings and the Egyptian reliefs lack a third dimension.

According to physiologists, when we are shown a moving spot on a screen, we at once perceive a two-dimensional object with fixed edges — and we perceive this before any perception of depth or perspective. Flat images then precede three-dimensional ones: a two-dimensional "screen" image is earlier, more primitive then a three-dimensional one. Evidently, both cinema and painting are indebted in no small way to our "flat screen" interpretation of the world — the former for its accessibility and popularity, and the latter for its stability of genre.

Pictures which have perspective, or even axonometry — that is, pictures with depth — are clearly much younger than "orthogonal" ones. However, probably the chief difference between "orthogonal" pictures and those with perspective lies in the constructive, non-static nature of the first. In contrast to perspective drawing, or models, plane drawings have always been, and always will be, the leading method of projection and construction. Thus, we cannot think of them just as reflections of reality, or as pure fictions.

So it turns out, paradoxically, that two-dimensional, flat drawings are in fact much more informative, have more scope, and possess much more content than all those different types of three-dimensional "expressions." Although the methods available to orthogonal drawings are more restricted and limited, this is certainly not an obstacle to revealing the structure of objects. On the contrary, these very limitations are much more effective as means of displaying precisely what is hidden beneath the surface, what is essential.

Different plane drawings of one and the same object often disclose different universals lying within it. The simplest geometric objects — for example, a cone, prism, or cylinder — leave traces of themselves in the form of circles, triangles, squares, and rectangles. This means that we can reduce at least twice as many well-known shapes to the circle, square, and triangle — which results in a clearer and more economic understanding.

In the majority of forms and spaces there is one projection which is dominant and in which events are unfolded. Blocks of apartments, parks, sky-scrapers, and towns are obvious examples of objects which are built upon a single and consistent base. Geometric universals do not only independently strive to become flat representations, they are also unfolded on a plane and themselves organize flat projections.

A flat plane is an intermediary between the world of man-made three-dimensional objects and the world of dimensionless universals, which are abstractions of themes, figures, and ideas. But it is also more than this: a flat plane can gather together the various geometric universals; it can compare them, relate them to each other, and present them as something coherent. In other words, two-dimensionality has the added virtue that it makes possible the classification and systematization of morphological beginnings.

CORPOREAL FORMS AND STRUCTURAL FORMS

In the gradual process of displaying universals, the most important step is to make evident the indicators of space and of form. We need to expose two paradigms, which could equally well be denoted by the terms "corporeal" and "structural."

On the one hand, physical reality is conceived by us in terms of mass, body, volume, capacity; or as spots, zones and so on; that is, as corporeal. On the other hand, physical reality may also be conceived in terms of structure or skeleton — as a totality or flow of lines, points, connections, and relations. Corporeality is something static and artistic, and it is in direct contrast to the tense, dynamic, and graphic concept of structure.

The familiar pair, "figure-background," is the essence of structural representations. Equivalent in some respects to this pair, and more understandable, is the pair, "mass-emptiness." Background and emptiness embrace and envelop pauses and intervals. Conversely, we could say that they glean through them, shine light through them. Just like a liquid, emptiness either forms some boundless reservoir in which bodies and masses float about, or it fills some empty space.

Corporeal models, in their turn, are made from points and lines, vectors and poles, which strive for immateriality and which are more reminiscent of a force-field, a net, or a web.

Structural and corporeal forms are to a large extent merely traces of a position, or a state of mind, which involve an elusive confusion of emphasis. The very instability of concrete representations — so beautifully demonstrated by M. C. Escher[10] in his drawings, where spaces imperceptibly turn into bodies and bodies become their opposites; the spatial backwardness of the modern mass consciousness; and, conversely, the very "obviousness" of everything visual — all these factors force us to conclude that the fundamental categories of space — including those listed here, simply lack a firm and generally accepted definition. In practice, everyone resorts to his own definition. In philosophical literature and in natural science, corporeal forms are sometimes associated with Demosthenes' school, and structural forms with that of Aristotle.

Without particular difficulty, we can give the title "artist" to anyone whose works exhibit some kind of vision — whether this is to be found in the images employed, in the techniques used, or in the subjects depicted. Pevsner[11] and Gabo[12] clearly preferred structural forms; Brancusi[13] and Moore[14] prefer corporeal forms. For several generations of architects, van der Rohe[15] and Le Corbusier represented polar approaches to the subject — not only because they were differently gifted, but also because of the way that each realized his own conception of space. Le Corbusier's work is characterized by its solidity, massiveness, materiality, fullness, and corporeality — all em-

[10] Maurits Cornelis Escher — 1898 - 1971, Dutch graphic artist, known for his prints that use realistic detail to achieve bizarre optical and conceptual effects.

[11] Antoine Pevsner — 1886 - 1962, Russian-French sculptor and painter. With his brother Naum Gabo, he was a leading practitioner of the constructivist style. He left Russia in 1922, living first in Berlin and then settling in Paris, where he remained until his death.

[12] Naum Gabo — 1890 - 1977, Russian-American abstract sculptor in metal. He was born Naum Neemia Pevsner in Russia; he later changed his name to Gabo to avoid confusion with his older brother Antoine Pevsner, also an artist. He left Russia in 1922, spending the years 1922-1932 in Germany and 1932-1946 in England and France . He settled in the United States in 1946 and died in Waterbury, Connecticut.

[13] Constantin Brancusi — 1876 - 1957, Romanian nonsubjective sculptor.

[14] Henry Moore — 1898 - 1986, British sculptor of large-scale abstract works.

[15] Mies van der Rohe — 1886 - 1969, German-American architect; one of the leading exponents of the international style.

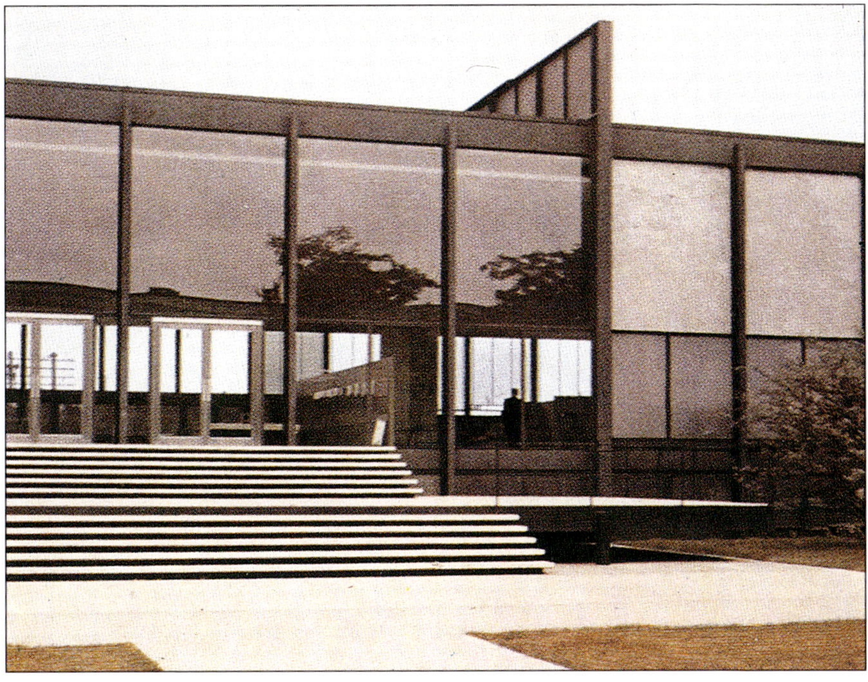

□□ *Illinois Technological Institute in Chicago.* Mies van der Rohe.

In spatial arts, the principle of complementarity is expressed in the structures of these representative specimens of structural (above) and corporeal (below) architecture.

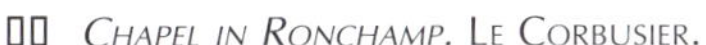

□□ *Chapel in Ronchamp.* Le Corbusier.

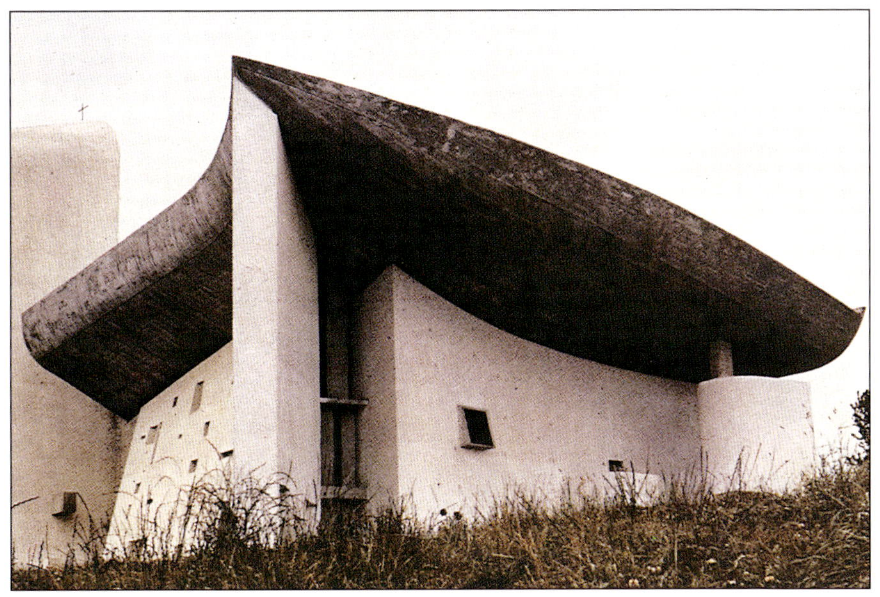

phasized by the huge blocks of reinforced concrete that he uses. And this stands in sharp contrast to van der Rohe's space, which is open and flowing, immaterial, transparent and ghostly, and revealing glass and elegant metal profiles. More modern versions of structural form include the Pompidou Center (Paris), with its escalator and network of tubes and constructions all on its outside wall, and Lloyd's Bank (London). The modern corporeal antitheses to these are the huge rectangular constructions made from concrete and glass.

The work of Pavel Florensky[16] reveals both the counterposition and the mutually fulfilling nature of the illustrative arts — both drawings and paintings — which emerge, above all, from the different technical methods employed (for example, daubs and spots, or lines and strokes). It is not individual personalities, but epochs and cultures which become the bearers of one or another vision of the world — and this vision may be depicted using lines as in structural models, or based on "spots" as in corporeal models. Corresponding to this idea, we have the culture of Germany and the Reformation, and the culture of Italy and Catholicism. Structural and corporeal forms can also be applied easily to the different methods in the left and right hemispheres which once acquired popularity — methods of formation of individual, group, or social consciousnesses — and which were applied to, among other things, towns and architecture.

Architects and architecture are traditionally bearers of a primarily corporeal

[16] Pavel A. Florensky — 1882 - 1937, Russian theologist, philosopher and scientist. One of his last writings appears on page 29 of this issue of geoGraffity.

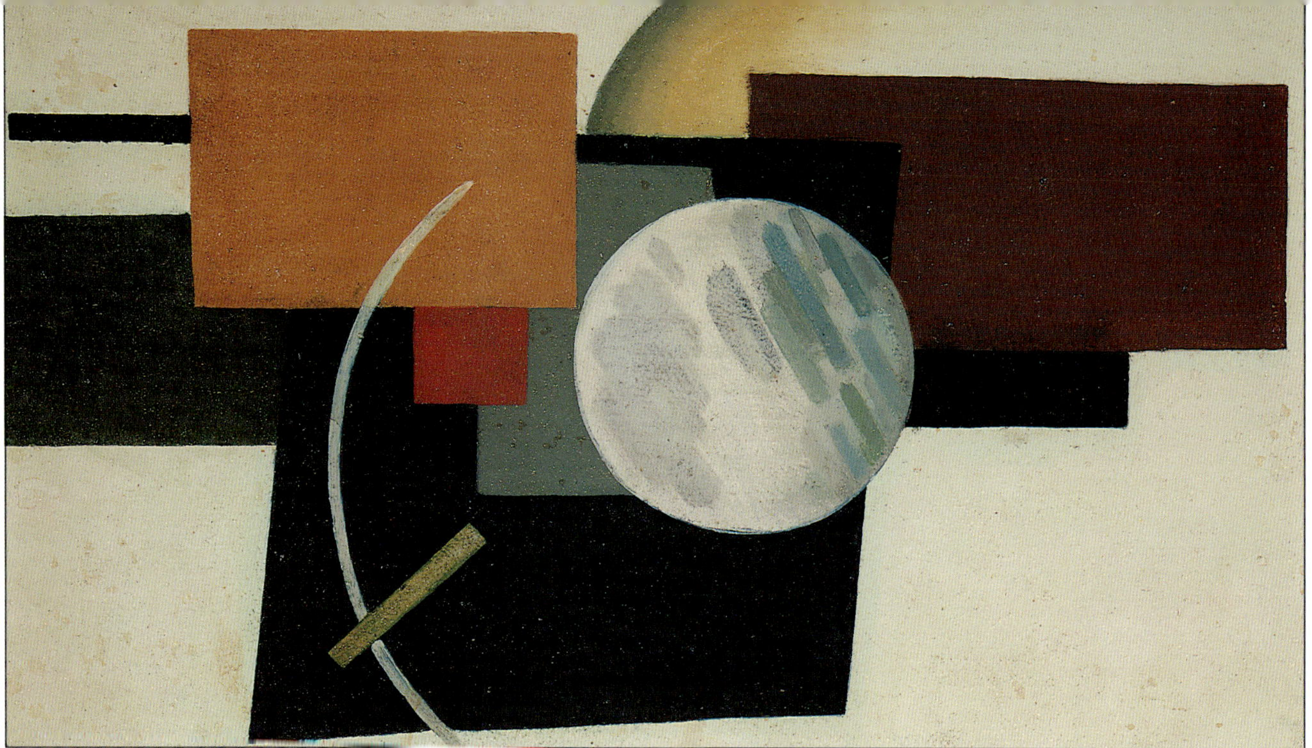

turn of mind: using separate substances and volumes they realize their potential in volumetric planning. The relatively new specializations, such as urban planning which is marked as a rule by structural characteristics, clearly do not fit easily into the usual boundaries which define the creation of things. The main achievements and the particular material of these new professions are best represented by such creations as linear towns, town networks, engineering networks and systems, town infrastructure, street lay-out, design of open space, and limits or borders of regions and zones.

CENTERED FORMS AND AXIAL FORMS

Geometric universals and their productions are the chief bearers of certain disappearing "family" traits which extend to give us two different geometries. These geometries can be defined on the basis of the opposition between, on the one hand, what is orientated, uneven, un-isotropic, and "centered;" and, on the other, what is isotropic, regular, and "axial."

SUPREMATIST COMPOSITION. I. CLUN
A DIALOGUE BETWEEN A SQUARE AND A CIRCLE. THE SQUARE AND THE CIRCLE TRIUMPH IN THE ART OF THE TWENTIETH CENTURY.

CHRISTIAN HIEROGLYPHICS. A CIRCLE INSIDE A SQUARE, A CROSS INSCRIBED IN A CIRCLE — AN ELEMENTARY MODEL OF THE WORLD. THE FOUR CARDINAL DIRECTIONS (NORTH, EAST, SOUTH AND WEST), THE ANCIENT T-O TYPE MAPS, AND THE FOUR ELEMENTS ACCORDING TO THE ANCIENT GREEKS ARE ALL PHENOMENA OF THE SAME NATURE.

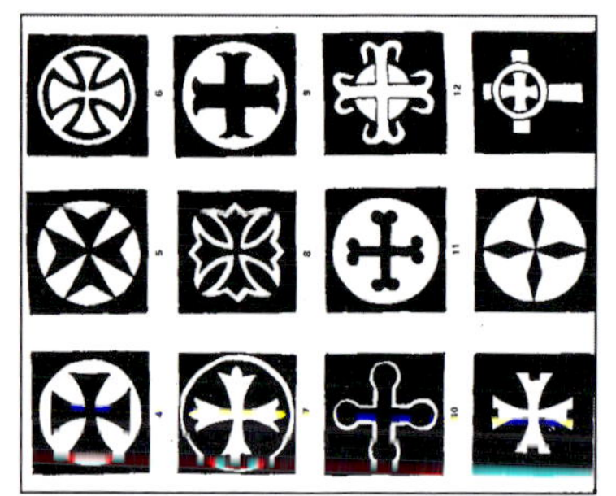

Some examples of isotropic orders built on the basis of axial forms are the fantasies of Hilberzeimer[17] and Koolhauss[18] about networks of American towns, or Candilis'[19] town plans, or linear towns, straight streets, rectangular mega-structures, multi-story apartments, offices, and hotels, skyscrapers with endless floors, church naves, and arcades. Examples of centered ordering are the radical circular plans laid down as designs for ideal towns —with enclosed circular streets and boulevards, communal buildings, and a nuclear organization.

However, centered forms and axial forms are linked not only by such twinning relations, which keep them on one level; they are also linked by relations of succession. A linear axis, in comparison with a point or the center of a circle, is

[17] Eugiwe Hilberzeimer — contemporary German urban designer.

[18] Rain Koolhauss — contemporary Dutch architect.

[19] George Candilis — contemporary French architect.

both more complete and more complicated. At the base of the chief differences between axial and centered forms is the category of movement. Movement can be depicted by points, strokes, spots, and blurs — that is , by positional, static, and scalar representations. Or we can depict it using extended, dynamic, vector representations.

The list of relations between axial and centered forms requires two final categories: first, the systems of measurement defined as "linear" and "angular"; and secondly, those most important space-time representations — such as those which are continuous, those which are marked by a beginning and by stages of a journey, and those which are cyclical and ringed by constantly changing trajectories.

Just like music, space and form have a two-fold nature. One side is based on instantaneous, simultaneous presentations, an original "one-ness"; and the other side is based on objects which are laid out, extended, and placed in succession. We are concerned here with different ways of ordering a mass of things: we can talk about what is simultaneous, or instantaneous, or what occurs at different times — or we can talk about what is continuing, lasting.

OPEN FORMS AND CLOSED FORMS

Turning now to the relations "point-line" and "figure-background," it is important to note the distribution of roles between the different elements of each pair. Lines and figures possess a particular type of activity; points and backgrounds are passive. Passive points and backgrounds are more like intervals, or fillers. When we isolate them at a particular level they can only be made to form, at best, their own type of negative depictions, or some type of constellation of points, or generalizations, which result in a picture with no rough edges. The conditions of "open-ness" and "closed-ness" are defined in the first instance by active material: they are defined by the position, the arrangement, and the orientation of lines and figures. Both position and orientation are given a very distinct topological meaning by familiar expressions — along an axis, across an axis, around a center, or from a center.

INTERPRETATIONS OF UNIVERSALS AND THE DECIPHERING OF REALITY

There is a particularly interesting interrelation between what is straight and what is curved, and between the square and the circle. In the ontogenesis of man-made forms, it is unquestionably the circle and the cycle which take first place. The circle, as the most complete embodiment of symmetry and centeredness, is much older, more primary, than axial constructions, crosses, squares, or rectangles. Axial forms are essentially more complex, appear later, and are undoubtedly more effective — both in the theoretical and in the practical sense — when it comes to solving the concrete problems which arise in the course of history. In a certain sense, the movement of material culture is a movement from the circular form to the square form. The antiquity of the circle is directly confirmed, first by the most rudimentary linguistic constructions — such as the expression "a circle of friends" — where the word "circle" has lost its original geometric-spatial content. Second, we find evidence when we look at successively changing cultural levels in traditional settlements: in the vast majority of cases, rectangular dwellings turn out to lie above ancient circular ones; and

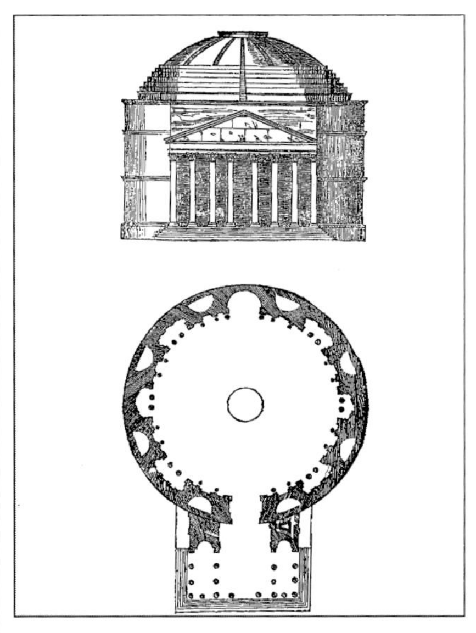

□□ THE PANTHEON IS BASED UPON A CIRCLE WHICH IS A PROJECTION OF AN IDEAL SPHERE, ONE OF THE SACRAL FIGURES OF ANCIENT GREECE.

in towns themselves, rectangular networks of streets are now taking the place of radial or circular forms. This generalization does not, of course, exclude the possibility of humans reacting against axial and rectangular forms; nor does it prevent the appearance of a number of marginal, in-between forms, "centaur-forms" which are simultaneously both circular and rectangular. Domes, cupolas, arches, apses, and vaults may all quite possibly be no more than reminders of the circular fore-runners of churches themselves.

A piece of string attached to a stick is much simpler and certainly much older than Egyptian triangles and squares. But it looks as though the true conception of a circle is older still than even the first compass. The first examples of circles — round dwellings and circular dishes — were much too curved and were more like ovals.

The archaic nature of the circle, and its "forgotten" presence, make it fully un-

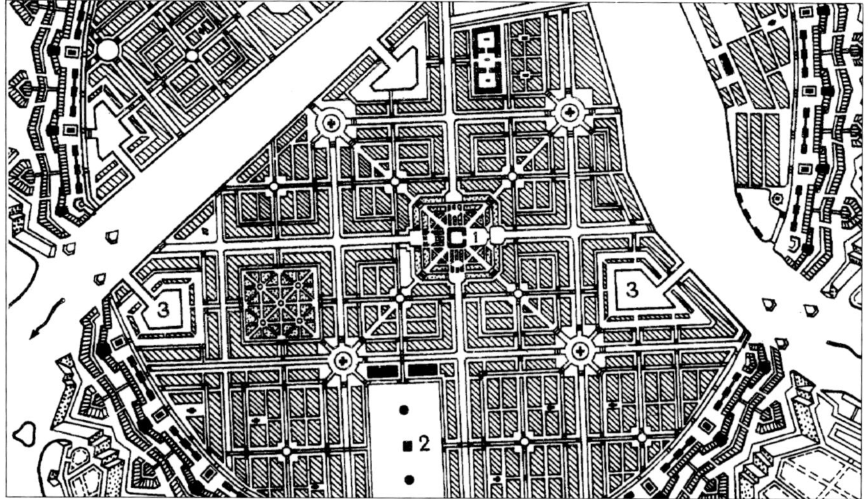

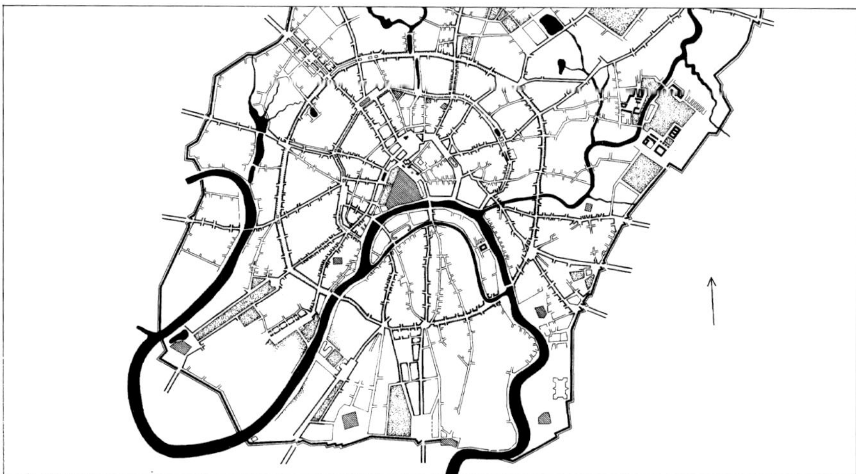

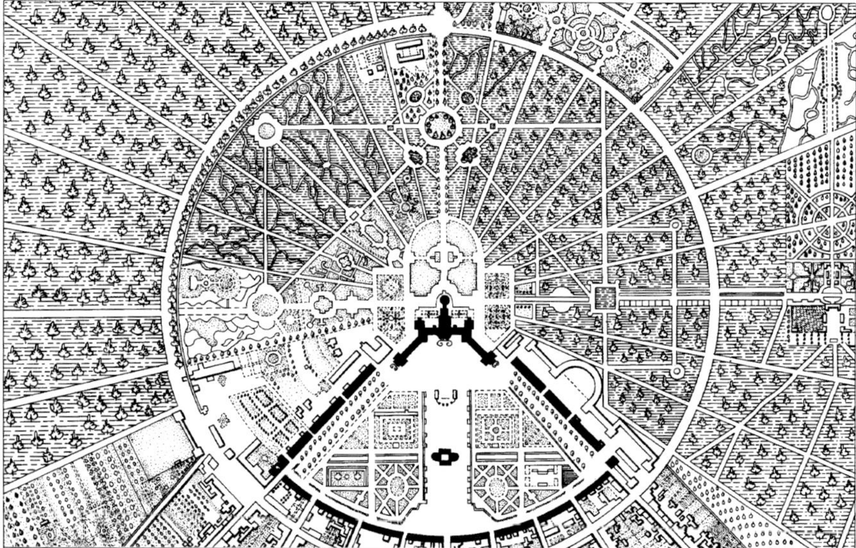

□□ The artificially synthesized crystal of St. Petersburg (top), the round Moscow (middle), shaped in harmony with the environment, and the perfect circle of Karlsruhe (bottom) as an infinite polyhedron.

derstandable that — paradoxically — it should be included in futuristic, fantastical ideas and pictures about a future or ultra-modern world, and that simultaneously it should preserve its position in the most conservative spheres and regions — in jewelry, details of clothing, money, crockery, and so on.

Despite the firm, two-way connection between the circle and the square, they nevertheless give rise to two different classes of reality — to radial-circular plans, or to rectangular plans; to centered cathedrals, or to basilicas.

Man's acquisition of the circle was just as difficult, just as long a process, and just as dramatic as the "straight and rectangular" revolution which followed. This second revolution led to the appearance of our own civilization — a civilization which rests on the artificially-synthesized, characterless square. The incitement to revolution was the discovery that the right angle and the straight line were more effective instruments than centers and points: a set-square and ruler were preferable to a pair of compasses and a piece of string. In one sense, we could define the whole of modern civilization as The Civilization of the Straight Line and the Right Angle.

The square and the straight line are firmly linked to a whole row of extremely labor-consuming human achievements — the perfectly straight line, perpendicularity, parallel lines, and equivalent angles. These are all materials which can be used to create an enormous family of figures that are independent of a geometrical center, and that can be defined as "rational." The rational square can be distinguished from the "irrational" circle in one instance at the level of mathematical description (the circle being based on the recurring number 3.14). Equally important is the practical matter of being able to tessellate blocks with each other (Alexander[20]), and being unable to tessellate spheres.

The opposition between what is rational and straight, and what is irrational and curved, is easily absorbed by the artistic consciousness. This consciousness produces whole classes of straight and circular forms — forms which belong to the world of architecture, and to the world of things, and which rest on their own geometric language or "jargon." The personal handwriting of masters like Gaudier[21] or Soleri[22] express a preference for what is curved, circular, flowing, organic, oval, and so do whole classes of manmade objects — means of transport, factories, instruments, etc. In relation to all these, curvilinearity can be understood as engendered by movement — among other things, by movement in symbiosis with man, in ergonomic mutual connections; by movement which is characterized by fluency of transition, uninterruptedness, lack of sharp borders, and lack of a clear expression of its constituents.

[20] Christopher Alexander — b. 1936, American architect, educator, head of Center for Environmental Structure, Berkeley, California.

[21] Henri Gaudier-Brzeska, original name Henri Gaudier — 1891 - 1915, French artist, one of the earliest abstract sculptors; an outstanding exponent of the Vorticist movement. He was killed in combat in World War I.

[22] Paolo Soleri — b. 1919, Italian-born U.S. architect, designer, and city planner, who coined the term arcology (architecture plus ecology) to describe his ideal construction, which would exist in but not disturb nature.

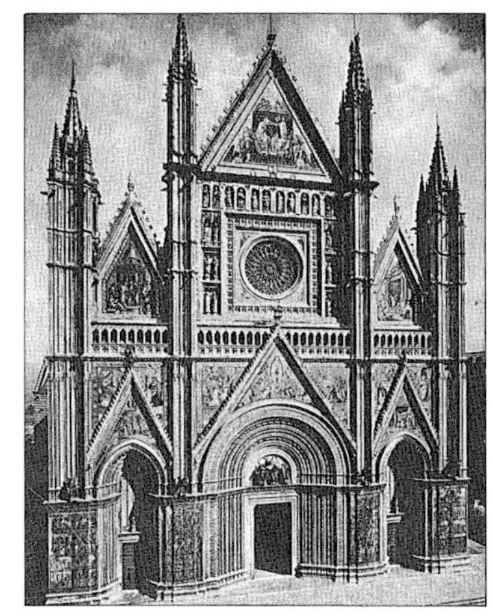

Images of the heavenly and the earthly worlds united in architectonics on the façade of a Gothic cathedral. The Trinity of the Divine Structure of the Universe is emphasized by the triune (triangularity) of the façade. Four pinnacles growing out of the folds of the cathedral accentuate the four elements and the four cardinal points.

On the other hand, if we want a clearer understanding of the language of "straight line and rectangle," it is more natural to look at discreteness, at the tendency of certain constituents to express themselves, whether this be looked for in modules of equipment, apartments, rooms, or houses, or in regions with rectangular outlines.

A discussion of the relations "straight-curved" and "square-circular" would be incomplete without mention of the places of triangles and the zig-zag lines. These are usually ranked along with, and on a par with, squares, circles, and straight and curved lines. The triangle is the most economical and the most appealing of figures: it is indisputably one of man's most brilliant discoveries. Nevertheless, it seems somehow to have found itself in the position of a pariah, of a discovery half-forgotten. It is purely exotic to make use of triangular or hexagonal forms. Our passionless evolution preferred the square to the triangle: for all practical purposes, it reduced the triangle to that infinite number of polygons having five, six, seven, or more sides. All these polygons in effect represent a chain of uninterrupted transformations between the square and the circle while the zig-zag line represents a transition between the curved and the straight line. In other words, polygons and zig-zag lines are, it seems, intermediate, marginal, mediating figures; and the clearest representatives of polygons and zig-zag lines are the triangle and the simple angle.

The decision to relegate both the triangle and the zig-zag to a class of less principal figures is based on two considerations: first, their lower popularity rating, which can be verified statistically. Second, both the triangle and the zig-zag line can be reduced to half of a square, cut down a diagonal; they can both be reduced to their own type of deformed square, one which has passed the trapezium stage; they can both be reduced to a generalized curve, and so on. If these considerations are unappealing, at least they complete the two relations "straight line - curved line" and "square - circle."

Axial and square forms, while co-existing with centered and circular forms, simultaneously alter them in the course of evolution. Today there is a distinct predominance of axial and square forms, both in everyday life and in architecture. Town planners, architects, and researchers rarely turn to radial or ring schemes, fan shapes, or other derivatives: round houses and ring schemes are thought to be too exotic.

At the same time though, it would be wrong to say that the circle has descended into oblivion. There is now a very evident interest in the circle as an antithesis to the square, as a means of contrast, something which completes and shows up the square and the axial. What is most important is the very possibility that there can be a generic, genetic lack of correspondence between first and last forms, between wholes and elements. Axial order can emerge from curved, centered constituents like the round towers of Marina City, parts of Canberra, or Tange's[23] megastructure. And, similarly, what is un-isotropic can be, and is, constructed using squares and right angles. For example, the mono-centered town of Le Corbusier was built on a rectangular grid, which did not in the slightest degree alter its morphological structure.

ABSTRACTED UNIVERSALS AND CORRELATED UNIVERSALS

It is obvious that geometric forms do not exist purely independently, self-sufficiently, and in their own enclosed region of space. Geometry is to be found arranged in reality, oriented and suited to the surrounding world; at the same time, it also orients and organizes that very world.

Essentially, we are speaking about some kind of supra-geometric construction, where phenomena and objects mingle. The simplest, or the first, of the ordered worlds, man builds around himself. The second, more complex world is created for everyone; it turns out to be more objective, and it is fixed by some center which is extra-personal — for example, the center of a town, country, or national territory.

Architectural space continues to work perfectly satisfactorily, not so much despite, but rather because of, the very archaism of its own mythological truth, its own common sense. In the system of these representations of the world, the world and the earth present themselves in the same way in which we see them. That is, for architects the Earth appears as flat, both in relative and in absolute presentations — just as it always has done.

Each of these presentations has its own particular characteristics. The relative world — with the observer at the center — divides into regions of upper and lower, left and right, as well as "here" — inside, near oneself, in front — and "there" — outside, beyond the horizon, behind. The natural upright orientation of man's body and bearing gives a sufficiently full structure both to personal space and to personal territory. The principal characteristics of the relative world are its tangibility and its secluded and introverted nature.

The absolute world possesses an absolute center, an absolute axis, and four "directions." The absolute world appeared after the relative world and was based on it, and today it preserves a number of the traits and characteristics of its predecessor. At the same time, this world is much more fully revealed, more extraverted, but finite.

Architectural space is conventionally defined as Euclidean and is described by three axes — the vertical, horizontal, and frontal. These three axes intersect at a point which lies at the center of the world and from which all measurements are taken. The axes may be transformed into a flat surface on which two versions of the single world are unfolded — the horizontal and vertical version, or the frontal version. Both versions have as their basis an identical pair of perpendicularly intersecting axes; but in one case these axes are oriented through the points of the compass, while in the other these axes appear as vertical and horizontal. The unreconcilable nature of mutually perpendicular axes is overcome, and somewhat mollified, by the introduction of diagonals. As a consequence, we are left with an eight-sided horizontal world and a whole family of slopes and oblique lines all laid down on a vertical plane.

Vertical and horizontal projections took shape even before the appearance of architectural projection, with its tradition of depicting plans and façades. The profession of architecture has successfully used such projections. This isolation of plans and façades is undoubtedly a mark of man's highly developed capacity to mold the environment. It results from an already formed capacity to construct imaginary models, pictures abstracted from reality.

Plans and façades, once formed, continue to exist for some time in relative isolation — outside the world of strong mutual connections. It is not easy, for example, to reconstruct the authentic façades of excavated buildings on the strength of their foundations alone. Nor does a photograph help us to construct a plan.

Pictures on the horizontal plane are more ancient than those on the vertical plane. But "verticalism," and the façades engendered by it, are a consequence of the application of many horizons — a consequence of the sensation of layer after layer on top of one another. Plans derive from the agrarian tradition: they are based on earthly figures, and first and foremost on the square. The erecting of the circle, the heavenly cupola, on a square foundation, thus forming a second, upper level, is a

[23] Kenzo Tange — b. 1927, Japanese architect, professor emeritus at Tokyo University.

characteristic theme in most cultures.

The importance of the plan is a natural consequence of the importance we place on the interiors of our homes. Caves and primitive pit-dwellings, tombs and graves, which all have a defined plan, do not really display any outside face at all. They are, then, a type of façade-less architecture. The plan was primary both in ontogeny, and in phylogeny — every construction begins from a plan, from a laying out of foundations. The foundations, then, remain as the parting speech of every house. To some extent, plan forms and façade forms — the latter of which become "panoramic form" in relation to towns — both define, and are defined by, two different levels, two tiers of our physical surroundings. Plan forms are the essence of the architecture of foundations and walls; façade forms are the essence of roofs and towers.

Given certain assumptions, we can talk about the predominance either of plan or of façade forms. We can talk of the silhouette-less, flat plan form of towns like St. Petersburg or Versailles; or of the panoramic façade towns like Moscow and Prague.

After centuries of human evolution, plans have become established instruments for the control of huge expanses of space, covering entire countries and continents. Such plans contain unquestionably constructive, active, potential, and distinct signs of successful application: it was precisely the plan approach which gave birth to Versailles, and to entire towns "under one roof."

Panoramas, or façades, on the other hand, are marked in the everyday, popular consciousness with the stamp of passivity. They are more instruments of reflecting what already exists, and not by any means instruments of transformation. Panoramas and façades prevail in the sphere of "natural" depictions of the environment, in semi-professional and amateur activity in art, above all in landscape painting. In contrast to the plan, where man degenerates into points and trajectories, the panorama permits clear human dimensions with which it is directly and graphically linked and correlated. Façade and panorama forms, at the end of a lengthy cultural evolution, are synonyms of self-assurance, self-awareness, man's upright position, possession of one's own home — feeling oneself to be a person.

Every correlated plan contains a totality of symmetric, counter-balanced coordinate axes, with a definite center, or origin. As a rule, a façade or panorama possesses a single, pronounced, and dominant horizontal axis, which creates the impression that everything has been cut in half. In contrast to the plan, where circles and squares are depicted without distortion, undamaged, in a panorama we may find halved circles, rhombi, squares, crosses, and so on. The horizon is, in its own way, an imaginary mirrored surface which tends to complete both the coordinate system itself and the universals in it — making them symmetrical.

The completeness of the plane matrix in effect both guarantees and explains the even and four-fold nature of the plane. At the same time, maybe the property of façades and panoramas that gives the impression of halfness both explains and guarantees their characteristic three-fold nature — that is, being made up from socles, with a central panel and ends. (A very rare exception to this canon was Melnikov's[24] Narkomtyazhprom[25] building, which extended in two directions from the horizontal axis — that is, not only upwards, but down below the ground as well — thus re-establishing geometric wholeness.)

The independent nature of plan forms and façade forms can be seen not only in the natural lack of convergence between the various elevations of one object (although exceptions to this exist in the form of those Russian churches where the contours of the façade coincide with the outline of the apses). There are even good grounds for speaking of certain qualities of universals which are characteristic either for plans or for façades. More than this, it is quite possible to construct a sort of "collective" façade-planar meta-construction; and then we find that the façade meta-geometry displays its triangularity and its impressions of halfness, and the planar geometry is marked by the presence of squares and circles.

Maybe it is precisely this predetermination, this pre-destination of certain universals, which makes geometrical inversions so provoking — for example, façade-like triangles on a plan, or planar spirals and circles on a façade (both again introduced by Melnikov). We may suspect some tectonic influence is at work when a figure in a panorama reminds us of a pyramid or a pediment. But there are no tectonic forces in the outlines of a plan or master-plan: here, at least, gravity is not the force to blame. The genetic kinship, the coherence of plan and panorama, only serve to confirm their innate geometric nature. The discussion of that nature I leave until a later date. ■■

[24] Konstantine S. Melnikov — 1890 - 1974, Russian architect, constructivist.

[25] Narkomtyazhprom — an abbreviation of People's Commissariat of Heavy Industry. The building was not constructed.

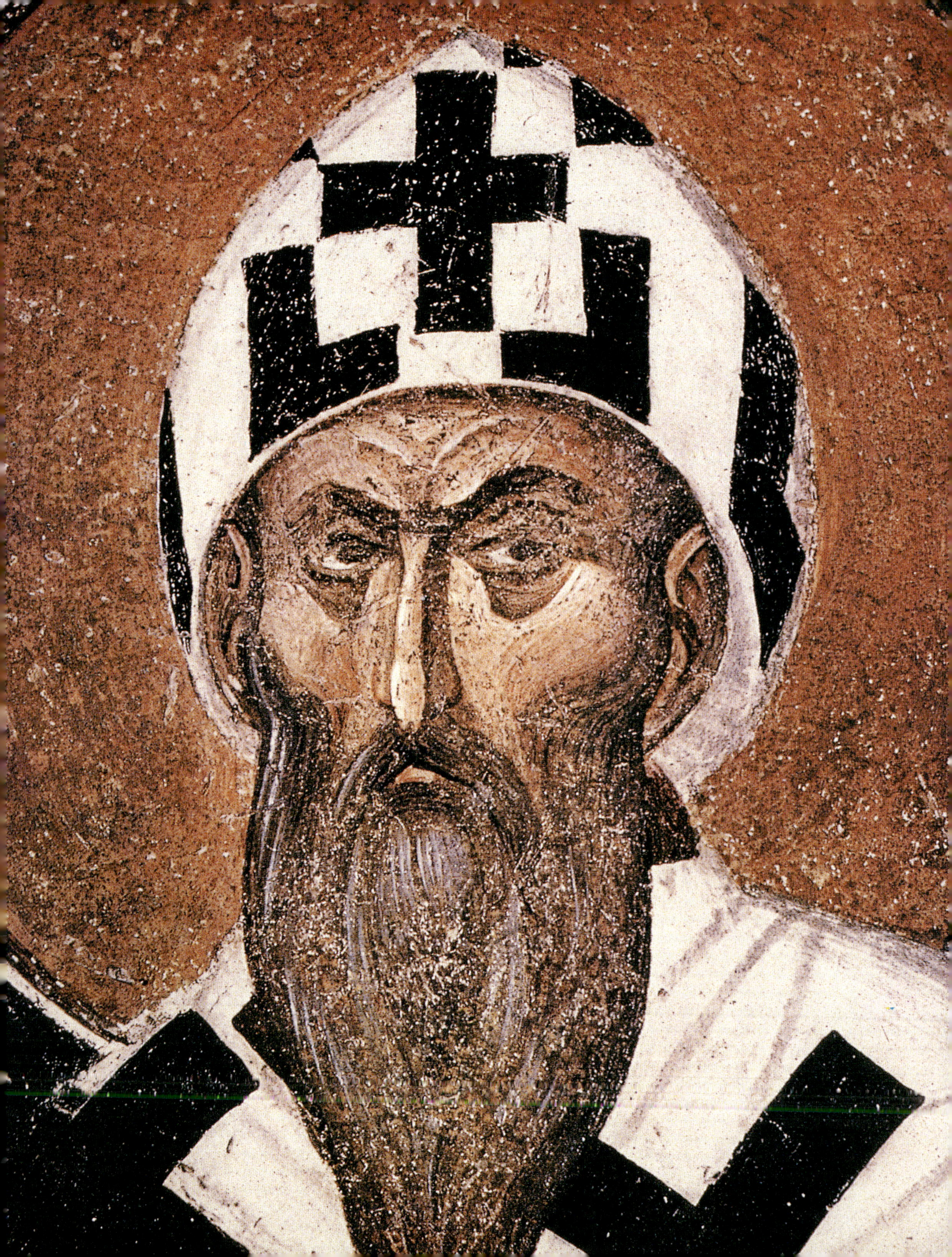

the point / pavel a. florensky

PAVEL A. FLORENSKY (1882-1937) — A RUSSIAN THINKER AND THEOLOGIAN. HIS CREATIVE WORK FORMS AN INTEGRAL PART OF THE INTELLECTUAL AND SPIRITUAL CULTURE IN THE EPOCH OF THE EARLY TWENTIETH-CENTURY RUSSIAN RELIGIOUS-PHILOSOPHIC RENAISSANCE. ACCORDING TO FLORENSKY, THE SPIRITUAL WORLD IS AS REAL AS THE PHYSICAL, AND HE SAW IN SPATIALITY ONE OF THE PROOFS OF ITS REALITY. TO KNOW A THING IS, FOR THE PHILOSOPHER, EQUAL TO CUTTING IT OUT, AS IT WERE, OF THE SPACE SURROUNDING IT. IN HIS WORKS FLORENSKY OFTEN USED METAPHORS BASED ON BRIGHT, VISUAL, SPATIAL IMAGES. HE WAS INTERESTED IN THE METAPHYSICS OF THE PICTORIAL PLANE IN PAINTING, INCLUDING ICON-PAINTING, AND IN THE CONNECTION OF DIRECT AND REVERSE PERSPECTIVE WITH THE SPIRITUAL SENSE OF THE THINGS DEPICTED.
THE WORLD ACCORDING TO FLORENSKY IS A REALITY OF IMAGES AND SIGNS, A KIND OF MAP. SEEING HIS PHILOSOPHY AS A COURSE IN PRACTICAL SYMBOLISM, FLORENSKY MADE UP HIS MIND TO COMPILE A UNIVERSAL DICTIONARY OF SYMBOLS — A SYMBOLARIUM — WHICH WOULD PLAY THE ROLE OF A LEGEND FOR HIS WORLD MAP. RECENTLY A DRAFT OF THIS DICTIONARY WAS PUBLISHED IN RUSSIA. THE HEAD WORDS ARE THE PRIMITIVE GEOMETRIC IMAGES (TRIANGLE, SPHERE, QUADRANGLE, ETC.) AND THEIR COMBINATIONS. IT WAS TO THOSE SPATIAL ELEMENTS THAT FLORENSKY'S BASIC VIEW OF THE WORLD BOILED DOWN. DUE TO THEM, FLORENSKY 'S WORLD MAP YIELDED TO DECIPHERING AND WAS FILLED WITH SENSE.THE FIRST SECTION IN THE SYMBOLARIUM IS DEVOTED TO THE "POINT" AS THE ELEMENTARY (INITIAL) AND AT THE SAME TIME THE MOST POLYSEMANTIC SYMBOL. BUT HIS GRANDIOSE PLAN WAS NEVER TO BE COMPLETED. IN 1933 FLORENSKY WAS SENTENCED TO TEN YEARS IN EXILE. IN 1937 HE WAS EXECUTED IN ONE OF THE GULAG'S CAMPS ON THE SOLOVETSKIE ISLES IN THE WHITE SEA.

By its significance in diverse spheres of thought, the point, the simplest of graphic symbols, is the *ab-ovo* beginning. As such, the point embodies the foundations of the antinomy of corresponding spheres: as the beginning of everything, the point is and is not. That is why it is made into a symbol, first, of the range of being in its most diverse meanings, and second, of the range of non-being. In the final analysis, the assertion that being and non-being can be related to the same symbol endows the point with a number of symbolic potentials capable of the most diverse applications.

The point's antinomic significance must be matched by a graphic antinomy, without which it would, naturally, remain sort of suspended in the air and be artificial and arbitrary. In fact, from time immemorial to our day, geometry has offered two lines of understanding the point. They are not reducible to one another and are antinomically interlocked; one may be confident that they will be projected in the mathematics of the future to the end of time, any later changes and improvements in mathematics notwithstanding. Either aspect of the point's antinomy may gain prominence at any period of historical thought, and claim the final triumph. But the other side only "plays possum" and, rather than being destroyed, simply takes a respite from previously experienced tensions. Then, coming into its own, it soon takes up its refurbished arms to regain its forfeited dominance, if only for a time. In the process, the structure of social thought as a coherent whole always prevents the traditions of either interpretation of the point from total rupture: the link of ideological genealogy stretches thin but never snaps, for any interpretation of the point means something else. The point and space are relative, and either may be logically accentuated; but that emphasis will only enhance — albeit as some kind of secondary emphasis — the nature of the link. Thus, from the beginning of time, the point and space have remained locked in a struggle for supremacy. A space of points is opposed by points in space; a set of points, albeit of an original structure, is opposed in thought by a whole continuum where points are but assumed to be arranged in a particular manner. In the former case, thought strives to turn space into an abstraction, into a kind of extra thought to be added to the true reality of points. But in the latter case, thought perceives as real only the continuum, the whole space, with points being dismissed as but thinkable fictions. In the former case, it is not possible to posit a set, for it is a "single" object of thought, without a uniting principle, which circumstance, given the purely spatial content of a set's presumed elements, can only mean a spatial medium. However, in the second case, the posited whole environment — continuum — would be absolutely impervious to thought if it lacked the elements actually locked within it. In addition, in an environment the substance of which is purely spatial, these sustaining supports of thought can only be spatial, that is, points. Points signify whole space, which in turn requires points.

Historically, the most succinct definition of a point was given by the Pythagorean school: "A point is a unit with a position" (μοναζ εχουζα θεσιν). So it is a unit which occupies a position in space; there has never been a happier and more precise definition, if one takes the point-space antinomy as a point of departure. It follows from this that a geometrical form is a set of points; any discussion of triangular, multiangular and pyramidal figures presupposes making geometrical forms out of points. Waiting in the wings is the use of points to build a physical world consisting of physical points: the Pythagoreans have never drawn a substantive distinction between a physical point and a geometrical point, between a physical body and a geometrical body.

According to P. Tannery[1] the Pythagorean idea that things are numbers was, before Zeno,[2] taken to mean that bodies are sums of physical points and that the properties of bodies are related to the properties of the appropriate numbers. This definition of a point was pre-eminent in the time of Aristotle and survived until the time of Euclid. After the critique by Zeno, howerever, the point began to be interpreted in a symbolic sense, which historians have related to the time of Philolaus.[3]

By contrast, the Eleatic school opposed the point, monad of the Pythagorean school, with the idea of a "single whole," by which was meant space. But the Pythagorean definition, by using the word "position" (*θεσιν*), already provided a hint of the spatial medium, without which one could not use the word "position." By contrast, the Eleatics described the notion of a single whole only in negative terms, through set elimination, separation, motion, etc. It follows that the notion of "single" can exist only until the set of units related to it has been expelled from it. In the extreme case, before disappearing altogether these units are perceived as points in the Euclidean definition — the last justifications of intellectual apperception. In the Euclidean definition, points are perceived as evanescent little bodies: a point is a body verging on self-destruction. Between the Pythagorean and the Euclidean definitions lies the entire history of mathematics; despite the seemingly irrevocable nature of Zeno's victory over Pythagoras's definition, and despite the Euclidean definition based on that victory, the Pythagorean concept re-emerged many times. Are not the people of our day inclined to regard the point as Pythagoras did, although with far less clarity?

In the seventeenth century, Pascal used to mock Cavalier de Meret, who, not being a mathematician, did not understand the notion of continuity and so thought of a line as consisting of points. In the seventeenth century, one could impute such naiveté, taking no trouble to adduce proof, and confine oneself to a mere grin. In the nineteenth century, however, we have witnessed countless attempts, apparently first plotted in the Herbert school and thoughtfully developed by Riemann,[4] to generate space by the motion of the point. Set in motion, the point creates the uni-dimensional form variety of a line; a line, by its motion, generates a two-dimensional form, a surface; the motion of the surface gives rise to a three-dimensional form, space; the latter provides the basis for quadri-dimensional form, and so on. The different nature of these motions, according to Riemann, is responsible for the different spatial structures of each respective number

[1] "Le concept scientifique du continu." *Revue philosophique,* 1885, No. 11

[2] "before Zeno" — Here, of course, Zeno is the disciple of Parmenides, born in southern Italy in the 5th century B.C., and not Zeno the Stoic, the founder of the Stoic school of philosophy.

[3] Philolaus of Tarentum — a Pythagorean, contemporary of Socrates and Democritus.

[4] George Friedrich Bernard Riemann — 1826-1866, German mathematician who conducted studies in the field of multi-dimensional differential geometry and the theory of complex variable functions.

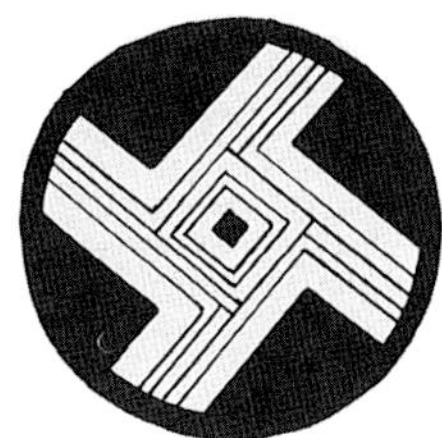

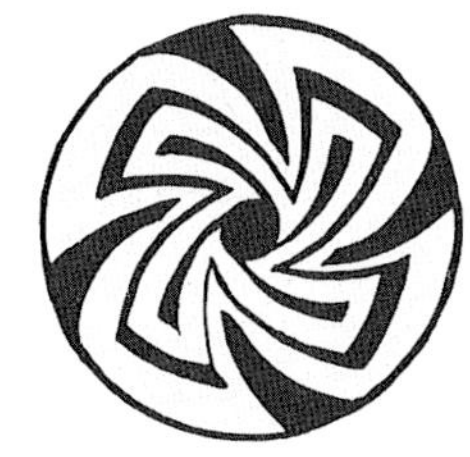

□□ Fragments of designs on ceramics from Peru. All the elements represent different interpretations of the so-called "solar" sign, an ancient ornamental archetype, which embodies the origin and the universal energy radiating out of a central point, as well as the sign of God and creation. However, the black dot in the center may be indicative of the symbol's negative "chthonic" nature.

of dimensions and the varying curvature of each point. Riemann's construction gained general acceptance, but no amount of improvements introduced into it could alter the basic concept that spatial formations, space itself, or spaces themselves are nothing but point variations. In other words, in mathematics and later in philosophy, the notion of space as consisting of points gained currency, so that points could no longer be regarded as units with a position of their own. But this attitude to the "position" problem was and remains well-nigh untenable, since people are apt to pretend that the "position," which eventually turns out to be purely spatial, may actually be determined outside space. The fact is that these points — units — possess no "qualitative" differences among them and so must either merge into a single point in our consciousness or gain a spatial distinction. The man who espoused the concept of space made up of points as units was Georg Cantor. According to Cantor, everything can be regarded as a set — totalities of quite different, individualized elements which yield units through abstraction, all mentally united into a single object. A set is the generic notion of cardinal and ordinal "numbers." Although forced to extend the natural numbers row beyond the finite limits to create trans-finite figures and types of magnitude, Cantor did not give up the old basic proposition that "everything is a set" (πολλα εστι τα ουτα), as with Zeno's formulation of the Pythagorean doctrine, or the Pythagorean idea that "things are numbers." Not only does Cantor not relinquish the proposition, but, for its sake, he devises his trans-finite numbers in order to continue asserting that everything is numbers. The chief thrust and true *raison-d'etre* of his work was to understand the continuous as a variation of the discrete, to put together a continuity of points, and to express the given set by a number. Cantor's and his successors' work on the problem of a continuum produced a whole system of finely-polished notions of infinite value in many diverse respects: the study of continuum-related notions probably made greater progress in the three decades of this work than it had in the previous three thousand years. But the principal task — the logical construction of a continuum toward points-units and the elimination of the environment in which these points have a "position" — is still where it was before Pythagoras: it is possible to construct a continuum only against the backdrop of an intuition of assumed wholeness, and when this intuition is honestly exorcised, no continuum is achieved. This is natural, for when we fail to see a hiatus, the gap between points which can be "beheld" only speculatively, we cannot construct a continuum, for we do not know whether what we have built has gaps or is "tied together," as Cantor put it; continuum or false continuum are no different, if we are guided only by our logical taste. Incidentally, the continuum "intuition" also deeply penetrates every set of points (*Punktmannigfaltigkeit, Punktmenge*), for the very distinction of points as space points is only possible against the backdrop of this space; and if we actually took them, with no quantitative difference and differing only by their position in space, outside space they would cease to differ from one another and surely merge together, for space is precisely their *principium individuationis*. This is an objection of substance, and historically, we are, doubtless, riding the crest of the Cantorean wave; this set of notions in mathematics has a future in the short term. Besides, as suggested by Boskowic[5] and Faraday, the notion of matter as a system of centers of force may apparently soon merge with the Cantorean understanding of space; and, after ether has dissolved in space and space has turned into ether, we are far from being inclined to associate points — the primary elements of space, or space-time, to be more precise — with *ab-ovo* matter.

[5] Roger Joseph Boscowic — 1711-1787, mathematician and astronomer who was born in Dalmatia but who spent most of his life in Italy and France.

So much for the development and strengthening of one aspect of antinomy. There has been, however, a parallel growth and strengthening of another aspect, that of negating point elements and proclaiming "wholeness" to be the reality. This is the chief message of Bergsonism and related schools of thought. Time, continued duration, and space are truly real, while sets in them are abstract fictions, inventions added to reality, an "opinion" (δοξα), as the Eleatics would put it. And thus, our thought returns to the Euclidean concept of a point as but negation of space-time, as nothing, zero, "the ghost of an extinct magnitude."

While the Pythagorean concept treated the point as a "unit," the Euclideans viewed it as nothing. Hence, one realizes the dual significance of a point or a number of points as graphic symbols in the most diverse spheres, meant either to denote unity, indivisibility, wholeness, and the relative self-containment of an object, or, conversely, the absence of an object or a negative, existentialist judgment about it. In the former sense, a point is a symbol of unit, like the beads of an abacus, like notched sticks, like tags or dots put down when things are counted, or like dots in mathematical formulas—for instance, in progressions that indicate that the matter is not confined to previously given members and that there are similar members, each being a certain mental unit designated by a point. Syntactical points indicate not that the started phrase is left incomplete, but rather that it has an end and that the speaker has in mind a further sequence of words as language units, which is certified by the dots. These dots are units which stand for words, and they could reveal their meaning at any moment. Dots

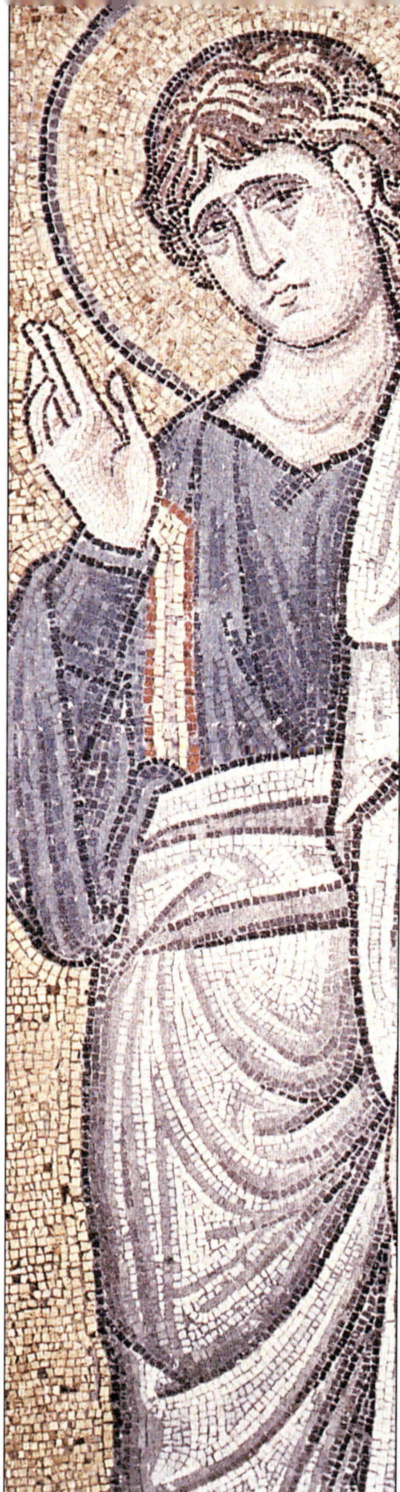

□□ The technique of Byzantine mosaic (a fragment—second century) bears a deep symbolism. "Material" smalter and tassarae, fitted together to form the picture and the golden background (the symbol of the light pervading the universe), acquire an additional significance. They are pieces of the absolute, the positive elements of the cosmic structure.

in the lists of contents in books, accounts, or inventories are used for a different end: they indicate the absence of things; they graphically denote emptiness or gaps or give you the idea that in the given place certain signs, figures, letters, words, etc., are absent, but that this should not be treated as omission, forgetfulness, or misprint. Dots, symbols of emptiness, are a guarantee that the empty space is never filled; thus, in financial documents dots are intended to prevent people from taking advantage of the gaps to add more figures. In this case dots secure the safety of empty space. A dot stands for the absence of something in the Hindu and Arabic number systems and in both cases is likely to have originated from the ancient Greek meaning of arithmetic zero. Our modern figure *0* increased in size with the centuries. Originally, it had the form of a minute circle. Incidentally, up until now, in certain foreign prints, zero is smaller in size than other figures. The ancient *0*, according to historians of mathematics, is both the graphic symbol of a dot and the initial *omicron*, *0*, as in the word ουεδν meaning "nothing."

One and zero, as dot values, are limits. But one can use a dot as a value striving to reach these limits. Then it is understood as a differential, and a "differential" in the dual sense: either as the "spirit of the arising value," Cohen's[6] Ursprung, a small brick with the likes of which a value is built or the way the notion of the differential is used in the mathematical study of history. Here the differential has a secret propensity to ap-

[6] Herman Cohen — 1842-1918, German philosopher, neo-Kantist, founder of the Marburg school of philosophy

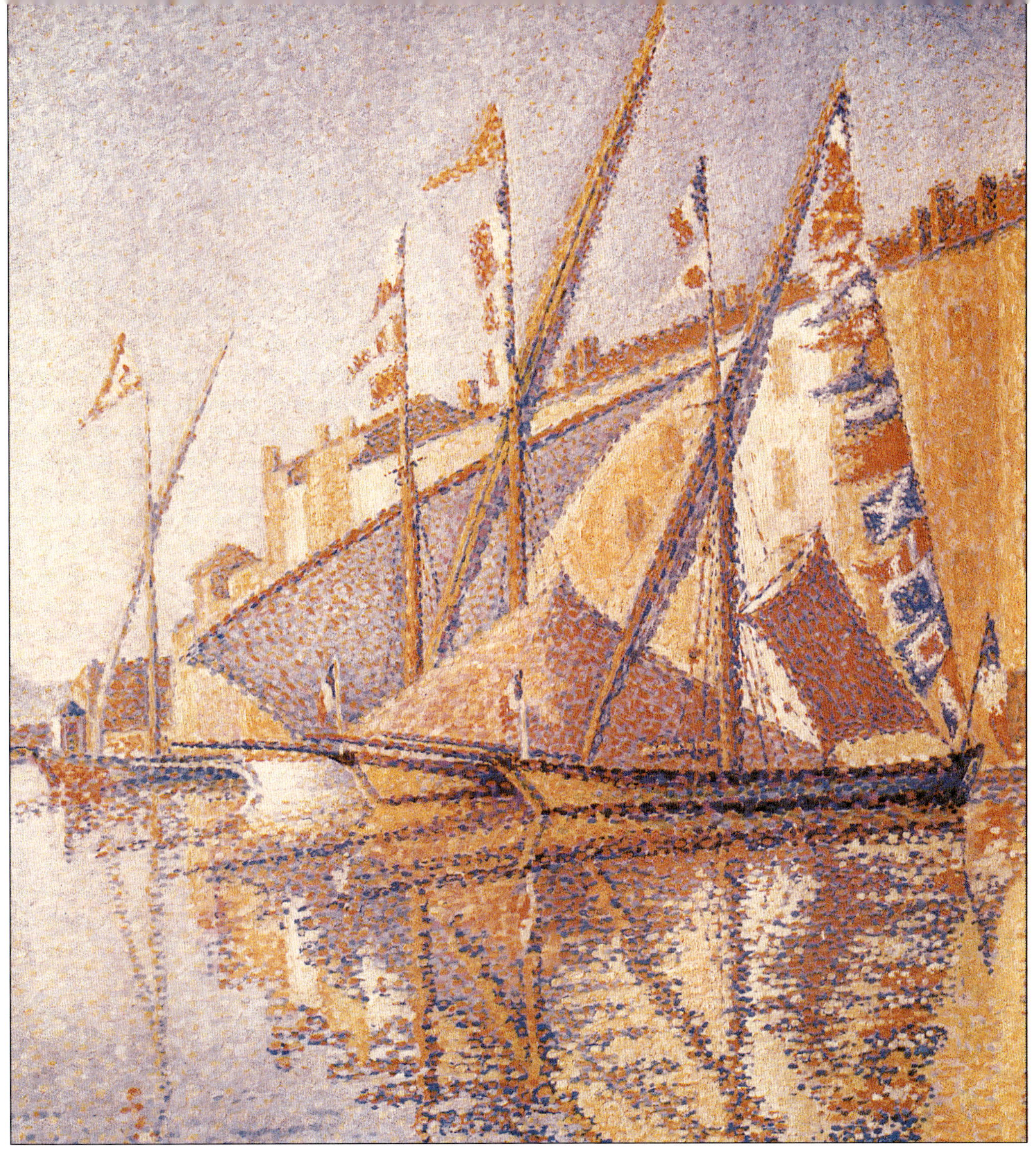

▯▯ LANDSCAPE BY P. SIGNAC (WUPPERTAL, VON DER HEYDT MUSEUM) IS A PIECE OF "POINTILISM" AND BEARS RESEMBLANCE TO A MOSAIC. HERE, THE POINT IS TREATED ESSENTIALLY AS AN AESTHETIC CONCEPT WHICH ADDS UP TO A PIECE OF ART. BESIDES THIS, IT RETAINS A PHYSICAL ATTRIBUTE DUE TO THE FACT THAT A MIXTURE OF DOTS OF VARIOUS COLORS PRODUCES A SPECIFIC COLOR .

proximate in thought (despite theoreticians' protestations to the contrary) infinitesimal values. In this sense, it is a unit; and it was not without reason that Leibnitz's differentials were twin brothers of his "monads," which were clearly units. Either a dot acquires the meaning of "the ghost that has disappeared" or of one about to disappear, in which case it is a kind of zero. It is Newtonian fluxion,[7]

[7] Newtonian fluxion — Newton's term for the derivative relative to a variable he called fluens; fluxion was designated by the same symbol as the variable itself with a dot placed above; e.g. X, the second derivative, was labeled with two dots and so on. Newton invented his fluxion method in 1665.

which, incidentally, was designated by Newton with a dot placed above the symbol of a corresponding magnitude. There is no fortuitousness, of course, in the different approaches of both infinitesimal-calculation founders toward understanding space. According to Leibnitz, the true reality is points-monads, metaphysical points (*metaphisiques* or *points de sustance*), and as to environment, space, it is nothing but *ordo rerum*, the order of existence of things, that is, something derived. According to Newton, the true reality in the world is recognized as its *sensorium Dei*, a Divine body that guides the world and ensures its existence.

This *sensorium Dei* is nothing but world space — whole and indivisible, the points of which are in reality zeros — something secondary and derived. Here one cannot but recall the words of Newton's latter-day compatriot who proclaimed Ether, the world medium, to be the true reality, while atoms and other primary elements of the material world are treated as empty spaces. I have in mind Lord Clifford's[8] theory of atoms — ethereal syringes — according to which in certain points of world space there are gaps and descents into quadri-dimensional space, and these, being points where Ether is discharged, are essentially points where it is destroyed, or disappears, or flows out of our world. The attraction effects of these "sinks" are perceived by us to be the force of gravity, while the ethereal turbulence arising here explains other properties of matter. The Universe lives solely by its continuous transformation out of existence, while the dot-like atoms are essentially its points of destruction.

Thus, one can accept the notion that true reality is environment, whole space, physical space with a structure of its own. The structure determines the existence of certain points, "sinks," and voids, which appear to be real, although they are essentially the negation of reality, the absence of it. Here, the structure of environment, by way of forming a secondary entity, determines a field of force, and the field, as something tertiary, determines a system of atoms, monads, and points. But these are not sources of force; the source of force is the environment, which applies its pressure to force them into the place where pressure is non-existent. Such a place is a zero, a fiction, and so it is natural to pass from here to the symbolic meaning of a point thus understood, as related to the notion of "*nihil*" (το ουχ ον), death, destruction.

Also possible is a notion which, albeit close to the above, is in direct opposition. In this case, points, or certain centers of action actually emanating from them, are recognized as true reality. A field of force is produced by these centers and, by virtue of its structure, assumes as a certain abstraction the formation of space, of world environment. This latter notion, however, is now thought of as an abstraction. As to the centers of force, we do, of course, imagine action emanating and spreading out from them. Thus, light streams out of a point of light, water bursts out of a subterranean spring. In the process, the source is perceived as a place where energies which have never been in the world before find their way into it. Does not our fascination for a little star lie in the fact that, to us, it appears to exude a beneficence of light from another world? Now, force is no longer thought of as the result of pressure *atergo*, from the back; it is traction, direct attraction toward the center, exerted precisely from that center as the source. A point thus understood is a unit, a differential. This notion of a point gives rise to a symbolic line, something, το ον, of birth, of coming into being.

A dot is a void and a fullness at the same time. Here and there, however, it is perceived to be on the borderline of being and non-being, or as a point of transition from what we regard as reality in our life here to its negation; or, contrariwise, as transition from an unworldly reality to nothingness here, but at any rate, as a nexus between two worlds, a world of the real and a world of the imagined. A point is a place of transcendence. Now a worthwhile observation is that in almost all of its symbolic applications, the dot can be interpreted both ways and still keep its function of linking two areas, while a particular view of the world may tend to emphasize the positive or, as the case may be, the negative interpretation of the symbol.

[8] William Kingdon Clifford — 1845-1879, English mathematician and philosopher. In 1870, Clifford proposed the hypothesis that matter was nothing but a space warp.

In ontology a point means the Beginning, a Unit, the *Ab-Ovo* Cause. It is the ontological Center which gives rise to everything. It is Active Principle, Spirit, Reason, God, Father of God, Jot in cabalistic philosophy — depicted by letter "j" containing a dot. So it is "maleness" which has yet to separate itself from its female adjunct, that is, something omnipotent and androgynous that itself gives birth to things. But this fullness of power, compared to which everything manifested and born is nothing, coming from a world of manifestations, is, from the viewpoint of that world, itself regarded as Nothing, *En-Sof*, as something understood only *via negationis*, an object for apophatic theology. A point is a symbol of the Un-nameable, the Incognitive.

In the same vein, in cosmology, a point is a solar speck or a solar atom on which rests the world, the atom, the electron, and other positive points of departure for transformation. A point is also the center of the world, that is, a perceived, but not real, hub of the world. It is both being and non-being, energy and nothing.

In pneumatology, a point — a star, a dot, a little spark — is, in the traditions of different peoples, up to the time of Funckelein of Meister Johann Eckhart,[9] a symbol of soul. Such traditions regard the soul as a positive center of reality, at the same time negated by the latter, because a star and a spark are symbols of light, which, having separated from Absolute Light and assumed individuality, becomes instantaneously extinguishable in its transience. Apparently closely related to the symbols just indicated is the notion of a spark as an external phenomenon, associated with the materialization of spiritual energies, as well as stories about miraculous happenings, such as the appearance of a holy person from a dot — a point of light unfolding as a bud and materializing into a whole figure.

In biology, a point is a symbol of a particular physical process concentrated on a certain life center: Goethe's living point; a grain in the symbolic notions of all peoples; a cell or a chromosome as a carrier of life; a sperm; a monad as a living organism perceived as material minimum, a posthumous carrier of life for future resurrection. It is the embryo of a body to be resurrected, *os sacrum* in Judaic theology; some minimal formation of bodily-composition monads, Leibnitz's posthumous carrier of bodily form; the navel as the hub and point of departure for the whole organism; the heart, or *plexus solaris*, filling the same function with respect to the spiritual body; *chakramas* of Hindu yoga and partly kindred nervous knots in anatomy and on and on — all these are perceived as "positive" meanings of the symbolic point. But it also has a subsidiary negative aspect, since, per se, it is nothing compared to what the thing is to become and what is to be concentrated within it. Besides, the thing must "get out of itself," cease to be its own self, die in order to realize its potential: "a seed will not come alive if it does not die"; a cell will not grow in the organism if it is not destroyed as the indivisible by dividing. A sacrum must rot in the grave before resurrecting into a new body; a sperm must dissolve in an *ovum* so as, by fertilizing it, to give rise to life; and concentrations of nervous energy must spread the energy over the entire organism, that is, cease to be concentrations, disperse before manifesting themselves and beginning to live. The common law is this: το μη ον (non-being which can materialize into being) becomes το ον (being) only by passing through το ουχ ον (non-being).

Where living things are at issue, prominence is given to the "positive" aspect of a point, with the "negative" serving as the background. But in building abstract schemes, the opposite is at work, and the point's negative meaning becomes prevalent. Thus, physically, the point fills a function which is *par excellence* an abstract one: gravity center, inertia center, the points of different physical conditions — melting, evaporation, the critical point of gas liquefaction, the focus into which rays, especially imagined ones, converge, etc. Being abstract, these points do not correspond to any reality, and a physical phenomenon occurs as if a given point were some real concentration: a gravity center is not something real; it may well position itself in the hollow void of a heavy object, but the object mechanically behaves as if its entire mass were compressed into that fictitious center. The same may be said of

[9] Johannes Eckhart — 1260-1328, German mystic who believed that God is cognizable to man because in man there is an *ab-ovo* spark cognate with God. In 1392 the Pope of Rome issued a special papal bull to pronounce Eckhart's teachings essentially false.

other similar points; thus, the imagined focus in geometrical optics is a point which, if rays emanated from it, would make their further progress precisely what it is in actual fact, although the imagined focus is no part of any physical reality. Points of physical states are also but our ways of our understanding reality and not centers of force application. The melting point is not the cause of melting, it is an imagined borderline between solid and liquid states of matter.

Some points in descriptive geometry, borrowed by the theory of fine arts, have become inextricable components of kindred notions in geometrical optics: a point of view in the sense of *locus standi*, the point of convergence of a perspective, etc., are artificial, ancillary techniques of speculation. The negative moment of a perspective convergence manifests itself with especial clarity. Converging in that point are the main straight lines of an image in perspective, and it becomes the compositional center of the picture. The composition is perceived as emanating and growing out of it. But by its spatial, depictive function, the convergence point is not the source but the "sink" of an image; not the beginning, but the end. A flat surface perpendicular to the central direction of view is thought of as being drawn into the infinite depth of Euclidean attraction in an ever uniform, monotonous fashion, without hitches, delays or stops. And, moving away, it grabs everything it meets on its way, utterly cleansing space of any reality whatsoever, while space, speeding on rails into non-being, is sliding along the descent lines without hindrance until it arrives at a point, that is, until the entire wholeness and variety of reality filling the space has petered out. Then space, devoid of quality, homogeneous, isotronic and indifferent to its own content, has become empty and thus turned into pure nothingness. The "perspective," that is, a "straight line," is a reality-destroying machine, a convergence point like some infernal jaws gobbling up everything. On the other hand, the "reverse perspective," as a fount supplying reality to the world, assists the birth of reality, its extraction from non-being, and its progress toward reality. A point of darkness and a point of light — this is the relationship of reverse perspective centers.

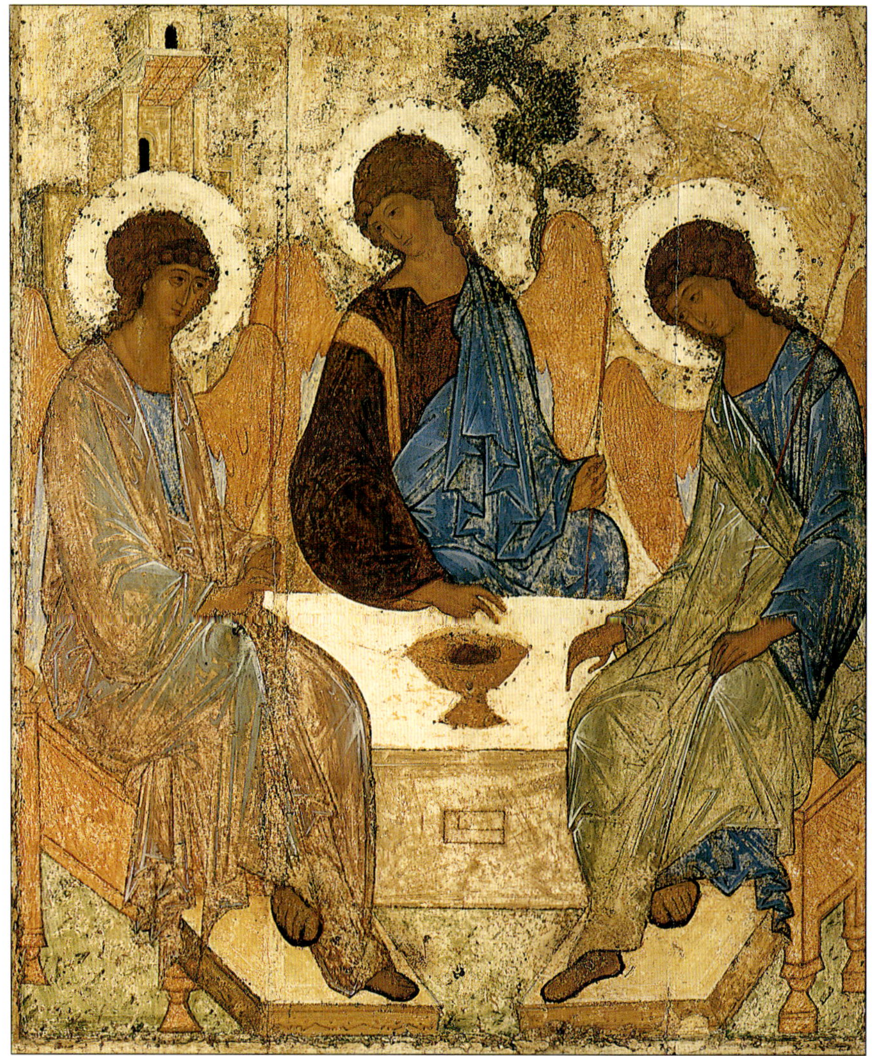

A multiple perspective is used as a technique of depicting spatial relations in the *Trinity Icon* by A. Roublev (Moscow, Tretyakov Gallery). Unlike a one-point perspective, multiple perspectives serve to create a representation of reality which "beams out of the world." The convergence points symbolize the points of darkness and light.

As symbols of darkness, we sometimes meet physically black points (although soot or ink do not always have color, and so an ink dot is not always synonymous with a center of darkness). Thus, a letter with a black dot brings news of a death sentence; the little black stone which the judges of the Areopagus threw into the urn meant condemnation; a black ballot ball was a sign of rejection. But a white pebble and a white ball meant the opposite, and a shining star or a guiding beacon stood for hope and assertion of life.

In ethics and orthobiotics, a point stands for the wholeness and intactness of a physical and, especially, spiritual, being, that is, its virginity, in line with the etymology and ancient understanding of the word σωφροσυνη (common sense) from σαυζ and φρονεω meaning spiritual health, fullness, and unspent energy. Such is the use of an asterisk, a little star, in its iconographic utilization, as on the forehead and chest of the Mother of God. Similarly, the sacred anointings of different religions — such as Hinduism and many ramifications of Christianity — include a ritual-graphic sign, looking very much like a set of dots, that underscores the integrity of the designated organ. The point's aesthetic meaning is similar when it serves as the vibrant unifier and centerpiece of an artistic whole. Such is the point of a golden section, both cutting apart and linking together a human figure, the body of an animal, a plant, a column, a building of a particular architectural style, a landscape, and, finally, a whole composition. Such is also the central point of a painting and, partly, of a poetic, dramatic, or musical composition. Achieving the same purpose is the rose in the portal of a Gothic cathedral. The artistic impression of the whole starts with and returns to the rose, which is the beginning and the repository of unity. In the aesthetic sense, a point can also acquire a kindred — albeit opposed in meaning — psychological use. In psychological usage, the point holds your attention and condenses apperception: spiritual forces are reduced to a dot, and the attention is brought into a focus. A hypnotist's sparkling ball with a light dot reflected in it; all kinds of contraptions designed to aid instantaneous concentration; big and small dots on billboards, advertisements, and publications; the beauty-spot as a tool of cosmetics; beads of rosaries and abacuses, etc.—all have the psychological function of concentrating and holding attention. In some cases, attention remains riveted to the point of attraction (a hypnotist's ball is one example), in consequence of which consciousness becomes empty and cleansed of everything else, receiving next to nothing in return. In other cases, a

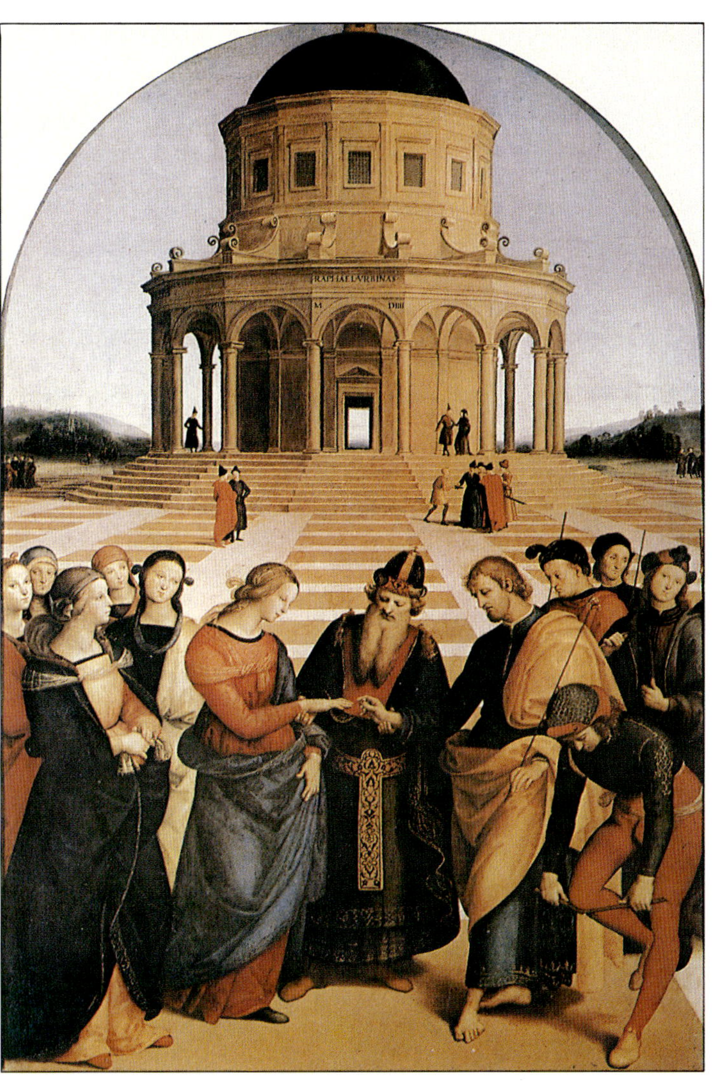

□□ The centric temple in *Mary's betrothal to Joseph*, by Raphael (Milano, Pinacoteca di Brera), embodies the Renaissance understanding of the perfect in architecture. The temple's base is a circumference taking its origin in a point. Here, the point takes on a new, aesthetic quality and acts as a concentration of the artistic whole.

point shifts consciousness onto some reality and, shielded from accidental impressions and the noise of life, the consciousness becomes filled with the chosen object and unreservedly accepts it (such is, for instance, the use of a dot in advertising). The function of this dot is to shift attention from itself to another object when the visual object receives a "cutting edge" or an arrow to mark the start of motion toward that object and, consequently, graphically combines to a slight degree with a line as a symbol of motion. In some cases, the dot's acquired linearity is hardly perceptible. Thus, the phonetic accent in French, old church Slavic language, Greek, and, to some degree, Russian, uses a dot or two (*accent circonflèxe*, *perispomenon*, etc.) to indicate that the letter below must stand out from the rest and that the sound it stands for gains emphasis — either by pitch or length. The logical stress, which makes a whole word in a phrase stand out, performs a similar function. In music, the emphasis has a kindred meaning, for an accent separates a note from the general fabric of sound (*staccato*) or makes it stand out by length (*fermato*). In other cases, the aspect of linearity becomes prevalent in a dot, and it clearly "goes out of itself," turning into a pointing finger, the fist becoming a graphic embodiment of the original symbol, the dot, or turning into an arrow, which, protruding and meandering, may itself assume the guise of some new object. More complex differentiations of a dot are also possible when there is a need to underline some specific aspect of its main function. Thus, paleographically, our entire punctuation has developed from a dot

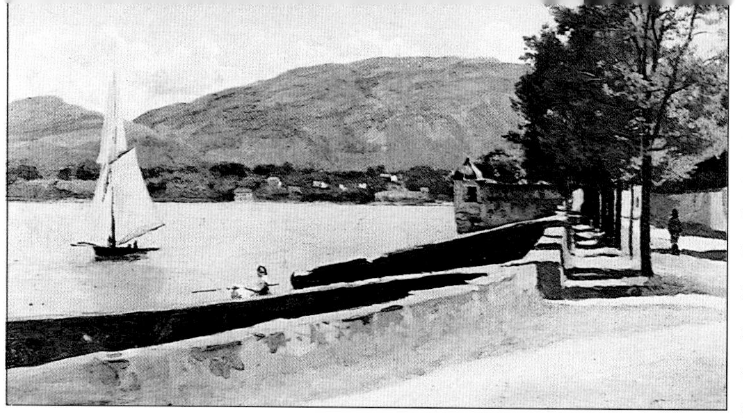

▯▯ In the landscape by C. Corot (Geneva, Museé d'Art et d'Histoire) space is a one-point perspective. The convergence point, located inside the picture, appears to devour the space around, draw it in, and thus destroy reality by turning it into visual and ontological fiction. In this way, the convergence point is both abstract and fictitious.

put between words. The dot served to denote a pause between words when, at the same time, the set of letters from period to period was perceived through a "single" act of apperception, that is, as "one" word. When it later became necessary to embrace a sentence as a single whole, by identifying a set of words in their general mass, man's attention, already schooled to activity, could, in order to identify words, do so with a mere blank between them, while the dot was endowed with a loftier mission — to serve as the basis on which apperception of a sentence could rely. The dot may also perform the function of a comma, that is, of an impure type of dot, in order to carry out an even greater apperceptive effort — the bringing together of several sentences. This is followed by the same process of differentiation, but all the signs are merely more complicated dots. The dot, originally some kind of a *nota bene* of the text, acquired even more diverse uses in Semitic languages, especially in Hebrew, gradually assuming the function of indicating a vocal "coloring" of the syllable represented by a consonant — its phonic, logical, and emotional emphasis, the nature of the consonant. As a punctuation mark, as the note of the accompanying melody (like Greek neumas and Orthodox Church "hooks"), and, finally, as textual-critical notes and exegetic explanations, the original dot of Hebrew manuscripts acquired uses of extraordinary diversity, depending on the place, the form, and the date of the manuscript. We have another dot-derivations system — an invented, artificial one — in the dot alphabet of the blind and in the telegraph code.

Despite its apparently artificial, derived, yet highly diverse, nature, a dot's legitimate status in mathematics does not go beyond common usage in combination with all kinds of other signs. It is a circumstance which warrants special attention, since every mathematician who uses a dot in some new sense pays no heed to the above status and believes that he uses a dot at random. In actual fact, however, although he may be quite original in using a dot for purposes unlike any other, this inventor of things novel unwittingly obeys the nature of the dot as a symbol, as well as the laws of symbolics. As a child speaks correctly without grammar, so the user of symbols — the nature of which he never ponders deeply — will not flagrantly sin against symbolics. Thus, the use of dots or accents with letters in their most diverse meanings aims on the one hand at the symbolic expression of a particular analogy of a letter emphasized by the same but un-accented letter, and on the other at setting it apart from similar letters and showing that they cannot be mixed up. Letter *a* with *accent aigue*, as related to *a* means: "it is the same as *a*, but (*nota bene*) not quite," or "be aware of the similarity but do not confuse them." Such is the denomination of fluxions, derivatives, transformed coordinates and variables in general, corresponding points of geometric forms, etc. In addition, the dot is used to combine thoughts into a single set and, consequently, to separate a whole set of signs from others. Thus, in logistics, dots separate inclusions which themselves serve as terms for a new inclusion. Such is the meaning of the dot between factors to indicate that the two numbers are distinctly separate and, at the same time, to state the need to form a certain new single object of thought — the product. Finally, the functions of a dot or dots as indicating continuation, or filling a certain space with interim members, or denoting the vacancy of a particular place, are quite in line with similar functions of general symbolics.

So much for the main aspects of the dot as a symbol. We do not claim to exhaust the entire content of the symbol, but even if we were to examine in the present paper many more aspects, the compilers of the dictionary would still have to make the same reservation. This would be no coincidence. A symbol is not an abstract notion or an artifact for which we can trace precise boundaries and even pass a legislation to prevent the symbol from overstepping its limits. As a living, spiritual product, a symbol is definitive and coherent, but inside, not as perceived from the outside. The study of actual symbol usages will give us some idea of a symbol's boundaries, but only a rough idea. We are confident that a living thing, all its movements notwithstanding, will remain true to itself and never go beyond the boundaries of its structure. Nevertheless, we never know in advance how the particular living thing will arrange itself in any given individual case. So it is with symbols. Even if we could gather all the known cases of dot usages in a "symbolarium," still each new day would furnish us with examples of "unauthorized" symbol usage, although we may confidently assert in advance that the new usage would find its place in the organism of the existing usages and would only serve to strengthen the relationships among them.

It is precisely for this reason that not only the cases of symbol usage but also their classification cannot be pronounced to be final — in the given symbolarium or in any subsequent one. As an organ of a living whole, of an organism, of a psychological constellation, a particular aspect of a symbol is not confined to a single feature; while exhibiting diverse characteristics, each characteristic is, to varying degree, correlated with all others . That is why the distribution of individual aspects is arbitrary and approximate. True, the links connecting a given aspect with others are in some cases direct and in others vicarious, in some leaping to the eye, and in others barely traceable. In the cognition of the living organism of symbols, however, all this can be stated only approximately. Today or tomorrow may bring a new aspect, a new case of symbol usage, which will create firm ties between things when previously the links between them were quite fuzzy. Let us cite two or three examples to demonstrate the lattice-like nature of symbol organization. An abacus bead is a point of apperception, but it also means a unit. The tip of the nose or the navel, in mystic practices, are attention-condensing points. But attention is concentration by a bodily organism, which then symbolizes world concentration — the Beginning of the World, Brahma. Then, as a vehicle of spiritual contemplation, the point may signify an entry into a different world, that point of light which unfolds in the mind of a mystic with a space of unworldly light. It may also mean the place of connection to the maternal organism, a feeding place. The same organ leads one to think about a link with the maternal bosom of the whole world, and then about a new birth by the universal Mother, and, consequently, about the thought of eternal life, etc., which again brings us to hailing the dot as the Beginning. This web of aspects linked together many times over could be discovered on a much wider scale. A rosary bead, also an attention-riveting point, stands for the Holy Name, and the name denotes the Named One and so on. The general convergence point, carrying away our eyesight and attention, is also a symbol of passive awareness of the world as illusory nothing, and of man as a theater spectator who can only watch the world spectacle from the sidelines, rather than work and live in it. Hence may unfold the whole spectrum of the point's negative meanings.

We have here examined several cases taken at random. Further comparison is provided in the text of the book.

The classification schemes and links proposed here must be taken as an appeal for spiritual self-reliance, as a kind of "for example," and not as a dogma or a strict system. It is a flexible and expandable net whose purpose is to catch the modern consciousness; and let those caught in the net do further netting. ■■

the heraldic "theater" of russian cities / sergei v. rogatchev

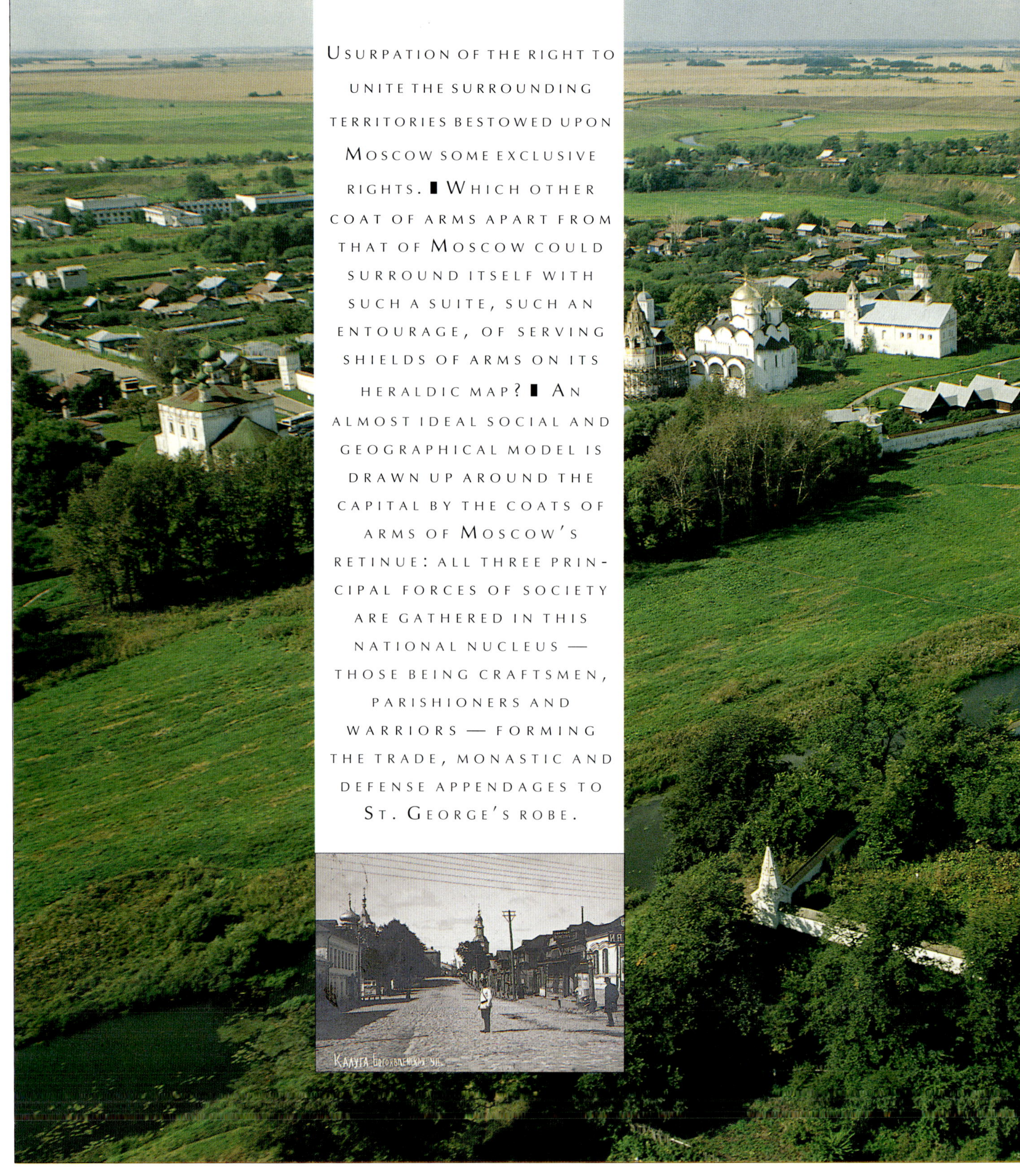

Usurpation of the right to unite the surrounding territories bestowed upon Moscow some exclusive rights. ▮ Which other coat of arms apart from that of Moscow could surround itself with such a suite, such an entourage, of serving shields of arms on its heraldic map? ▮ An almost ideal social and geographical model is drawn up around the capital by the coats of arms of Moscow's retinue: all three principal forces of society are gathered in this national nucleus — those being craftsmen, parishioners and warriors — forming the trade, monastic and defense appendages to St. George's robe.

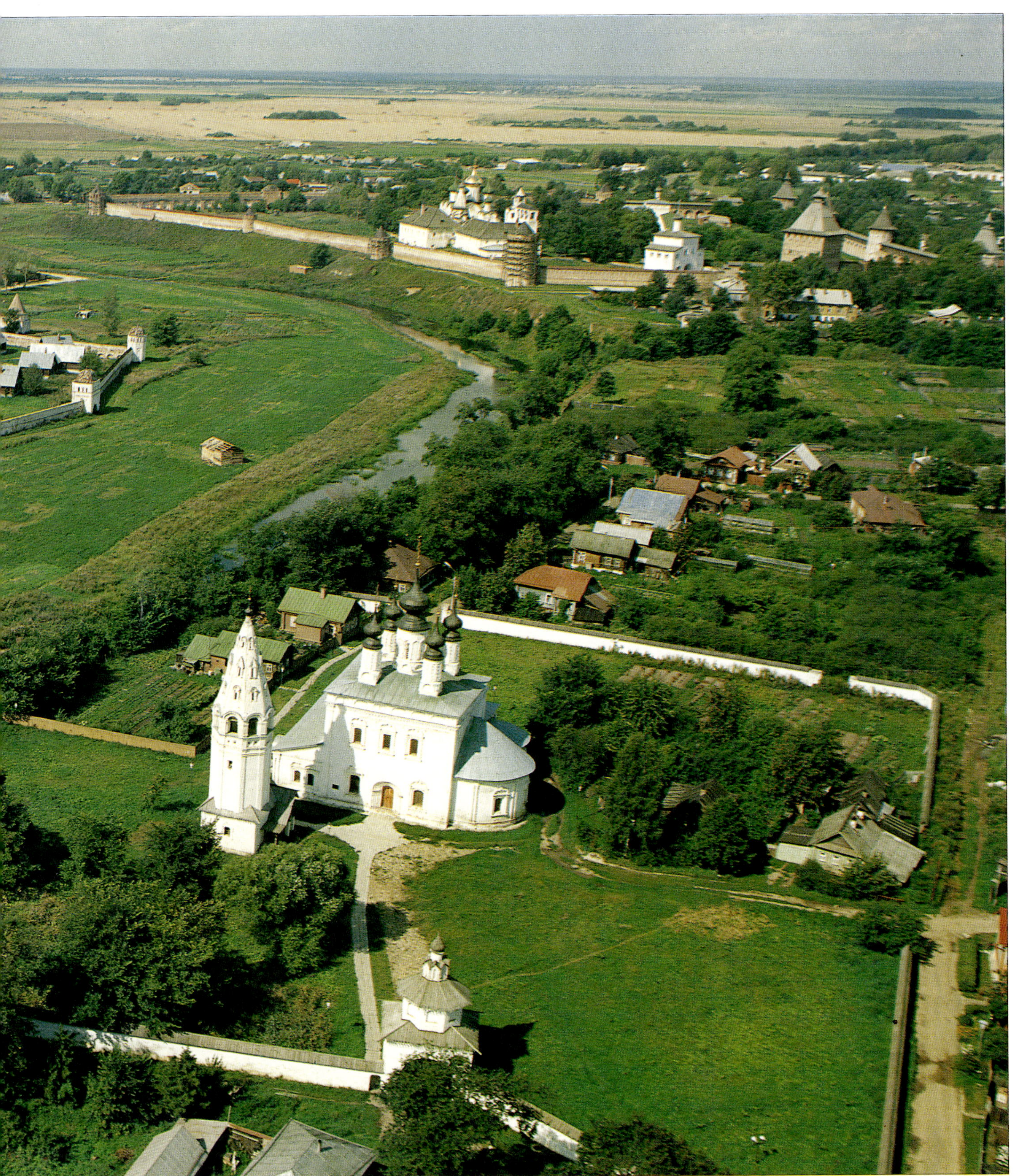

□□ *Suzdal'* (photo by Victor Kornyushin)

THE HERALDIC "THEATER" OF RUSSIAN CITIES / SERGEI ROGATCHEV ▮▮ I. Moscow

THE WONDER OF ST. GEORGE AND THE DRAGON

Saint George is striking the dragon lying prostrate at his horse's feet. This image of slaughter, placed in the center of Russia's heraldic map, is uncommon among the Russian regional coats of arms. Moscow's "wonder of the dragon" looks an absolute wonder alongside some of the routine and humdrum subjects which constitute most ancient Russian heraldic symbols. One comes across such imagery of violence perpetrated against another solely in the coats of arms of Archangel'sk,[1] Novogeorgievsk, and Yegor'yevsk. However, on these coats of arms such themes are merely illustrations interpreting the city names, the heraldic readings of place names. The suggestion of massacre on the coat of arms of Moscow seems, however, to be deliberate, for the capital proclaims through this heraldic bearing its exclusive right to both execution and mercy.

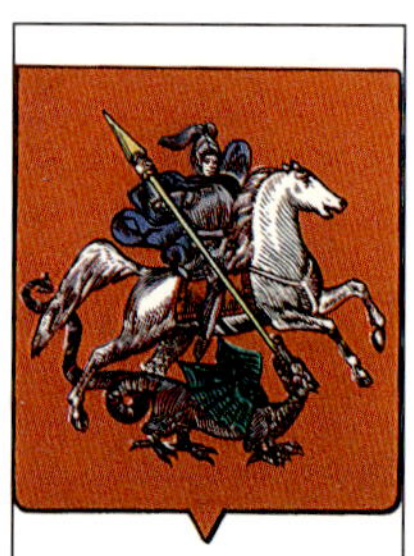

The ancient seal of Kiev also bore a heraldic composition depicting a saint striking the dragon. When it brought the former South Russian capital under its power, Moscow deprived the Kiev warrior of his challenger, and the monster disappeared from Kiev's coat of arms. Recognizing the historical merits of Kiev, Moscow's authorities left an armed archangel on the armorial shield of Kiev, yet wrested from him his right to choose and castigate the enemy independently. The dragon deserving the spear's agonizing thrust could be decided upon only by George the Victorious bearing the gilded shield of Moscow.

Before the unambiguous language of Moscow's heraldry brought the spear-bearing horseman to Kiev,[2] some nearer provinces had found themselves in the role of the dragon under the onslaught of the Center's spear. The Moscow horseman assumed the right to govern and speed up the centralization process, which, in spite of the internecine wars among the local princes, started its development in the area between the Volga and the Oka rivers. When in the 13th century the princes of Tver', Pereyaslavl', Vladimir, and Moscow arrived at a concord of unity and their princely crowns came together onto the ermine background of the coat of arms of Dmitrov — "to commemorate the famed reunion of the four Russian princes in this town,"[3] their crowned heads never imagined that the "confederation" shield of Dmitrov would soon be headed by Moscow's mounted ruler.[4] Dmitrov's coat of arms was a testament to the "democratic" alternative to Moscow's sweep across Russia, a monument to an unsuccessful attempt at centralization from below.

SUITE OF ST. GEORGE

Usurpation of the right to unite the surrounding territories bestowed upon Moscow some exclusive rights. Which other coat of arms apart from that of Moscow could surround itself with such a suite, such an entourage, of serving shields of arms on its heraldic map? The town of Podol'sk is cutting and trimming the

[1] Though according to the coat of arms of Arkhangel'sk, the Warrior is not killing the devil (at least, the heraldic scene tells nothing about it) but merely shaming this mystical enemy of the human race.

▯▯ Above. Moscow's coat of arms.
▯▯ Opposite page. Detail of Russian icon of 15th century.

[2] The author alludes to the proverb: "The tongue will lead one to Kiev," i.e., a very well-known place in ancient Russia. But later the understanding of the proverb changed, and it started to mean that by asking people, one can learn the way to a very remote point.

[3] The late 13th century abounded in princely feuds aggravated by the princes' support by rival groups in the Golden Horde. In 1299, Andrew Great Prince of Vladimir, Michael Prince of Tver', Ivan Prince of Pereyaslavl', and Daniel Prince of Moscow came together in the town of Dmitrov to make peace. Andrew and Daniel succeeded in working out their mutual problems, while Ivan and Michael parted to feud. *[All quotations in this article are taken from N. A. Soboleva, Starinnye gerby Rossiyskih gorodov (Ancient coats-of-arms of Russian cities), Moscow, 1985.]*

[4] Generally speaking, the regional coat of arms is found in the upper part of the heraldic shields of regional centers, the smaller settlements normally playing a quite formal part and telling us about their administrative subordination. The "upper figure" has nothing in common with the local heraldic figure either in terms of composition or plot. We have removed (except for some special cases) the local "headers" from regional coats of arms featured on the heraldic map here. Yet the position of the Moscow victor on the coat of arms of Dmitrov is so expressive that one is tempted to regard the whole coat of arms as an integral composition. The Moscow horseman is aiming its centralizing lance not only at the conventional dragon, but also at local equality shimmering feebly at the foot of the shield.

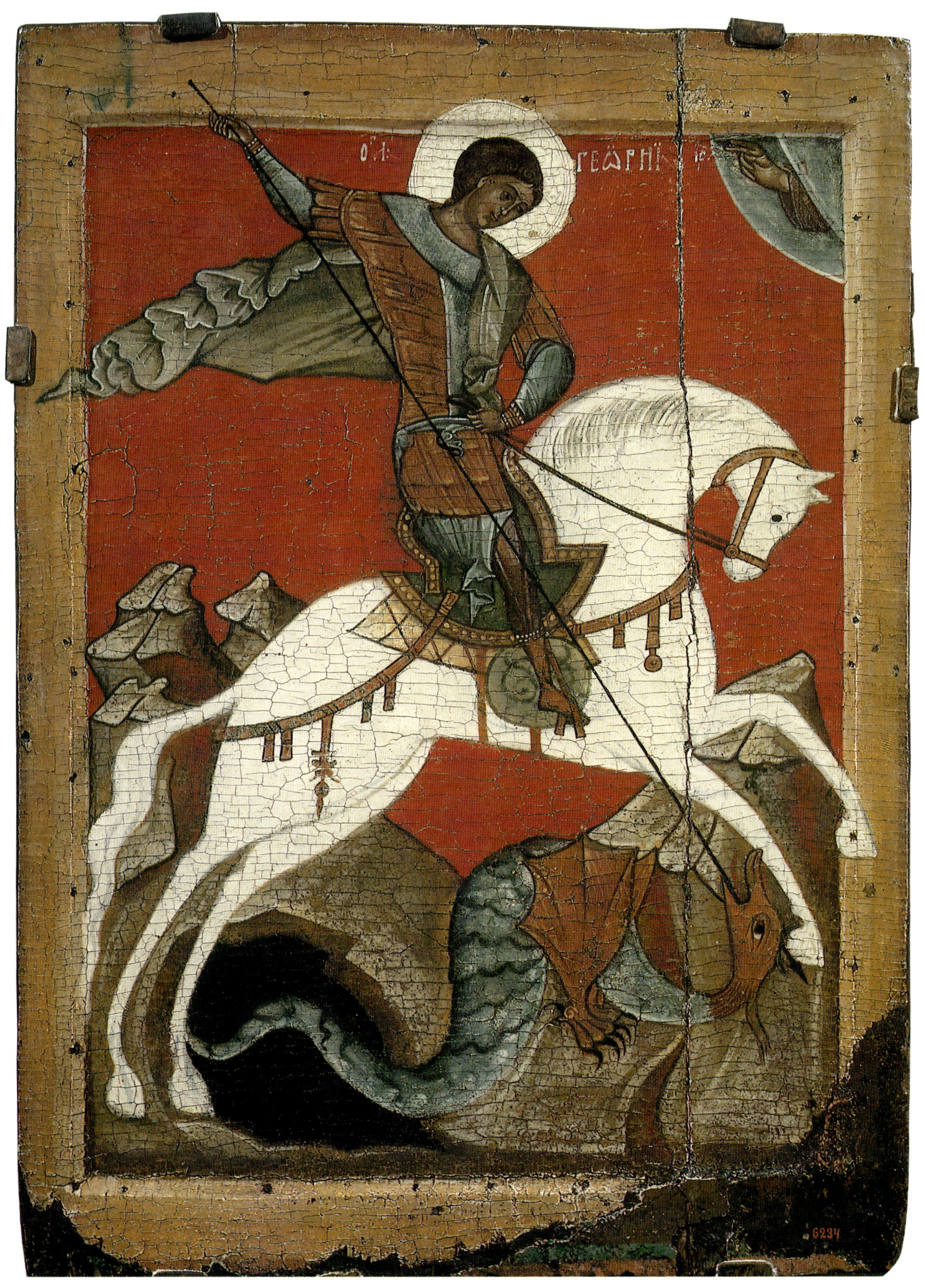

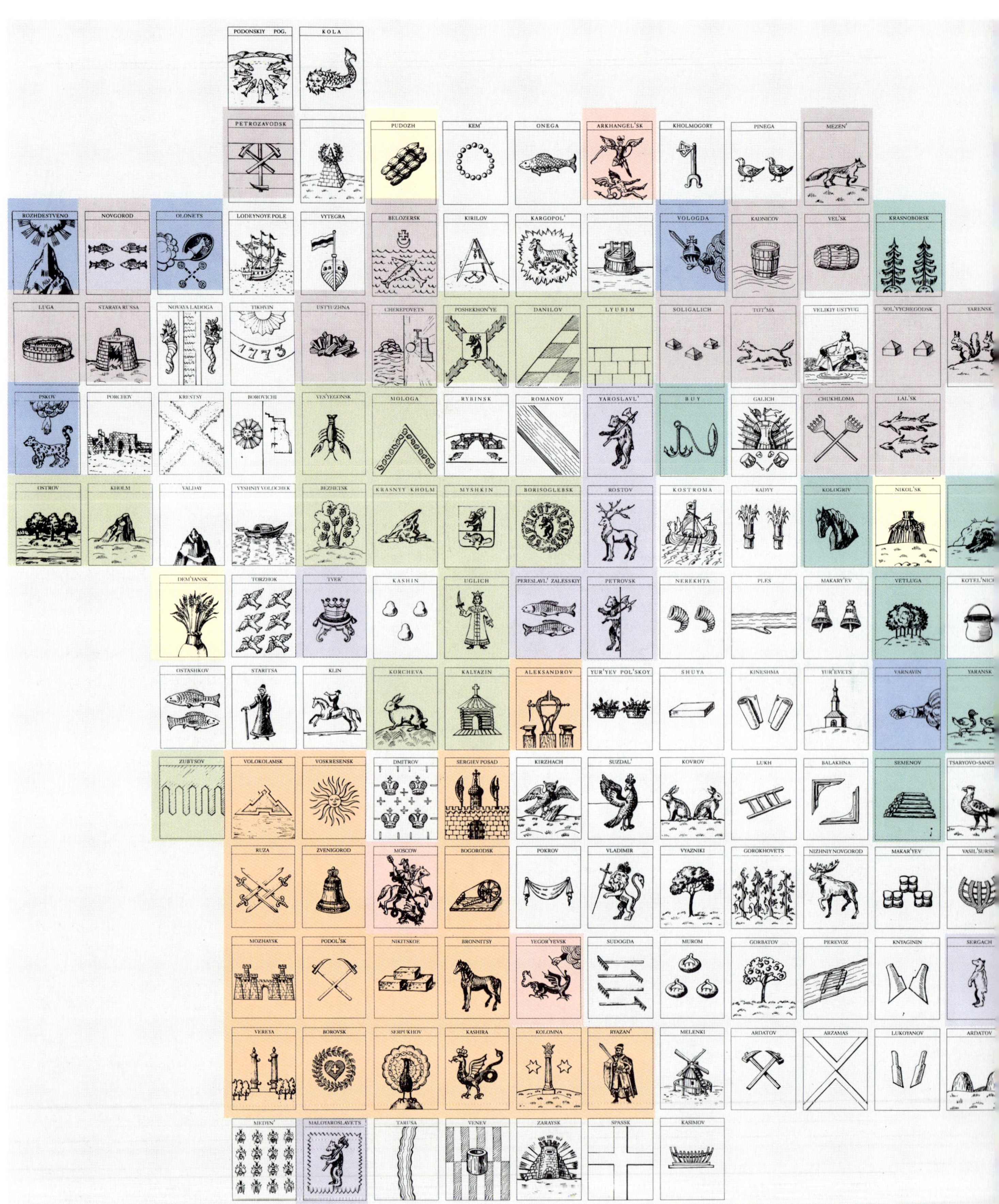
PODONSKIY POG.
KOLA
PETROZAVODSK
PUDOZH
KEM'
ONEGA
ARKHANGEL'SK
KHOLMOGORY
PINEGA
MEZEN'
ROZHDESTVENO
NOVGOROD
OLONETS
LODEYNOYE POLE
VYTEGRA
BELOZERSK
KIRILOV
KARGOPOL'
VOLOGDA
KADNICOV
VEL'SK
KRASNOBORSK
LUGA
STARAYA RUSSA
NOVAYA LADOGA
TIKHVIN
USTYUZHNA
CHEREPOVETS
POSHEKHON'YE
DANILOV
LYUBIM
SOLIGALICH
TOT'MA
VELIKIY USTYUG
SOL'VYCHEGODSK
YARENSK
PSKOV
PORCHOV
KRESTSY
BOROVICHI
VES'YEGONSK
MOLOGA
RYBINSK
ROMANOV
YAROSLAVL'
BUY
GALICH
CHUKHLOMA
LAL'SK
OSTROV
KHOLM
VALDAY
VYSHNIY VOLOCHEK
BEZHETSK
KRASNYY KHOLM
MYSHKIN
BORISOGLEBSK
ROSTOV
KOSTROMA
KADYY
KOLOGRIV
NIKOL'SK
DEM'YANSK
TORZHOK
TVER'
KASHIN
UGLICH
PERESLAVL' ZALESSKIY
PETROVSK
NEREKHTA
PLES
MAKARY'EV
VETLUGA
KOTEL'NIC
OSTASHKOV
STARITSA
KLIN
KORCHEVA
KALYAZIN
ALEKSANDROV
YUR'YEV POL'SKOY
SHUYA
KINESHMA
YUR'EVETS
VARNAVIN
YARANSK
ZUBTSOV
VOLOKOLAMSK
VOSKRESENSK
DMITROV
SERGIEV POSAD
KIRZHACH
SUZDAL'
KOVROV
LUKH
BALAKHNA
SEMENOV
TSARYOVO-SANCH
RUZA
ZVENIGOROD
MOSCOW
BOGORODSK
POKROV
VLADIMIR
VYAZNIKI
GOROKHOVETS
NIZHNIY NOVGOROD
MAKAR'YEV
VASIL'SURSK
MOZHAYSK
PODOL'SK
NIKITSKOE
BRONNITSY
YEGOR'YEVSK
SUDOGDA
MUROM
GORBATOV
PEREVOZ
KNYAGININ
SERGACH
VEREYA
BOROVSK
SERPUKHOV
KASHIRA
KOLOMNA
RYAZAN'
MELENKI
ARDATOV
ARZAMAS
LUKOYANOV
ARDATOV
MEDYN'
MALOYAROSLAVETS
TARUSA
VENEV
ZARAYSK
SPASSK
KASIMOV

A schematic map of cities. Each city is represented by its coat of arms. The location of each city on the scheme in relation to any other location approximately corresponds with the real location of the city on the topographic map. Only distances between cities have been distorted, but neighbours and orientation are maintained.

- Clouds in the sky
- Bears and raspberries
- The wonder of St.George
- Suite of St.George
- Bear's corner
- The sanctuary of wild birds
- The industrial North
- The northern limit of agriculture
- For the description of these coats of arms see next issue

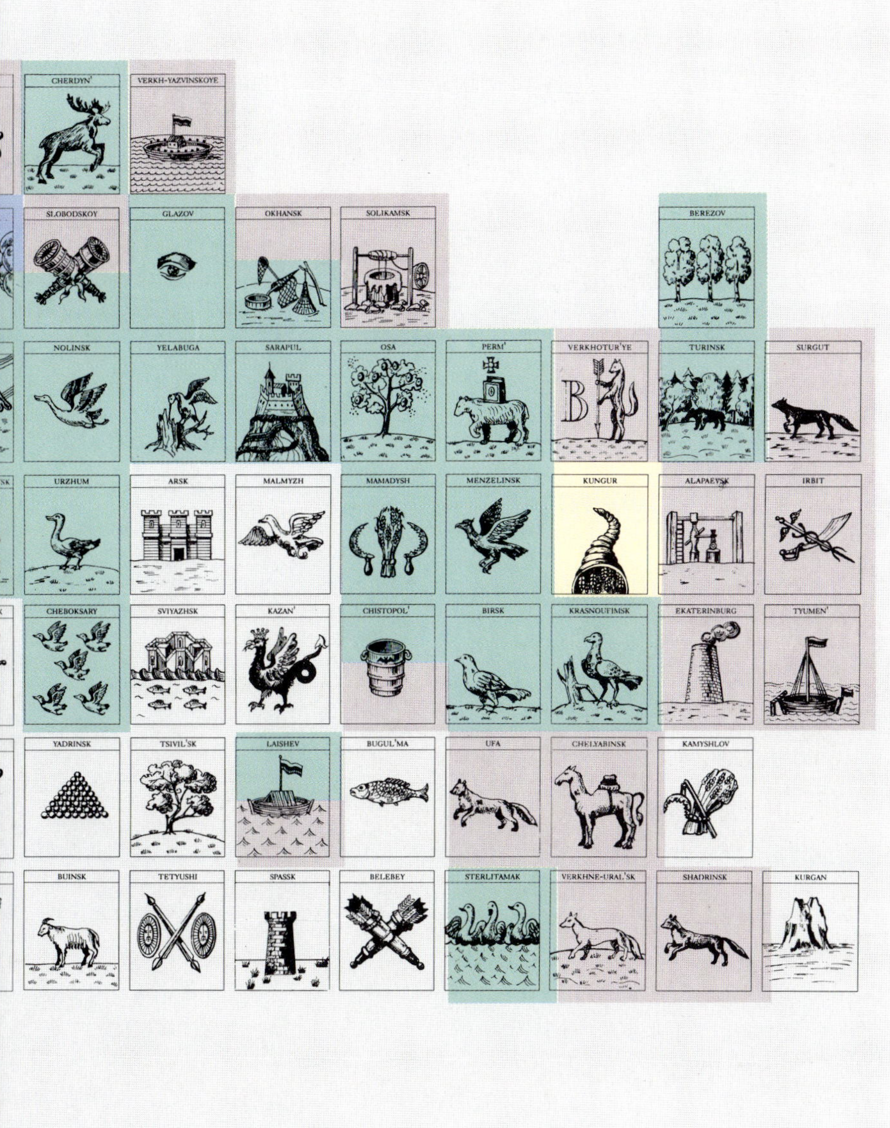

stone for Cyclopean Kremlin buildings with its crossed stone hammers. The silk-spinning wheels of Bogorodsk are turning tirelessly; Aleksandrov is working in metal; the horse-breeders of Bronnitsy are raising "golden horses in green fields" for the court of Tzar Theodor Ioannovich.[5]

Volokolamsk, Ruza, Mozhaysk, Vereya and Borovsk[6] repel the blows of Western Europe aimed at Moscow with their symbols of fortification and martialism, while Serpukhov, Kashira, Kolomna and Ryazan' guard the southern borders from marauding nomads. Intimidating potential

[5]Theodore Ivanovich, tzar of Russia, last of the Ruriks' dynasty (to say nothing of Basil Shuisky), who reigned in 1584-1598.

[6] Here is the description of the coat of arms of Borovsk. In the times of the Second Pseudo-Demetrius (in 1607, the Second Impostor, whose real name is unknown, but who is commonly known as the Thief of Tushino, declared himself Demetrius, son of Ivan the Terrible, and headed a party of insurgents for Moscow, where he held his ground for two years and was killed in 1610), Borovsk and Pafnutyev, a monastery abiding in Borovsk, were the site where the defenders of the town betrayed their Motherland and surrendered the town and the monastery to that villain Pseudo-Demetrius. However, Prince Volkonsky, one of the defenders, did not stop fighting and, pierced by dozens of arrows, was slain at the left-hand choir in the monastery church. To recall this honorable feat the coat of arms has a silver background (which stands for innocence and a kind heart) and a reddish golden heart (evidence of faithfulness) which is emblazoned with a cross. The heart is surrounded by laurels signifying the strength and honorable resistance that brought fame to this leader and many others who perished in the name of justice.

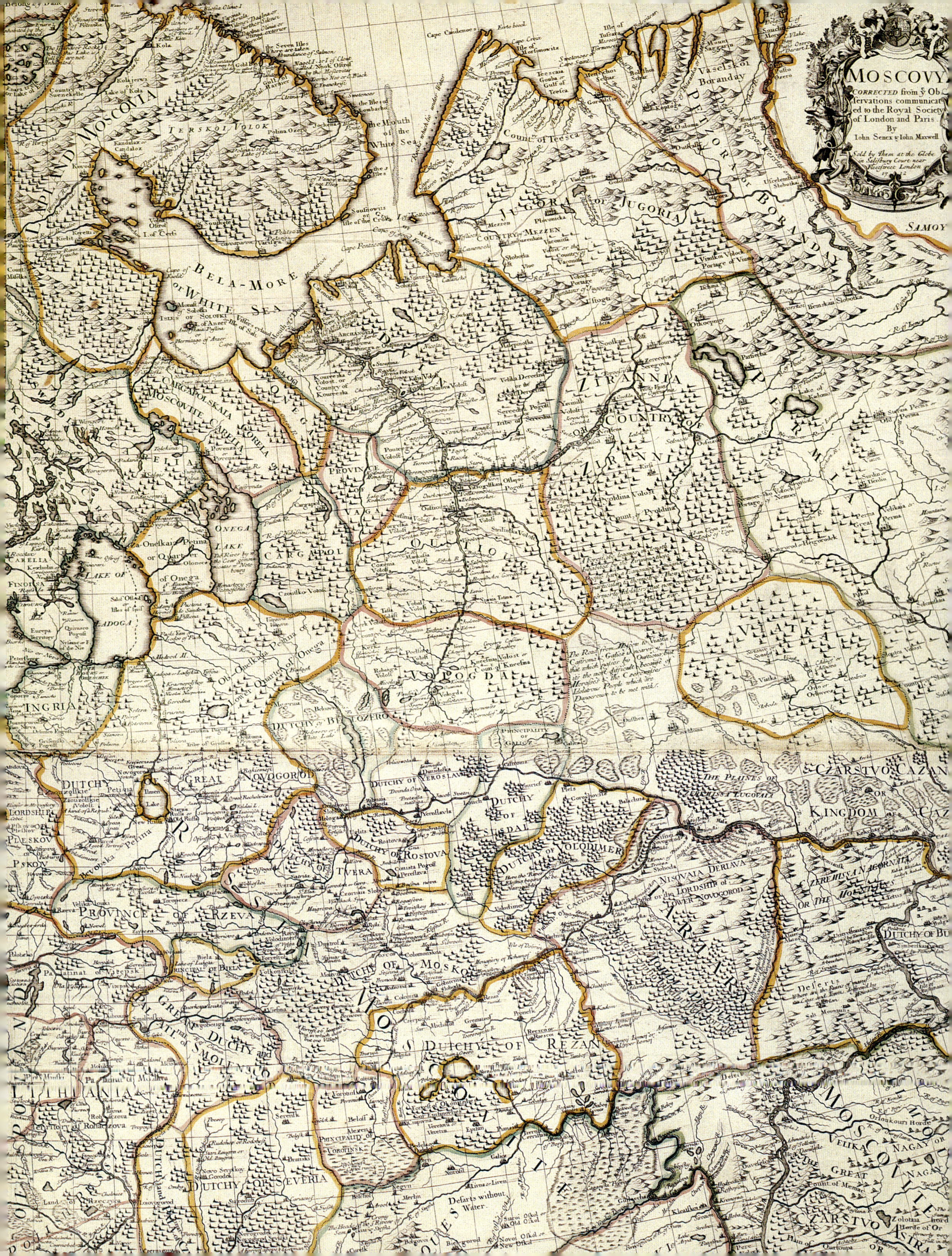
MOSCOVY
CORRECTED from ye Ob-
servations communicat-
ed to the Royal Society
of London and Paris
By
John Senex & John Maxwell
Sold by Them at the Globe
in Salisbury Court near
Fleetstreet London
17 12
SAMOY
BELA-MORE
or WHITE SEA
TERSKOI VOLOK
JUGORIA
BORANDAY
ZIRANNIA
PERMIA
CARGAPOL
ONEGA
VOLOGDA
VIATKA
INGRIA
LAKE OF LADOGA
DUTCHY OF BELOZERO
GREAT NOVOGOROD
DUTCHY OF VEROSLAW
DUTCHY OF SUSDAL
DUTCHY OF ROSTOVA
DUTCHY OF TVERA
DUTCHY OF VOLODIMER
PROVINCE OF RZEVA
DUTCHY OF MOSKO
DUTCHY OF REZAN
DUTCHY OF SMOLENSKO
DUTCHY OF SEVERIA
PRINCIPALITY OF VOROTINSK
LITHUANIA
KINGDOM
CZARSTVO CAZAN
THE PLAINES OF
LORDSHIP OF PLESKOV
PSKOV
Desarts without Water.
MOSCOVITE
CZARSTVO ASTRA

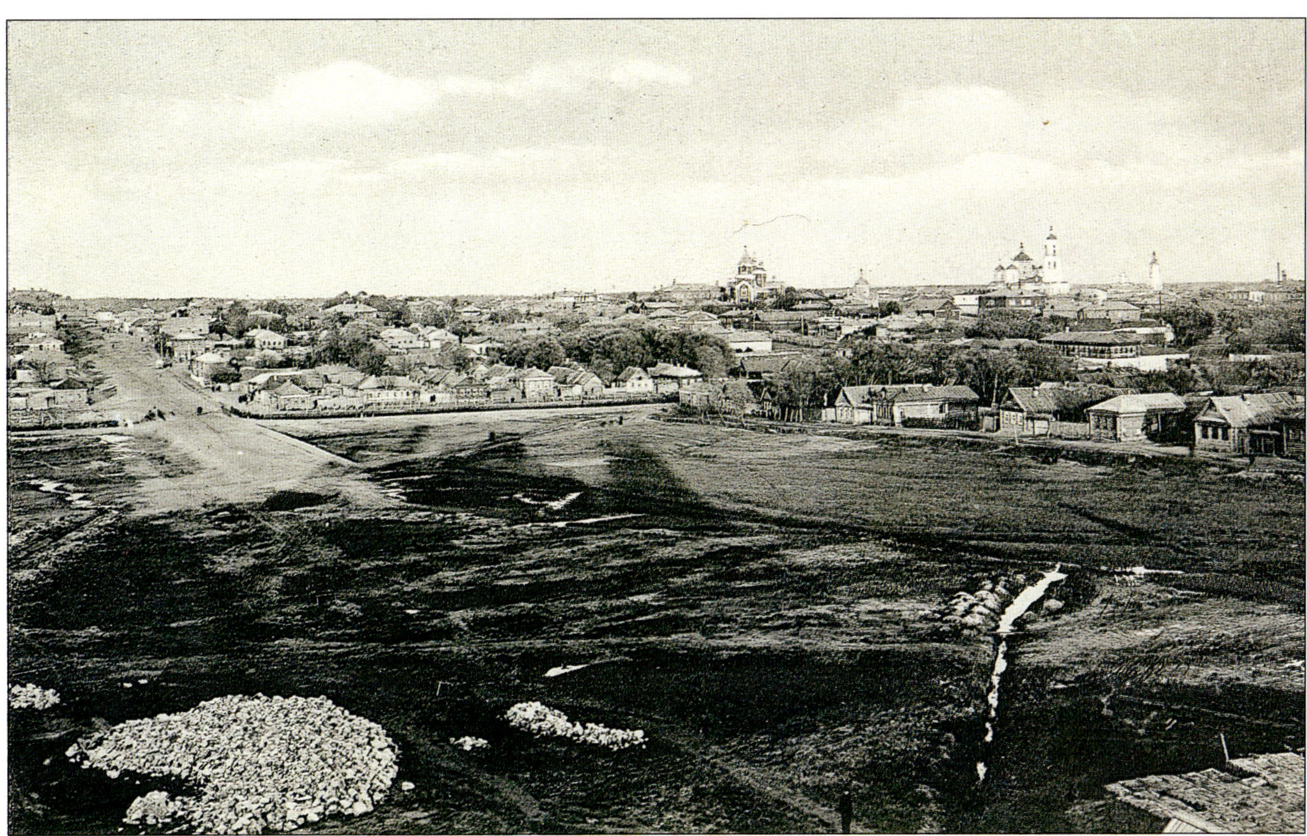

□□ Panorama of Egor'yevsk. Postcard 1916. The town was founded in Meshchera Land (not far from Moscow) and is known for its swamps, formed on glacio-fluvial sand. One can discern several drainage canals in the foreground.

□□ British map of Muskovy (Russia), 1712.

enemies, the Serpukhov peacock spreads its tail as a barrier; a glorious border sign is raised high in Kolomna — "in sky-blue field a white post with the crown at its top." Two stars on the sides of the Kolomna post threaten trespassers of the lord's Rubicon with heavenly fire. The prince of Ryazan' who, like the saint on Kiev's seal, was for determining the enemy independently, guards the Oka border of the Center, his sword in hand.

Prayers are offered for the Moscow emperor in the monastery cells of the towns of Sergiev and Voskresensk (New Jerusalem); *ex occidente* — an ancient bell — tolls either joy or danger at the monastery named after "Savva the Vigilant" (Storozhevskiy) in the town of Zvenigorod.

An almost ideal social and geographical model is drawn up around the capital by the coats of arms of Moscow's retinue: all three principal forces of society are gathered in this national nucleus, — those being craftsmen, parishioners, and warriors — forming the trade, monastic and defense appendages to St. George's robe.

At first, the hostile West and South — whose attacks Moscow's feudal sovereign beat off with the aid of his vassals, relying little on his own spear — could not take easily to the tranquil elevation of Moscow. The silver horse of St. George could run north and east with much more audacity. Practically no heraldic military symbols were encountered in this wide and spacious area, from the castles of the Baltic knights and bishops up to Sviyahzsk and the Simbirsk steppe.

II. Bears' corner (God-forsaken places)

Yaroslavl' bear at service

Moscow conquered easily the lake lands of Pereyaslavl' in the North and thus provided the tables of its citizens with "golden herrings." Afterwards, Rostov and Yaroslavl' joined, and with due obedience, as if from a zoo's cages, their animals too stepped out onto the heraldic shields. Rostov's deer allowed the gilding of its hoofs and mane to look like a wrought metal collar. And Yaroslavl's bear shouldered an axe, with which Prince Yaroslav the Wise,[7] the leader of all Novgorodians, once killed this animal sacred to the Finns living in the Upper Volga.

It is notable that the scene of this symbolic hunting was never depicted on the heraldic shield of Yaroslavl', when in this particular instance the scene of butchery would be more historically justified than that on Moscow's coat of arms. The bear is neither lifeless nor blood-soaked, for the exclusive right to execution and mercy no longer belongs to Novgorod's leaders, but to the horseman "in silver armor and sky-blue cloak." The authors of Yaroslavl's heraldic coat of arms revived the animal, and as a comical clown he walked onto the shield doomed to humiliation, carrying a pole-axe on his shoulder — not so much as a reminder of his slaying at the hands of Prince Yaroslav, but as his "sword of Damocles,"[8] a sign of his subordination to Moscow.

Bears' clumsy assistance

Striving for power, Moscow was very sophisticated in finding different ways of pursuing the heraldic struggle with rival towns. In the South the authors of Russia's heraldic emblems overthrew the Prince (formerly Grand Prince) of Ryazan' and forced him to stand at attention before the Moscow horseman and guard the peace of Moscow at its unsafe southern borders. But in the not so dangerous North, Moscow's heraldic conclave preserved the throne of Tver's Grand Princes on the field of Tver's coat of arms — as a pleasant gesture toward the suppressed grandeur of the rival — while the Tver' prince was mercilessly dislodged from his throne.

After Tver' it was the turn of "Lord Novgorod the Great." On Novgorod's heraldic shield the stepen[9] was replaced by the monarch's throne. The throne is va-

[7] Yaroslav the Wise, prince of Kiev 1019-1054; in his youth he was designated prince of Novgorod by his father, Saint Vladimir.

[8] In 1918 "the sword of Damocles" would hit the rebellious people of Yaroslavl'. Demidov's Lyceum, burned down by Moscow gunners (this is a reference to a mutiny (see next column) stirred up by the opposition and suppressed by the Bolsheviks), became for Yaroslavl' as irreplaceable a loss as the killing of its furry totem had been for earlier pagans. The pagans' domain disappeared, as did Yaroslavl', famous for the first theater and the first provincial magazine. But the bear is still doomed to carry the instrument of its murder, and the axes of smoke from Yaroslavl's plants, fixed on the poles of their chimneys, are rising high over its head.

[9] Stepen is a raised seat for posadniks (designees). The political system of Novgorod was notable for the weak power of the prince. The greatest power was vested in the veche, the assembly of free citizens (the word was also used for the meeting place itself). The veche elected a posadnik, who would administer the city and judicial system.

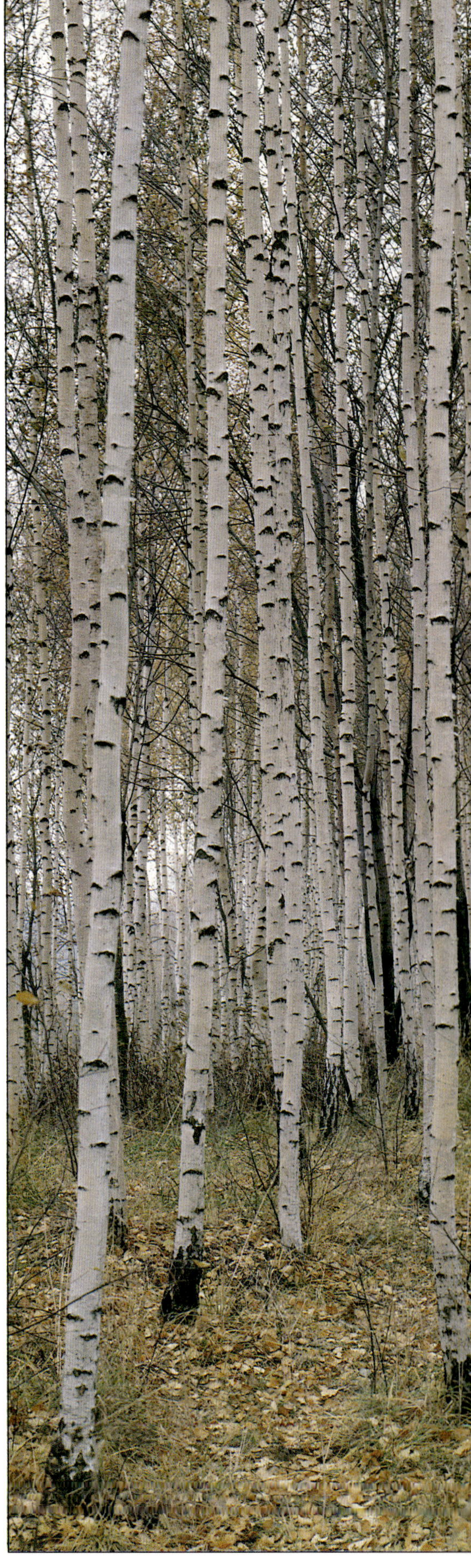

▯▯ *Birches*, Victor Kornyushin.

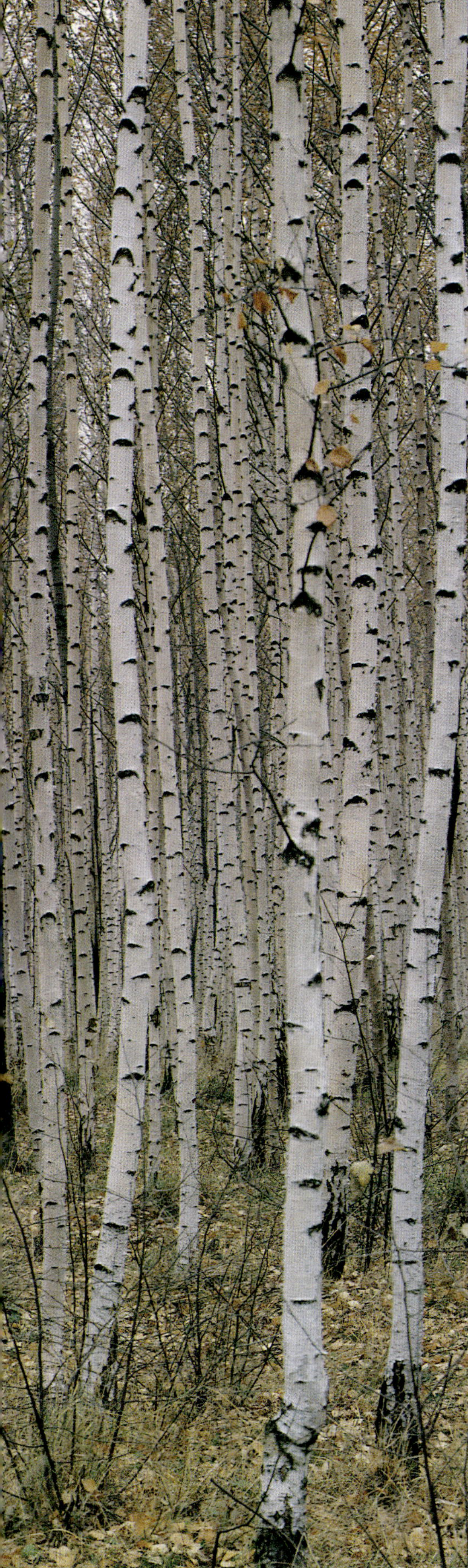

cant, but the scepter placed on it speaks clearly about the presence of an autocratic Moscow. (Remember the witty observation from *Dead Souls* by N.V. Gogol — the district police officer needn't go personally to calm down his rebellious peasants, it being sufficient just to send his police cap.)

Neither the snow leopard nor the bear is guarding Novgorod's throne, as they did on the ancient seal of Novgorod. Since that time there have appeared two bears symmetrically placed as though holding the Novgorod symbol with their elbows. The snow leopard is a far too independent symbol to bow to the heraldic influence from the West. The bear is simpler and safer. Sending a bear-governor to replace the snow leopard in Novgorod, Moscow both "strengthened the local administration"[10] and deeply humiliated Lord the Great: the bear that was placed on Novgorod's heraldic shield as the master and the Yaroslavl' pagan who earlier gave fealty to Novgorod are as like as two peas. That explains why those who devised the coats of arms in Moscow decided to revive, tame, and arm Yaroslavl's beast.

The practice of sending out heraldic bears was not confined to the correction of Novgorod's coat of arms. According to the formal similarity of two place names, the heraldic conclave would deliberately move the Yaroslavl' bear onto the coat of arms of the town of Maloyaroslavets. The bear from the northern woods was placed forward to persecute the steppe eagles that overflowed the shields of Mosal'sk and Odoev, as heraldic replicas of the shield of the town of Chernigov.[11]

The bear was also lifted onto the heraldic shield of Sergach. Unlike his Yaroslavl' and Novgorod brothers, who have lost their animal nature and have become purely symbolic figures, the bear of Sergach is living and natural. He has no other heraldic burdens and is absolutely "naked." His at service posture was chosen by the Sergach people without the influence of any heraldic canons, for they were able pupils of Moscow's herald masters and famous bear tamers as well. They caught and trained bears; the trainer of "General Toptygin"[12] was undoubtedly from Sergach.

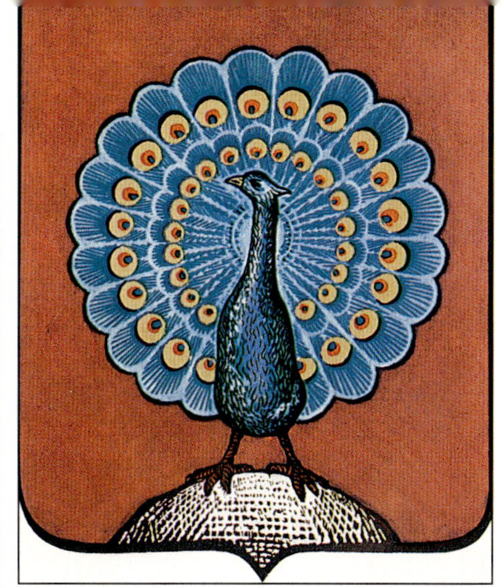

ПП SERPUKHOV'S COAT OF ARMS.

Export of the ancient Yaroslavl' bear in the new Sergach version (the strong bear knew the mysteries of the Volga left bank woods but was absolutely tame;[13]he was wild, though easy to train) contributed a

[10] A communist idiomatic cliché.

[11] Chernigov's coat of arms, with minor additional detail, is depicted on the coats of arms of Mosal'sk and Odoev. The eagle on the coat of arms of Chernigov signifies that, earlier, those towns were drawn into the Chernigov domain.

[12] General Toptygin, a bear, the character of a satirical poem of the same name by Nikolai Nekrasov.

[13] "Is the bear with you?" "Don't worry, ours is tame and quiet." N. Nekrasov, "General Toptygin."

great deal to turning this heraldic protagonist of the Russian North into the informal national symbol of Russia — especially for foreigners.

BEARS AND RASPBERRIES

The heraldic area situated to the north-north-west of the heraldic ingot of Moscow, between the far-flung bears' routes to Novgorod and Yaroslavl', looks a veritably god-forsaken place. In this remote corner, lost between the colonial routes of the Moscow horseman, the ideas of heraldry are at slumber.

The author of the coats of arms for the Yaroslavl' region became the victim of doubts; he thus failed to devise any individual and specific attribute for the towns of Danilov, Lyubim, Poshekhonye, Borisoglebsk, and Petrovsk. Here he found no food for his heraldic thought and succumbed to trifling with the regional bear.

We run up against a very rare situation for Russian heraldry with the coats of arms for the towns in the Yaroslavl' region. They broke the custom according to which the regional symbol, usually placed at the top of the local shield, served as a universal crest for all the local coats of arms. The upper, regional figure never interfered in the affairs of the independent figures located in the lower, local part of the shield.[14] But this is absolutely different for the Yaroslavl' region. Only a few local coats of arms independently carry their own meaningful figures. Yet the bear of Yaroslavl' is given a free hand, and he becomes a protagonist in half of the coats of arms of the Yaroslavl' region. Each time, he acquires arbitrary size and background color. The choice of position on the shield is also left to the bear: one can find him in the center, upper, or left-hand part. At times he is depicted to the local people as a whole form, at time its top half; he may face fully or half-face his audience.

No other regional heraldic hero in Russia could afford such an unruly behavior as the famous General Toptygin could in his heraldic domain. Toptygin went on a spree, for localities subordinate to him could put forward no worthy symbols of their own. Even in recent documents and papers about the local towns of the Yaroslavl' region, we come across only humiliating definitions such as "Although an administrative district, Poshekhonye is a mere rural area, without a town."

Could the small mouse of Myshkin (*Myshkin* in Russian means *that of a mouse*, for *mysh* is the Russian for *mouse*) struggle even with a small bear? All rights of the mouse to appear on the heraldic shield come down to the interplay of the place name and heraldry. Similarly, the red hill on the coat of arms of Krasnyy Kholm in the Tver' region (in Russian *krasnyy kholm* stands for *red hill*) could never be an obstacle for the bear's expedition to Novgorod.[15]

Oh, no! Instead of trying to resist the advance of General Toptygin it is much better to welcome him with some delicious food. The Tver' province welcomes the bear with a cane of delicious raspberries placed on the tray of the Bezhetsk's shield. It is better to do the bear such a favor than to let him step onto the field of the regional coat of arms and the throne of Tver', as happened in Novgorod.

The passive suffering and geographical lack of expression of this area are built up by the picture of the crawfish of Ves'yegonsk and the hare of Korcheva. Both animals became a delicious dish recently, but in earlier times, when coats of arms were being formulated, such symbols denoted the dull banality of the places to which they were awarded.

The most expressive symbol of the suffering and passivity characteristic of this Upper Volga "bears' corner" is the coat of arms of Uglich, which depicts the innocent Prince Demetrius[16] holding the knife of his murderer.[17] What other role could be played by Uglich, which be-

[14] In later local coats of arms the regional symbol is placed in the upper "right-hand" corner (actually meaning left-hand corner, since heraldic terminology uses mirror images.)

[15] This group of coats of arms is based on place names and extends further into the southwest of the Moscow-Novgorod line: an aged nun (Russian: *staritza*) in Staritza, an isle (*ostrov*) In Ostrov, prongs (*zubtzy*) in Zubtsov, a hill (*kholm*) in Kholm.

[16] Demetrius, son of Ivan the Terrible, was murdered in Uglich in 1591. An official commission appointed to investigate the murder included Basil Ivanovich Shuisky. The commission reported Demetrius to have stabbed himself in an epileptic fit. In 1606, Basil Shuisky headed a plot against the First Impostor, known as Grishka Otrepyev, who had declared himself as Demetrius Ivanovich. After the First Impostor had been murdered, Shuisky was crowned tzar in Moscow. Written statements were circulated by Shuisky, who now testified to the violent nature of Demetrius' death, thus backtracking his own words, but proved to be to no avail in precluding the appearance of the Second Impostor, the Pseudo-Demetrius II.

[17] Naturally, there is no murderer on the coat of arms. The figure of *(see next page)*

longed to the land of mice, hares, and bears fed with raspberries, and which used to be the nearest destination from Moscow for political exile, as well as the place of secret political murder?

Where could an outcast find asylum here? Behind the monastery gate of Kalyazin or the ground city wall of Mologa, which was to remain the protector of monuments of archaic times for posterity? Could these museum strongholds be taken seriously by the Moscow horseman, who had surrounded himself by the stone castles of Mozhaisk and Sergiev, by the traditions of Vereya and Kolomna, and by the modern fortifications of Volokolamsk, and who demolished everything, even the eternal stones of Podol'sk and Nikitsk?

The coat of arms of Uglich echoes that of Yaroslavl'. The last fortress of the pagan's domain, cut down with an axe, resembles the last tzar from Rurik's dynasty, murdered with a knife six centuries later. Together with the empty thrones of Tver' and Novgorod they give almost eschatological meaning to the whole heraldic area, where, along with the ending of the pagan realm and of Rurik's dynasty, of the independence of Tver' and of Novgorod, Vladimir-and-Suzdal' Russia came to an end; blood flowed freely everywhere (probably, the ancient earthen wall around Mologa is somehow connected with the battle at the river Syt'[18]). Both the long-eared hare of Korcheva and the small unarmed bear of Mologa seem to foresee their end, listening carefully for the roar of bulldozers, as if the author of the coats of arms had read the future plans of "Hydroproject"[19] and deliberately gave Korcheva and Mologa these symbols that are so poor in vitality!

But we cannot say that the heraldic "bears' corner" of the Upper Volga region looks senseless or that it passed without purpose. Its sufferings teach us a lesson. On the heraldic map of Russia, the victim of Uglich on his blood-red shield is the first (on the heraldic map of Russia) reminder of morality in politics. The frightened figures of Korcheva's hare, drowned in the artificial lake, and the unarmed bear from Mologa, who in vain hid himself behind the city wall ruined by the waters of "the Big Volga," should be regarded as a revelation about a morality in economics that is only nowadays approaching us.

BEARS' CORNER IN THE SANCTUARY OF WILD BIRDS

In 1812 the Moscow prizefighter would trudge the road to Paris fairs with the bear of Sergach through Kovno (a monument to Russia's victory in the Napoleonic war rises high in Kovno's coat of arms). Not all the bears of heraldic Russia want to walk on their hind legs as performing clowns beyond the Kovno milestone.[20] Not all of them want to wear on their shoulders the uniform attributes signifying service to the Center.

The bear of Great Perm would only agree to carry the Bible and the cross laid on its back for the famous educator, Saint Stephen of Perm.[21] Moscow's heraldic conclave, trying to disturb the bear of Ust'-Sysol'sk, faced open resistance. This bear was unwilling to become a human being, either through heraldic symbols or through the training of Sergach, and would hide deep in his den, exposing his white fangs.

The bear of Ust'-Sysol'sk is literally cornered, driven to the upper corner, which "collapsed" between the economic axes of the Volga and the Urals. His perilous roar prevents men from feeling free deep inside these areas. They dare hunt only with heavenly help, and in the coat of arms of Vyatka a hand appearing from the clouds holds the bow, while the shield itself is emblazoned with a cross. This land is bountiful, not with things of human concern, but with the twitter and song of many different birds: hawks, wild duck, geese, wood-peckers, and even an eagle are placed on the heraldic shields of the Vyatka region. The elk of Cherdyn',

the villain placed near the innocent boy would have inspired respect for the memory of the Prince. Nevertheless the hand that lifted the knife could never appear on the heraldic shield of Uglich. Only the Center can execute and show mercy, which it did — either by the hand of noble Basil Shuisky, who signed the investigation document about the casual suicide of the boy or by the same tzar's hand pointing at the murderers.

[18] The battle of the river Syt' took place in 1238. Here, Khan Baty defeated the armies of the Vladimir princedom.

[19] Hydroproject is an organization which draws up land melioration and hydro engineering projects. In particular, it managed the Volga reservoirs that inundated a considerable number of old villages and towns including Korcheva and Mologa.

[20] Besides its literal meaning, "beyond the western border," the phrase "beyond the Kovno milestone" means "far." It is analogous to "the Kolomna milestone," an expression that is synonymous for something long and that derives from the belief that the Moscow-Kolomna road was marked out with milestones set extremely far apart.

[21] Stephen of Perm preached the Gospel to the local Finnish peoples.

which has gone to lick salt at the Solikamsk mine, is galloping back to the safety of this nature's asylum. At the southern end of it his mate of Tzarevokokshaysk remains prone, trembling with each new knock of the logs rolled by the Volga timber cutters to the stack of Semenov. There is no room for wild animals in the hearth of life active on the Volga. Only the wild ducks, soaring high in the heavenly blue in the coat of arms of Cheboksary, feel temporarily safe from men. They can find sublime peace only in the depth of Vyatka of Yaransk's heraldic shield.

The essence of this heraldic area, forgotten by proud man, is very well expressed in the allegorical description of the coat of arms of Nolinsk, of "the flying swan, because birds fly by, never stopping near the town." Yet the human eye of Glazov (*glaz* is the Russian for *eye*) has shrewdly pierced this remote corner. It will be very, very soon that the ministries, avoiding every stranger's look, will set their eyes on these territories. The bears, birds, and elk are ideal spectators for the future defense constructions.

In the west, "the land of peaceful birds" is trimmed with a strip of heraldic impersonality. Interpretations of place names — the white willows (*vetla* in Russian) of Vetluga, the horse's head with a large mane (*griva*) of Kologriv, the buoy (*buy*) of Buy, the red pine forest (*krasny bor*) of Krasnoborsk — link the corner of Vyatka with the remote areas of the Yaroslavl' and Tver' regions both geographically and semantically.

In the East the chatter of Vyatka's birds is drowned in the active clatter of the Kama shipbuilding industry of Laishev (like that of the Volga in the South); the bread trade of Chistopol; the corn growing of Mamadysh; the colonial castle of Sarapul; the fishing of Okhansk; the educated bear of Perm'; and the salt works of Solikamsk. The woodpecker of Elabuga, in the vicinity of the Kama, is also affected by the sound of the woodcutter's axe, since the ax has already touched the banks of the Kama (like those of the Volga in the town of Semyenov), and the woodpecker is now pecking at a tree stump. Yet beyond the Kama one again finds oneself in the kingdom of birds, recurrent in the coats of arms of Menzelinsk, Birsk, Krasnoufimsk and Sterlitamak, and on to the very Urals.

The river sparrow of Birsk and the geese of Sterlitamak appear as heraldic water pointers on the left tributary of the Kama — the river Belaya. Like the wild goose of Urzhum, the blue ribbon of Orlov and the fishing nets of Slobodskoy suggest the existence of a hidden valley around the Vyatka, the right tributary of the Kama, deep in the bird wilderness of Vyatka.

CLOUDS IN SKY

This kingdom of impersonal and passive towns, with its animals that are of little use to the people, forms an expansive belt over Moscow's heraldic bar from the Pskov boundaries to the Urals — from the island (*ostrov* in Russian) of the town of Ostrov to the cauldrons (*kotyol*) of Kotel'nich and the wasps (*osa* in Russian) of Osa[22]. The northern economic border of this barren belt is the northern limit of agriculture, signified on the heraldic map by the rye sheaves of Demyansk and Nikol'sk (in Vologda region), protruding to the North,[23] between them the linen of Pudozh and, continuing the line to the east, the not so abundant horn of Kungur rye.[24] Naturally Kungur, where it is possible to grow and harvest corn, seems absolutely abundant to the bear of Perm' and the sable of Verkhotur'ye, surrounded as they are not by fertile cornfields, but by the woods of Osa and Berezov.

Running almost parallel to this rational economic boundary of agricultural poverty, one can see on the heraldic map a borderline displayed in a different way, which is either climatic or semimystical. This is a heraldic chain of clouds connecting the shields of Pskov, Olonets, Vologda, Varnavino, and Vyatka. This line of heraldic water suspended in the sky resembles the isohyet of maximal precipitation in the Russian plain. But the heavenly hands appearing out of the clouds reveal on the obscure horizon the cover of Providence, Moscow's cloak covering the ancient Russian lands that since olden times have been under the temporal and absolute tyrannical influence of the Center. Development is suppressed under that cloudy and gloomy halo of prestigious Moscow in this land of withering agriculture. Place names and their mean-

[22] The insects of Osa are called bees in the description of its coat of arms. This is apparently conditioned by the desire to bring more sense, to retouch the offensive picture that depicts these useless and harmful wasps on the coat of arms of a small, harmless, and remote town.

[23] This northern protrusion corresponds to the actual curve northwards around the lakes of the Beloozero and the Ladoga, which used to be the limit of Russian agriculture.

[24] The rye ears inside the horn of plenty seem an embodiment of heraldic irony, for normally the horn is depicted full of all the exotic fruits imaginable.

ings are monotonous and artificial, and the remote bears' and birds' heraldic shields are only disturbed by glimpses of lakes, the vision of St. Demetrius, and the ghostly vacant thrones of Tver' and Novgorod.[25]

III. The industrial North industrial colonization

Desperate bears with axes go wandering through the Yaroslavl' North, near the boundary of withering agriculture, and are searching for their best application. Not all of them can join the administrative service to hunt for the outcast ounce of Novgorod or travel — through Maloyaroslavets's stirring eagles — to the desirable hives of Sosnitsa (we will speak about the hives later). Few of them are ready to choose the path of a Sergach dancer.

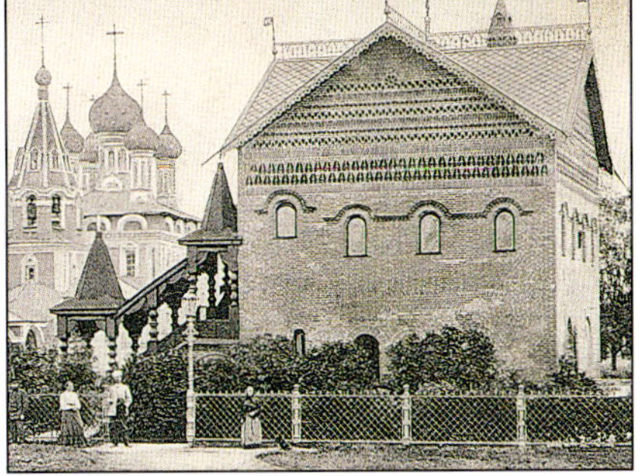

Uglich. This church was build on the spot of tzarevich Demetrius' assassination; his palace is in the background.

Leaving the orbit of immediate subordination to Moscow, breaking the harshness of poor agricultural soil, the bears head for the industrially colonized North, where, above the clouds, St. George's spear of Moscow will never reach them. It is in the depth of their adored woods that they create an amazing and versatile range of trading activities, without comparison among other parts of the heraldic map.

With their ready and speedy axes, the forest inhabitants are hired to make the vats (*kadka* in Russian) of Kadnikov and to produce wood-tar and fill barrels with it in Vel'sk. In the woods they hunt for fox (Mezen'), marten (Lal'sk, Shadrinsk and Ufa), squirrel (Yarensk) and in the taiga, up to the Urals, and further — for Siberian sable (Verkhoturye) and ermine (Verkhneural'sk). The hunt for trivialities becomes so attractive that Tot'ma's hunters spread their trade as far as Russian America. And it was from the American is-

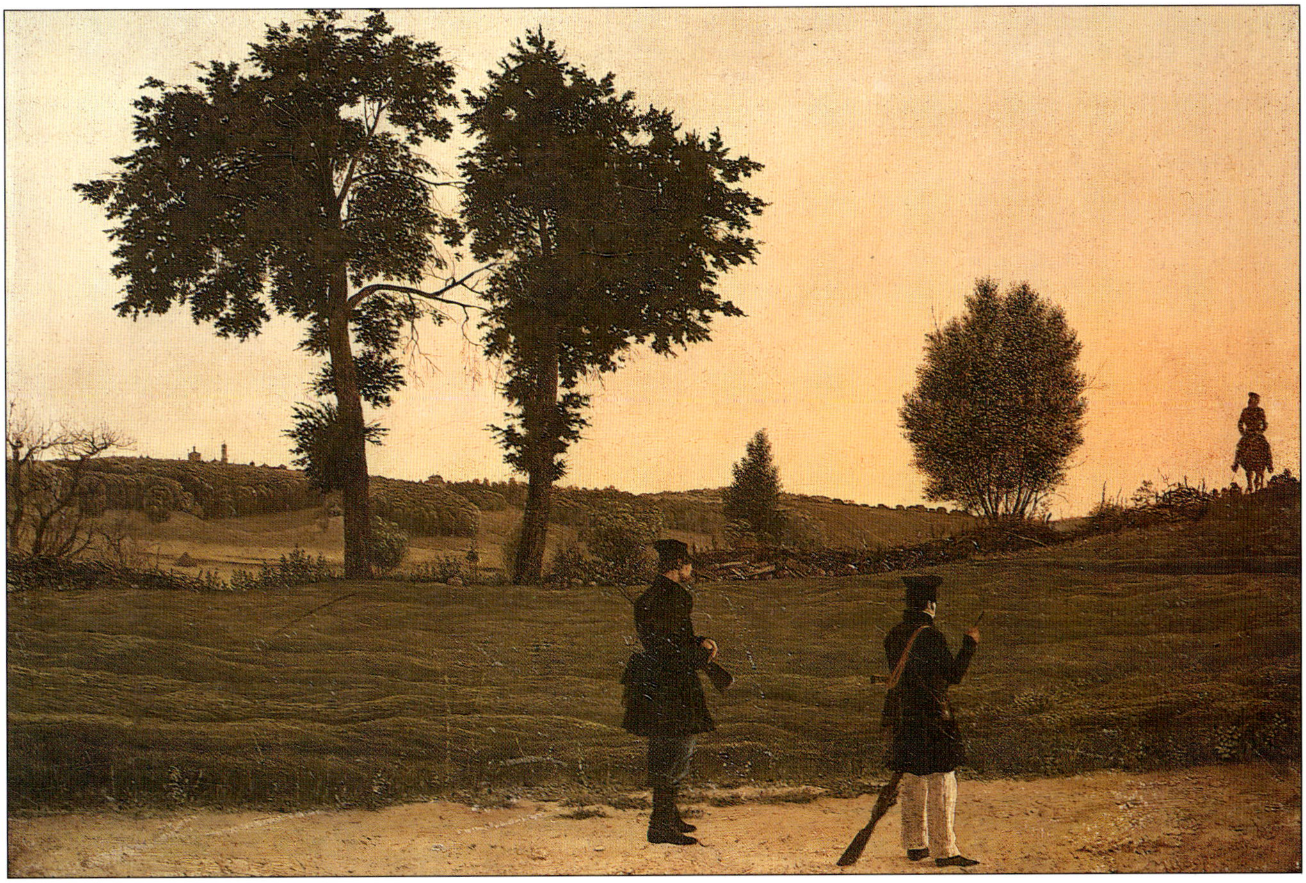

[25] For the moment we will disengage ourselves from the transport symbols of Moscow and St. Petersburg fighting their way through these virgin heraldic areas. We will come back to them later.

Landscape with hunters. Area of Kolomna. I. Shchedrovsky.

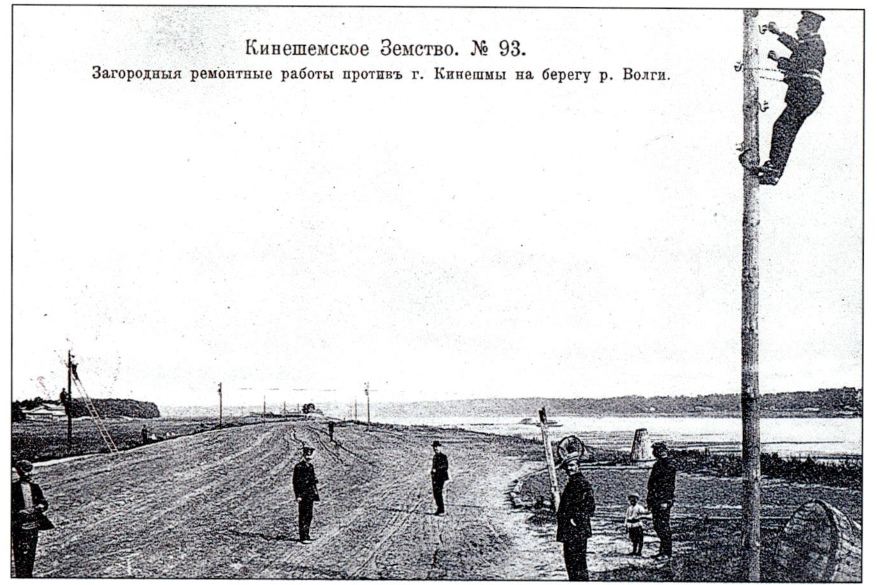

□□ Kineshma. Repair works on a telegraph line. The town is located in the Upper Volga, where people have always been noted for their industriousness. In the eighteenth century, peasants would often go off to town in search of a living; by the late nineteenth century, the region's agriculture as such was finally relegated to the background. The region has primarily been developed industrially, because of its poor soil.

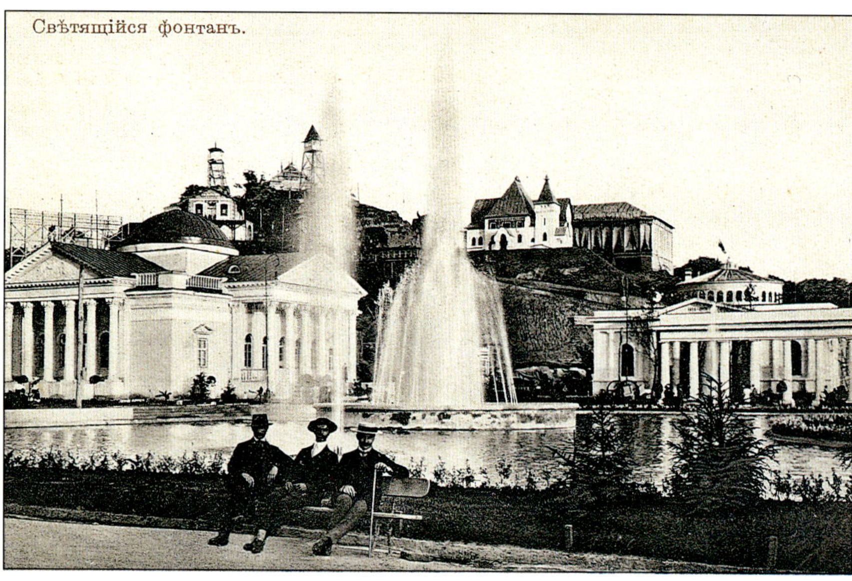

□□ Kostroma. "An illuminated fountain." The postcard anticipates the creation of a festive mood but for the strikingly lonely streets, a sure sign of provinciality.

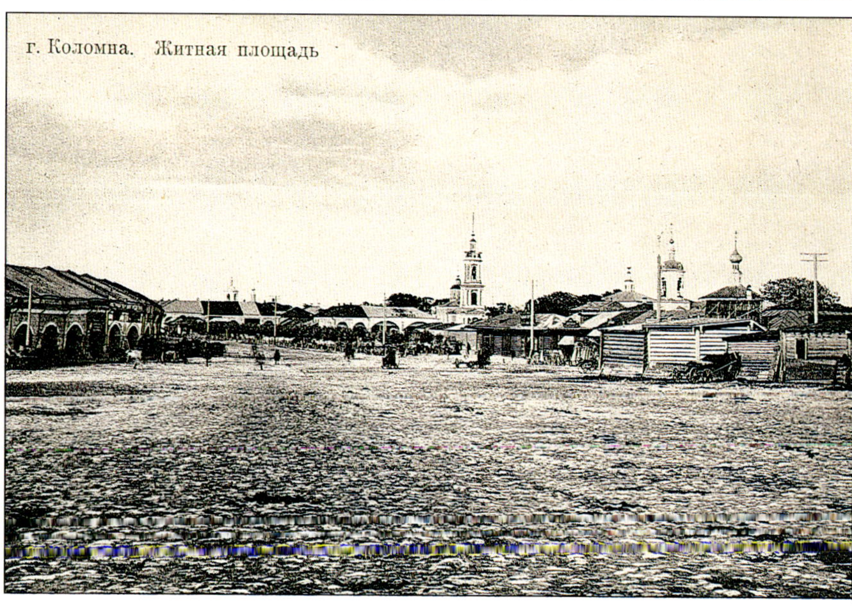

□□ Kolomna. Zhitnaya Square. Southern provinces used to supply Moscow with bread. The size of the square, formerly used as a marketplace, speaks for the scale of the bread trade.

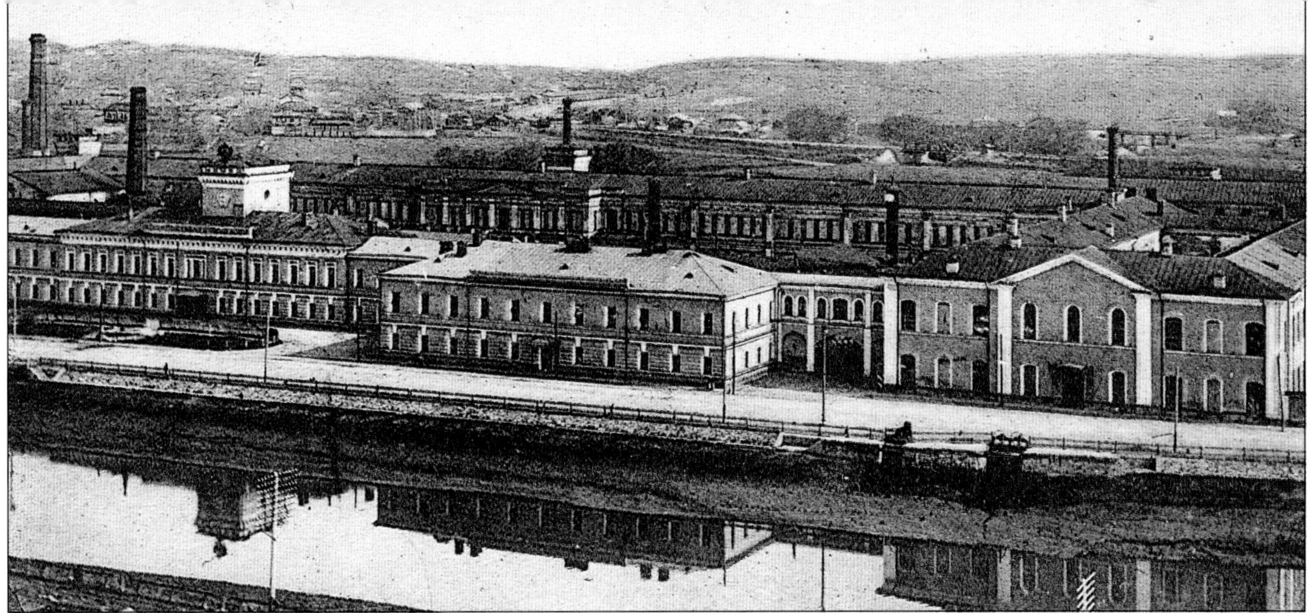

lands that the silver fox stepped onto the Tot'ma and Surgut coat of arms, for it was never seen in those places before.

With the golden harpoons borrowed from the shield of Chukhloma, these northern animals go fishing not only to the Chukhloma Lake, but also to the Beloye Lake (fishes are on the coat of arms of Belozersk) and Il'men' Lake (four silver fishes make the base of the Novgorod throne). The residents of Okhansk and Slobodskoy get their fishing nets, rods, and other tools, "with the help of which different species of fish can be caught there in great abundance." In this vicinity the people of Kaigorod boil fish to make "fish glue." The silver river salmon fill the tubs of Luga. There is also enough salt there to pickle it.

The second golden currency after furskins in the bear's Russia — salt — is boiled off at the salt works of Staraya Russa and falls in geometric crystals onto the shields of Soligalich and Sol'vychegodsk. The old salt sources are running out, yet a new salt mine is dug out in Solikamsk — "with a bucket for lifting the salt to the surface."

Salt was not the only reason for penetration into the northern forests. The

▯▯ Tula. The emperor's arms factory. Iron ore deposits found in the town's environs made Tula the birthplace of Russia's metal-working industry. Tula's symbols are arms and a samovar. It was from Tula that factories began to spread towards Petrozavodsk and the Urals.

coats of arms of Ustyuzhna (Ustyuzhna of the Iron Field) and Cherepovets draw attention to the significant — for those times — marsh resources of iron ores. Soon three iron hammers covered with a forked branch[26] thump at the shield of Petrozavodsk, indicating the abundance of ores and the different workshops abiding in the area. The North passes the baton of iron-processing on to the Urals, where Ekaterinburg is extracting ores from its "iron mine" and smelting them in "the silver furnace," while Alapayevsk is forging iron with its mechanical hammer.

The Urals are rightly seen as so attractive in terms of economy that the heraldry sees them neither as mountainous (all attention to the Urals' heights is limited to "the three green hills, which are actually situated nearby" on the heraldic map of Kostychy), nor as an impenetrable border obstacle. The Russian crossing of the Urals is marked off by no milestone or monument, by no kind of "Kolomna milestone"; the first milestone in the East appears only in the pyramid of Tobol'sk, much further to the East of the Urals. On the contrary, the heraldic heart of iron works in the Urals (Ekaterinburg and Alapayevsk, bordering Solikamsk in the North) is on all sides surrounded by blood vessels of transport and trading symbols (Laishev, Chistopol', Verkh-Yazvinskoye, Irbit, Chelyabinsk, Tyumen'). This will be discussed further on.

It is beyond the Ural mountains that the bear, who had gone through the purgatory hearth of metal-forge drudgery and toil, who had escaped Yaroslavl' and Sergach slavery, Novgorod gendarmery, Perm' humiliation and Ust'-Sysol'sk bondage, started a free and natural life, going without a care onto the enchanting clearing of the coat of arms of Turinsk.

(to be continued)

[26] Quite often, metal deposits and water-bearing strata used to be found by the divining method, with the use of a forked branch. The branch, when held in the diviner's hands, would rotate over the deposit.

the crimea: culture, art, landmarks / max voloshin

Maximilian A. Voloshin (1877-1932) — A significant figure in early twentieth-century Russian culture, Voloshin was a poet and watercolor painter. His life and creative work were inextricably linked with the Crimea, where he spent his adult life. For Russian culture, Voloshin opened up the Eastern Crimea — Cimmeria — which served as the theme for many of his poems and drawings. In Koktebel, a small village not far from Theodosia, he founded what resembled an artists' colony. There, many famous people of the artistic community often came into contact with those novices who were later to become the leading figures of twentieth-century Russian culture. "Max" — as he was known to his friends — was a caretaker, a kind of *genius loci* for that tract of land, saturated with cultural meanings, that furthermost outpost of the Mediterranean world.

◘◘ All the watercolors by Max Voloshin reproduced in this publication are deposited in Moscow's Pushkin Museum of Fine Arts.

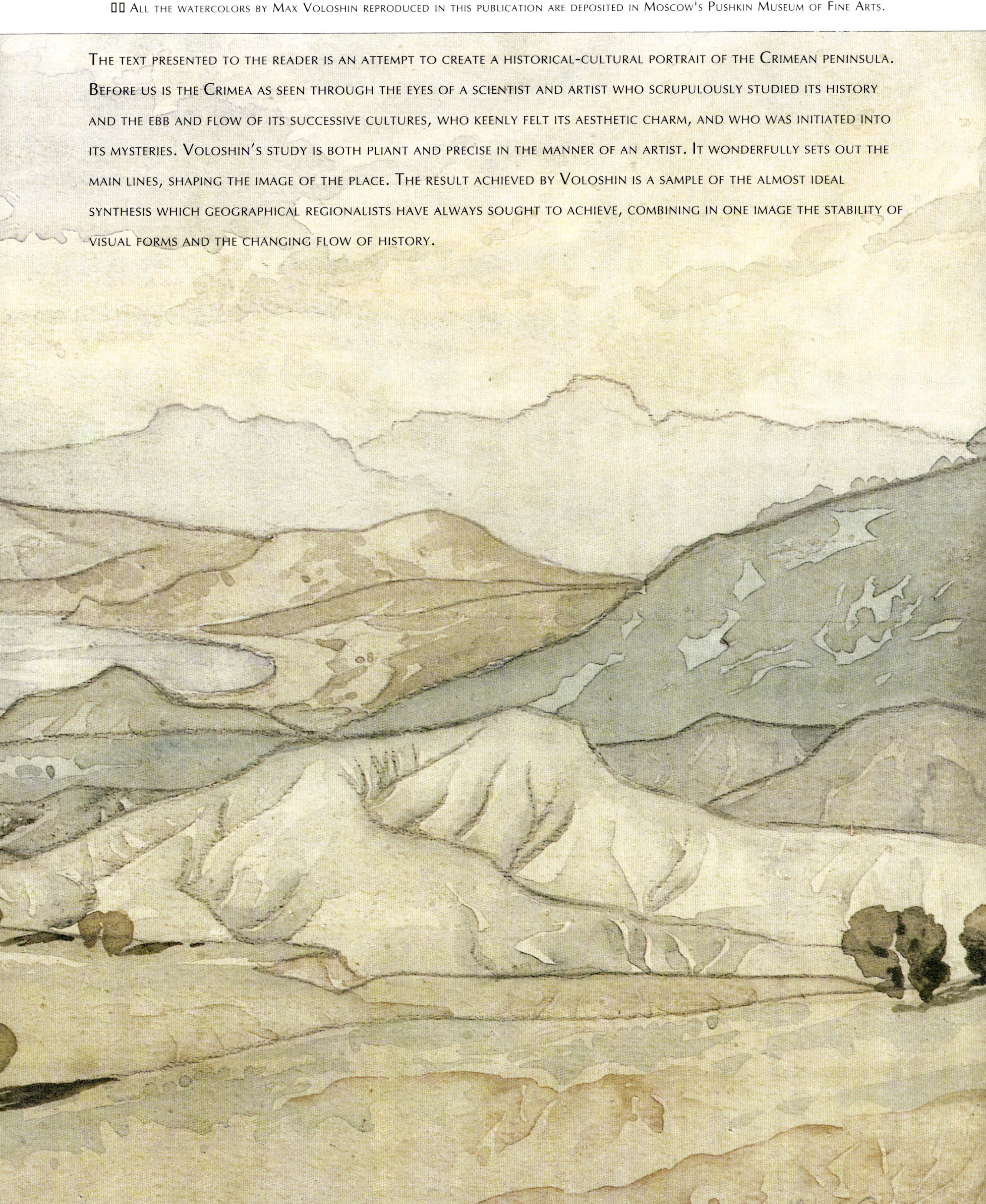

The text presented to the reader is an attempt to create a historical-cultural portrait of the Crimean peninsula. Before us is the Crimea as seen through the eyes of a scientist and artist who scrupulously studied its history and the ebb and flow of its successive cultures, who keenly felt its aesthetic charm, and who was initiated into its mysteries. Voloshin's study is both pliant and precise in the manner of an artist. It wonderfully sets out the main lines, shaping the image of the place. The result achieved by Voloshin is a sample of the almost ideal synthesis which geographical regionalists have always sought to achieve, combining in one image the stability of visual forms and the changing flow of history.

THE CRIMEA: CULTURE, ART, LANDMARKS / MAX VOLOSHIN ■■

Crimea, Cimmeria,[1] *Kerman,*[2] *Kremlin.* All these words have the same root, *KMR*, which in Hebrew means "sudden dark and gloom" and which carries connotations of castles, enclosed spaces, dangers, and mist and mystery.

The Crimea is an island separated from the mainland by stagnant, stinking *Maeotic* marshes,[3] salt lakes, and narrow sandbanks; its coast takes in the sea in the guise of deep harbors, straits, and bays. The mainland in its eyes has forever been a flowing, heaving mass, the bed of a great ocean across which glaciers and avalanches of human tribes flowed from the depths of Asia to Europe. The sea, on the other hand, was a more stable element, with the constant ebb and flow of Mediterranean culture. The Wild Field[4] and *Mare Internum*[5] defined the history of the Crimea.

For The Wild Field, the Crimea was a quiet backwater. During human floods, The Wild Field overflowed its banks. The neighboring Caucasus was a comb against which peoples scratched themselves, leaving patches of fleece and skin of every color — specimens of all races. This makes the Caucasus a veritable ethnographic museum.

The Crimea is less of a museum. It was only occasionally reached by the streams of humanity which came to rest in the backwater, settling like silt on the harbor bottom, overlaid and mixed with each other. Cimmerians, Tauri, Scythians, Sarmatians, Pechenegs, Khazars, Polovtsy, Tatars, and Slavs all formed the sediment of The Wild Field. Greeks, Armenians, Romans, Venetians, and Genoans formed the commercial and cultural yeast of the *Pontus Euxinus*.[6] This was a dizzying conglomerate of racial alloys and hybrid forms, a preserve of the human species exposed to powerful cultural currents.

This flow and mixture of humanity accounts for the dual role of the Crimea. On the one hand, it was a remote, anonymous, provincial part of vast Asia, a wild peninsula. On the other hand, it was Mediterranean Europe's outpost in the East and, as such, caught some of the historical limelight of antiquity.

The Crimea derived its special significance from lying at the intersection of the sea lanes and ancient caravan routes to India. Today, if you drive along the highway from Theodosia to Simferopol, you will notice a row of sturdy iron poles next to the ungainly slapdash wooden telegraph poles. This used to be the Indian Telegraph line from London to Calcutta built by Britain across the Crimea under an agreement signed after the 1856 war.

If you turn off the present highway and follow the line of the Indian telegraph, which skirts Mount Agarmysh in the north where the old highway used to be, you will cross two valleys named, respectively, the Dry Indol and Wet Indol.

Yol is the Tatar for "road." *Ind-Yol* means "the road to India." Ancient linguistic facts converge with reminders of the recent past.

This was the old caravan route that went across the Crimean steppes to the *Cimmerian Bosporus*[7] and continued across the Caucasus and Persia. The route ceased to be used during the fifteenth century when the Ottoman Empire blocked all the roads leading to Asia Minor and when Vasco da Gama discovered new sea routes from Western Europe to India.

But the need for the land route did not entirely cease. England, the colonial power, eventually came to need it more than anyone else. Access to it was one of the conditions England set to Russia after the seizure of Sebastopol in 1855. England had been planning to build a railway along the forty-fifth parallel before the start of the European war in 1914. During the war the project was launched by Russia at England's request.

The route to be followed was from Bordeaux to Mont Cenis, Turin (or, alternatively, from London to Paris, Lyons, Turin), Lombardy, the Venice area, Trieste, Yugoslavia, Romania, Odessa, Nikolayev, Perekop, Dzhankoi, Vladislavovka, Kerch, the bridge across the Kerch Strait, the Taman Peninsula, and the Caucasian coast whence, by one of several possible routes, via Turkey and Persia

[1] *Cimmeria* — the ancient name of the north shore of the Black Sea stretching from the Danube River to the mouth of the Don River, formerly populated by the Cimmerians.

[2] *Kerman* — a province in the south-eastern part of The Persian Empire; called Carmania in ancient times.

[3] *Palus Maeotis* — the Sea of Azov, named by the Greeks after the tribe of Maeots which populated its shores.

[4] The Wild Field — the vast southern steppes of the Eastern European Plains across which passed a great number of nomadic waves during the first millennium A.D.

[5] *Mare Internum* — the Latin name for the Mediterranean Sea.

[6] *Pontus Euxinus* — the Greek name for the Black Sea.

[7] *The Cimmerian Bosporus* — the Greek name for the Straits of Kerch, which separate the Crimea from the Caucasus so connecting the Sea of Azov and the Black Sea.

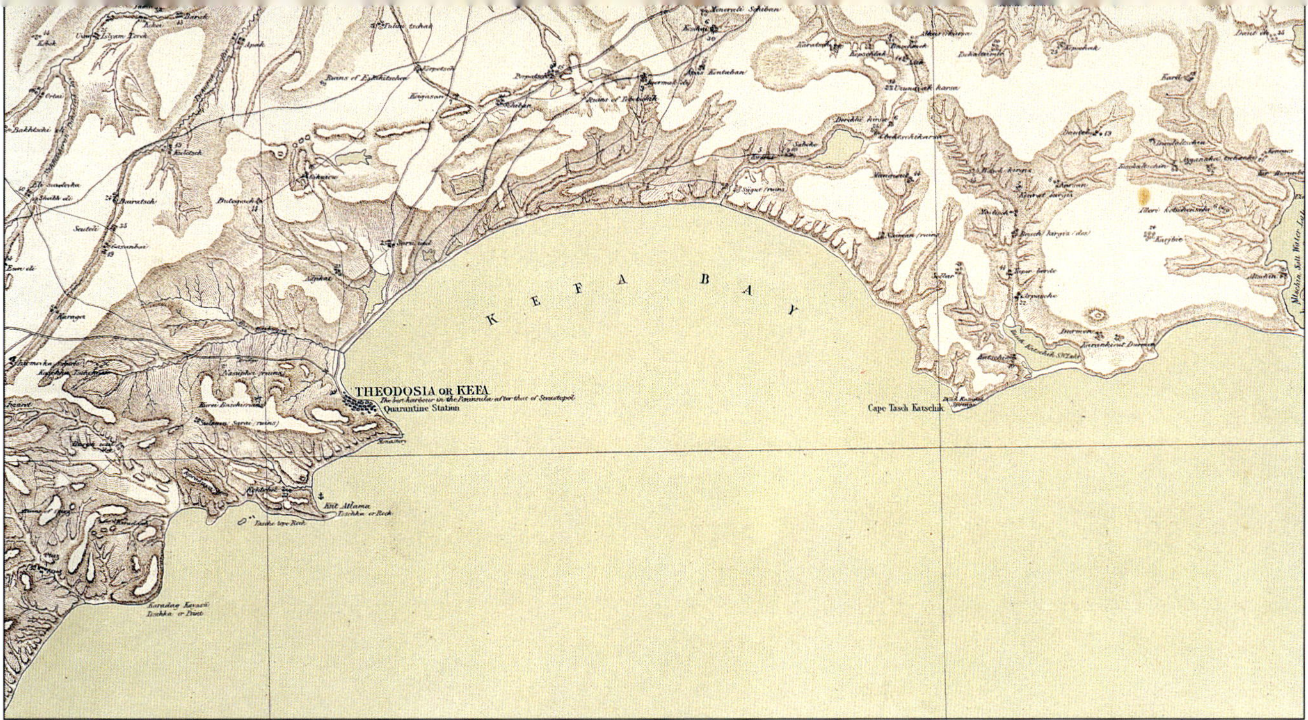

Crimea. A British war map of the nineteenth century.

Crimea. Times atlas.

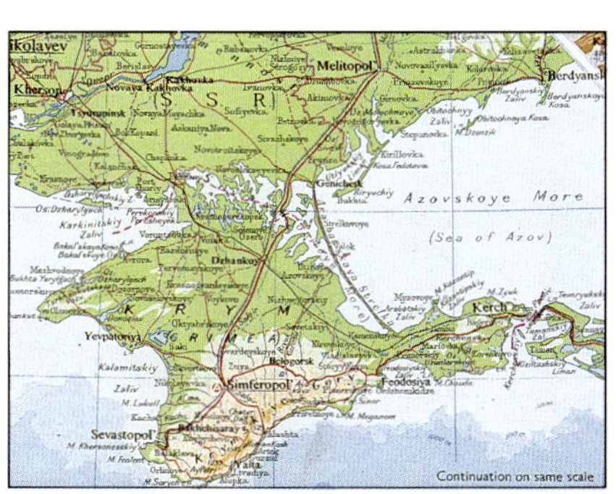

to India.

During World War I Russia completed feasibility studies for a bridge across the Cimmerian Bosporus, discovering in the process that its bottom was an active mud spring. Construction was under way on many other sections at the time, but the Civil War and new political combinations put an end to that work. There is no doubt, however, that sooner or later a railway track will run along the old caravan route, when the Crimea will again be at the center of a great European way to Asia and will acquire immense trade and political significance.

The future of the Crimea is linked much more closely to its past than might appear at first sight. Human settlements have existed in the confluences of the earth and the sea in the Crimea since prehistoric times. Cimmerians and Tauri, of whose history nothing is known for certain, undoubtedly built cities and fortresses and had large settlements beside the deep harbor of the *Thrachaeic Peninsula*,[8] along the Cimmerian Bosporus, and at the wide Theodosian bay. These might well date back to the early second millennium B. C. The role of the trade ferment was undoubtedly played in those times by the Phoenicians.

In the early fourteenth century B. C. the Crimea was overrun by the Scythians, and in the sixth and seventh centuries Greek colonization began, bringing Crimea within the orbit of world history.

The Greek cities built in the accessible harbors — *Chersonese*,[9] *Panticapaeum*,[10] *Theodosia*[11] — were to become important foci and centers of propagation of Hellenism for many centuries. Their individual roles differed widely. Initially Chersonese (the Doric pronunciation is Chersonas) was the outpost of Greek culture. Its colo-

[8] *The Thrachaeic Peninsula* — the Greek name of the Tarkhankut Peninsula in the western Crimea.

[9] *Chersonese* — an ancient Greek colony near Sebastopol in southern Crimea.

[10] *Panticapaeum* — an ancient Greek colony in eastern Crimea, presently the city of Kerch.

[11] *Theodosia* — a city in eastern Crimea, formerly an ancient Greek colony.

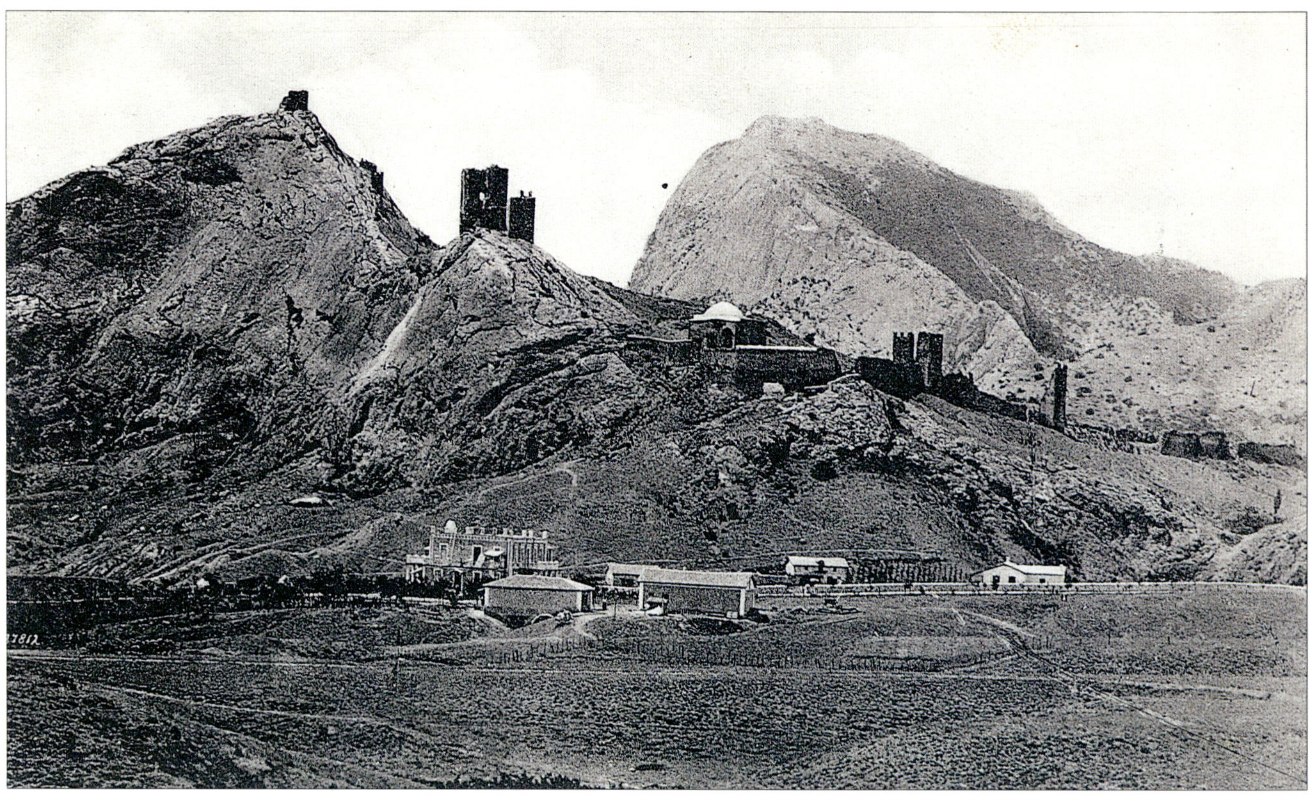

▯▯ *Genoan fortress in Sudak. Postcard 1913.*

nial pedigree relates it to Heraclea and Megara. Its cultural significance for the whole Black Sea was immense. Situated close to the colonies of Asia Minor, more remote from The Wild Field, and at the crossing of Black Sea routes running from south to north, it was better placed than other Greek colonies to uphold its political independence. The role of Chersonese in the Crimea was, albeit on a smaller scale, similar to that of Babylon and Rome — that is, the cities that likewise took in conquering races, digested them, and carried their cultural traditions through a series of world catastrophes and collapses of empires.

Although it was but one outreaching tentacle of Greek culture, Chersonese withstood the onslaught of The Wild Field for 2000 years, Hellenizing wave after wave of conquerors who settled in the Crimea. Scythians, Sarmatians, Allans, Goths, Huns, Ugrians, Varangians, Slavs, Pechenegs, Khazars, Polovtsy, Tatars, and Turks — all of them over the ages appeared at its walls with their armies. Only Rome and Byzantium had enough stamina and muscle to resist their attacks. Chersonese, however, was just a free trading city with only a tenuous link with its metropolis. It had neither a large population, nor a large and rich territory to fall back on, nor the natural protection of mountains or gorges. It was welded together only by the civic oath of the Chersonasites, an oath which was discovered recently. This oath represents a fine specimen of ancient incantation and civic poetry:

I swear by the Sun, Earth, Zeus and the Virgin,
The Olympian Gods and Goddesses and Heroes,
Who own the city and the land
And the fort of Chersonasites:
I will be faithful to the freedom of the city and the citizens. . . .
I will not betray Chersonas, nor Kerkinitida,
Nor the Beautiful Harbor,
Nor the fortifications nor the land of Chersonasites. . . .
Nothing to anyone: a Greek or a Barbarian.
But I will preserve them for the people of Chersonas. . . .
I will serve the Demiurges and the Council Members.
In the best and justest way for the city and the citizens.
I will not betray, in words, any secrets,
That may harm the city, neither to a Greek nor to a Barbarian,
I will sell the grain brought from the valley to Chersonas,
But not to any other place.
If I keep my oath, may I and my tribe be blessed.
If I break it — may neither the land
Nor the sea, nor the wives bear fruit

Judging from the works of art excavated in Chersonese and now located in the Hermitage Museum, Chersonese cultivated and disseminated an austere classical style. This reflected the ebb and flow of great historic changes — Ancient Greece, Rome, and Byzantium. Even in later Byzantine time, Chersonese appeared fabulous to Kievites and Novgorodians. This cultural richness brought Prince Vladimir [12] to its walls in pursuit of the romantic glory of Korsun. [13] To the Prince, Chersonese was simultaneously what Constantinople was for the Crusaders and what Amsterdam was for Peter the Great.

Chersonese provided Rus with many imports, including religion, priests and artisans, monks and craftsmen, relics, icons, fashions, furniture, prayer-books and secular luxuries. Its exports to the south, throughout its existence, were from The Wild Field, mainly slaves, grain, and salt fish, as well as timber, wool, leather, and furs.

The first people to be Hellenized in this area were the Scythians who occupied the Crimea for about 1,500 years. Towards the end of that period the Scythians were to Greece culturally what Gaul was to Rome. But the peoples magnetized by Chersonese constantly threatened its independence. Such was the case with the

[12] Prince Vladimir —?-1015, Kievan ruler who introduced Christianity into Ancient Russia (Rus) in 988.

[13] Korsun — the Slavic name for Chersonese.

[14] The Bosporus Kingdom — a state of united Greek cities north of the Black Sea Basin with its capital in Panticapaeum. The Kingdom reached its prime under Mithridates IV Eupator (132-63 B. C.). The Roman army defeated him in Asia Minor.

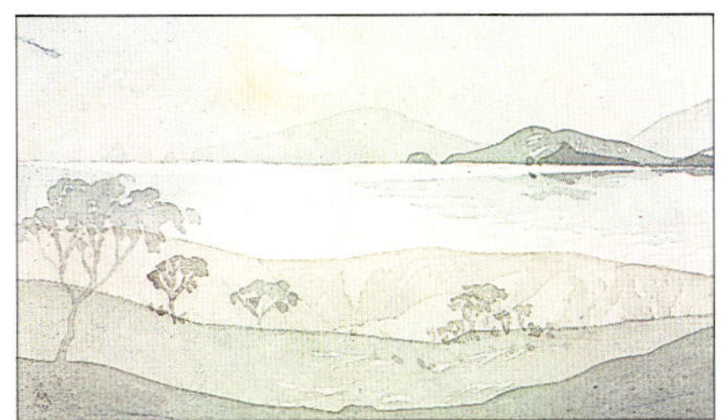

□□ *Crimean Landscape.* Max Voloshin. 1922

Scythians in the second century and the Bosporus Kingdom [14] at the times of Mithridates.

Later, Chersonese fell within the orbit of Rome, which did not challenge its self-rule and even helped it to defend itself against the Goths and the Huns. By the fifth century it was referred to as the strongest state in the Crimea, a disseminator of Christianity, an important trading post, and, for Byzantium, a particularly important outpost in the struggle against The Wild Field.

Under its influence, the Crimean Goths were Christianized, Hellenized, and dissolved, while the whole southern coast, peopled by Greeks and Goths, long retained the name of Gothia in the stretch of territory between Sudak and Balaclava . [15]

In the fifth and sixth centuries, when the Huns conquered the lowland Crimea, the Goths joined the Greeks in defending the highlands. In the seventh century the Huns were succeeded by the Khazars. In the eighth century Chersonese was deeply involved in the internal Byzantine struggle between iconoclasts and icon-worshippers, taking the side of the latter. To this epoch belonged all the Crimean cave monasteries founded by the icon-worshipping monks who had fled from

[15] Sudak and Balaclava — the outer eastern and western reaches of the south coast of the Crimea.

the empire. These included Inkerman, the Assumption Monastery, Kachikalen, Cherkes-Kermen, and Mangup-Kale.

From the ninth century Chersonese was the target of attacks by Varangians and the Rus. Prince Vladimir's expedition to Korsun was part of that saga.

The whole of Gothia was part of the Chersonese *theme.* [16] The Avars, Magyars, Pechenegs, and Polovtsy swept through it.

In the thirteenth century, after Constantinople fell to the Crusaders and the Latin Empire emerged, the Crimea experienced Italy's influence. Genoans settled in Theodosia and Venetians in Sudak. They proved a more formidable rival than the Tatars who occupied the Crimea after the Battle of Kalka (1224). By the end of that century, the whole of Gothia passed from Chersonese to the Genoan Kaffa [17] under a treaty between Genoans and Tatars, and before long Chersonese itself fell under the rule of Kaffa.

Towards the end of the fifteenth century, when Kaffa fell to the Turks (to be revived as Little Istanbul), Chersonese had been reduced to ruins, its walls and towers razed on the orders of the Kaffan consul.

While Chersonese, throughout its two thousand-year history, was the carrier of the pure Greek spirit without any admixture of barbarism, the Bosporus culture was a complex mix of many barbarian races, although the Hellenistic element was constantly present.

Initially, Panticapaeum and Theodosia,

[16] Theme — a military and administrative division of the Byzantine Empire.

[17] Kaffa — name of a Genoan colony created where the Greek colony of Theodosia had been located.

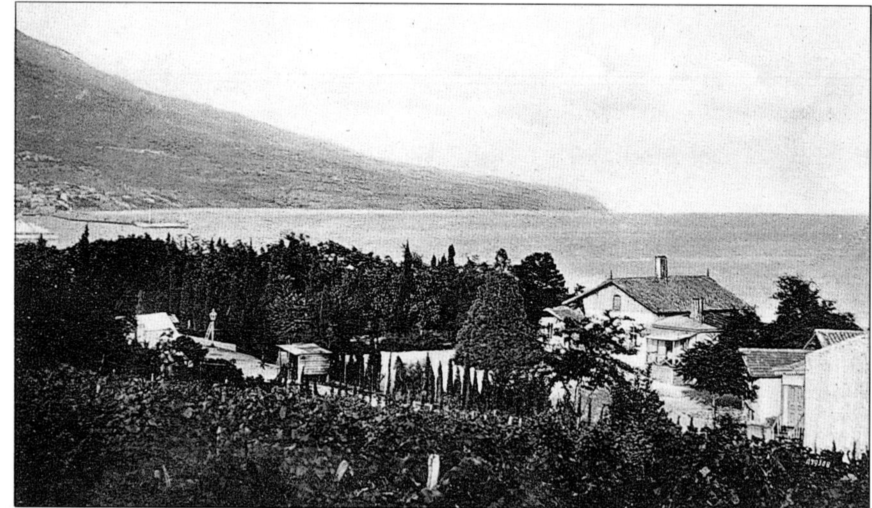

Crimea. Chukurlar. Postcard 1913.

Opposite page. *Crimean landscape.* Max Voloshin. 1923.

founded like Chersonese in the sixth century B. C. by Ionic Greeks, played no small part in the destiny of Athens. These colonies provided Attica with grain and took part in the Peloponnesian War, and their names were mentioned by Demosthenes. But they were not strong enough to uphold their independence in the whirlpool of barbarian tribes flooding from The Wild Field. Overwhelmed by the peoples that invaded them, they formed Greco-Sarmatian, Greco-Iranian, Thracian-Armenian-Hun, and Khazar-Tmutarakan-Hellenistic alloys. Yet, the Bosporus Kingdom, with its seven Hellenized dynasties and its moment of glory at the time of Mithridates Eupator, lasted for 800 years.

Theodosia's fate was even more fickle. After reaching its peak of prosperity in the fourth and fifth centuries, it became part of the Bosporus Kingdom. Its name was hardly ever mentioned in the first twelve centuries of the Christian era, but it reappeared in the early thirteenth century as Genoan Kaffa, to play a brilliant role in the destiny of the Crimea. For two hundred years, the Tatar invasion notwithstanding, it was the focus of Black Sea culture. Kaffa's trade significance at that time was greater than that ever achieved by either Chersonese or Panticapaeum. It withstood the Turkish conquest and the fall of Genoan colonies. Under the Turks, it prospered as a trade city for another three centuries. The Turks, who came from Constantinople, were basically representatives of the same Mediterranean culture, though somewhat diluted; they had reached the Far East via other routes. But for the Middle East, the Turkish Keffe remained Kuchuk-Istanbul.

We have now reached the layers of Crimean human history that lie close to the surface. The vast conglomerate of all the races that had ever passed through The Wild Field, overlaid by strong Hellenistic, Roman, and Italian elements, was inundated by Tatars.

The Tatar-Mongol population turned out to be highly malleable; it quickly mixed with the local races and assimilated their culture. Greek and Gothic blood transfigured the Tatars. The Tatars became a synthesis of the country's checkered history. Under the spacious and tolerant umbrella of Islam, the indigenous Crimean culture flourished.

The whole country, from the Maeotic marshes to the southern coast, became a flowering garden; fruit trees were grown in the steppes and vineyards in the mountains, while in the cities there were bubbling fountains and soaring white minarets. Among the stone and wood arcades, in the architecture and decorations of houses, and in the design of fabrics and embroidered towels were the echoes of Byzantine mosaics and Italian ornament.

After a turbulent period of Tatar history under the Golden Horde came the Golden Age of the Gireis,[18] under the protection of the magnificent, powerful, cultured Turkey of the times of the Solimans, Selims and Ahmets.[19] Never — before or after — did this land, its hills, mountains and valleys, its bays and plateaus, experience such riotous flowering, such peace and serenity.

But in the eighteenth century The Wild Field sent another wave of barbarians against the Crimea. This time it was to be a prolonged period of domination because these barbarians were Russians, and they had behind them not transient nomadic tribes, but the solid foundations of the St. Petersburg empire.

[18] The Gireis — a dynasty of Crimean khans that reigned from 1427 to 1788.

[19] Solimans, Selims and Ahmets — Turkish Sultans who reigned during the sixteenth and seventeenth centuries.

Times and reference points changed. To Kievan Rus, the Tatars were, of course, associated with The Wild Field; for Moscow, the Crimean Khanate was a nest of robbers who badgered it with raids. But for the Turks, the heirs to Byzantium, and for the Girei kingdom, who had assimilated the complex legacy of the Crimea with its Greek, Gothic, and Italian undercurrents, the Russians were but a new tide from The Wild Field. They behaved like all other invaders from The Wild Field: they were ruthless and destructive.

Beginning in the first half of the eighteenth century, with the expeditions of Minich[20] and Lassi,[21] Crimean orchards and villages were destroyed by fire and sword. After it was annexed under Catherine the Great,[22] the Crimea was stifled, cut off from the Mediterranean, denied access to the Bosporus, and suddenly by-passed by trade routes.

The change in the fortunes of the Crimea had deep effects on its internal life. In the south, water was the basis of the economy. Tatars and Turks were great experts in irrigation. They could collect the tiniest streams of ground water and channel it by clay pipe into large reservoirs. They could use the temperature variation to extract moisture from the air and to irrigate their hillside orchards and vineyards. Even today if you plunge a pick at random into the barren hillside, you are sure to uncover the remains of water conduits. At the top of a hill you can find oval polished stone vessels for collecting dew; in any clump of trees you can see a feral pear tree or a degenerated grapevine. All these are signs of the blossoming garden this barren desert was only a hundred years ago. This paradise has been razed to the ground. Instead of the sumptuous cities out of the "Arabian Nights," the Russians built a few drab provincial towns to which they gave pseudo-classical names — Sebastopol, Simferopol, Eupatoria — partly due to Potemkin's[23] romanticism and partly due to Catherine's penchant for self-aggrandizement.

What used to be Gothia, from Balaclava to Aluston,[24] was built up with

[20] Burhard Christoph Minich — 1683 -1767, a general, commander of the Russian troops in the 1735-1739 Russo-Turkish war.

[21] Peter Lassi — 1678 - 1751, a Russian general and an army commander involved in invasions of the Crimea in 1737 and 1738.

[22] During the reign of the Russian Empress Catherine II (1739-1791), the Crimea entered into the Russian Empire as a result of a series of wars with Turkey.

[23] Grigori Aleksandrovich Potemkin — 1739-1791, a Russian statesman and favorite of Catherine II who played a major role in the annexation of the Crimea and the northern part of the Black Sea Basin by Russia.

[24] Aluston — an ancient Greek fortress, now the town of Alushta, on the southern coast of the Crimea.

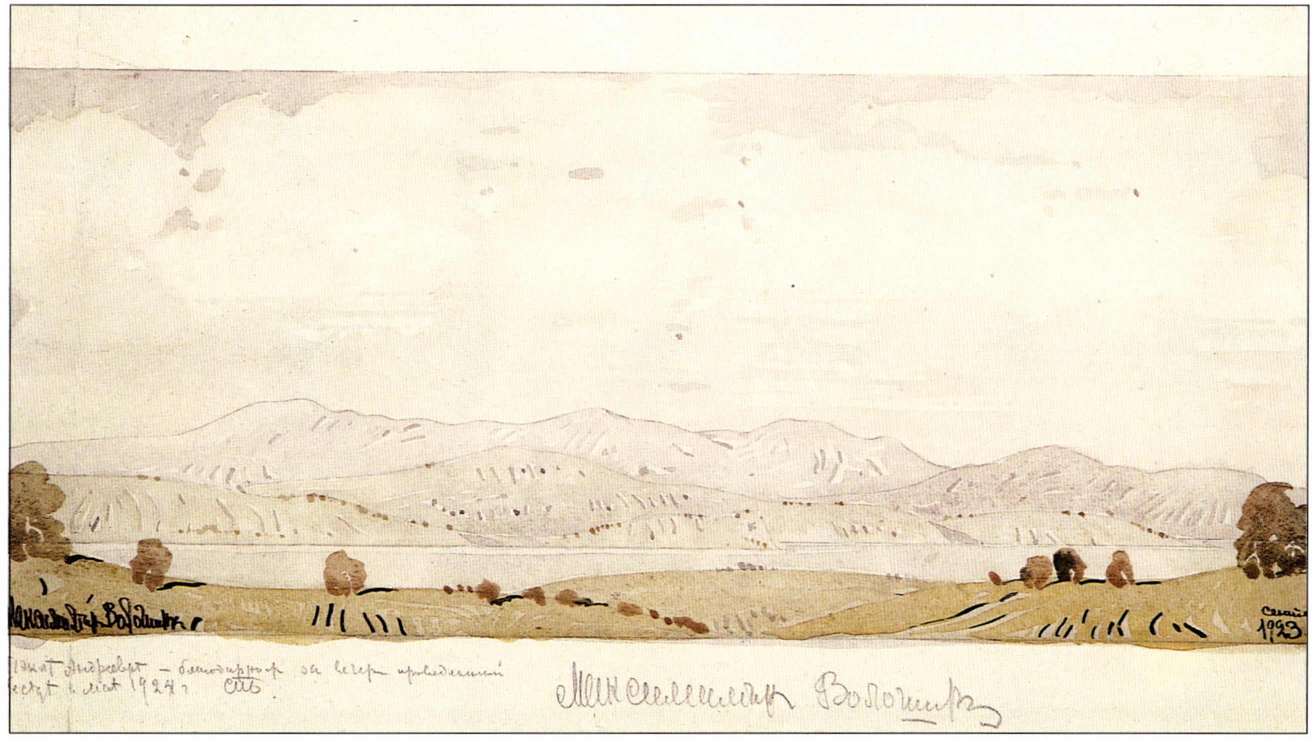

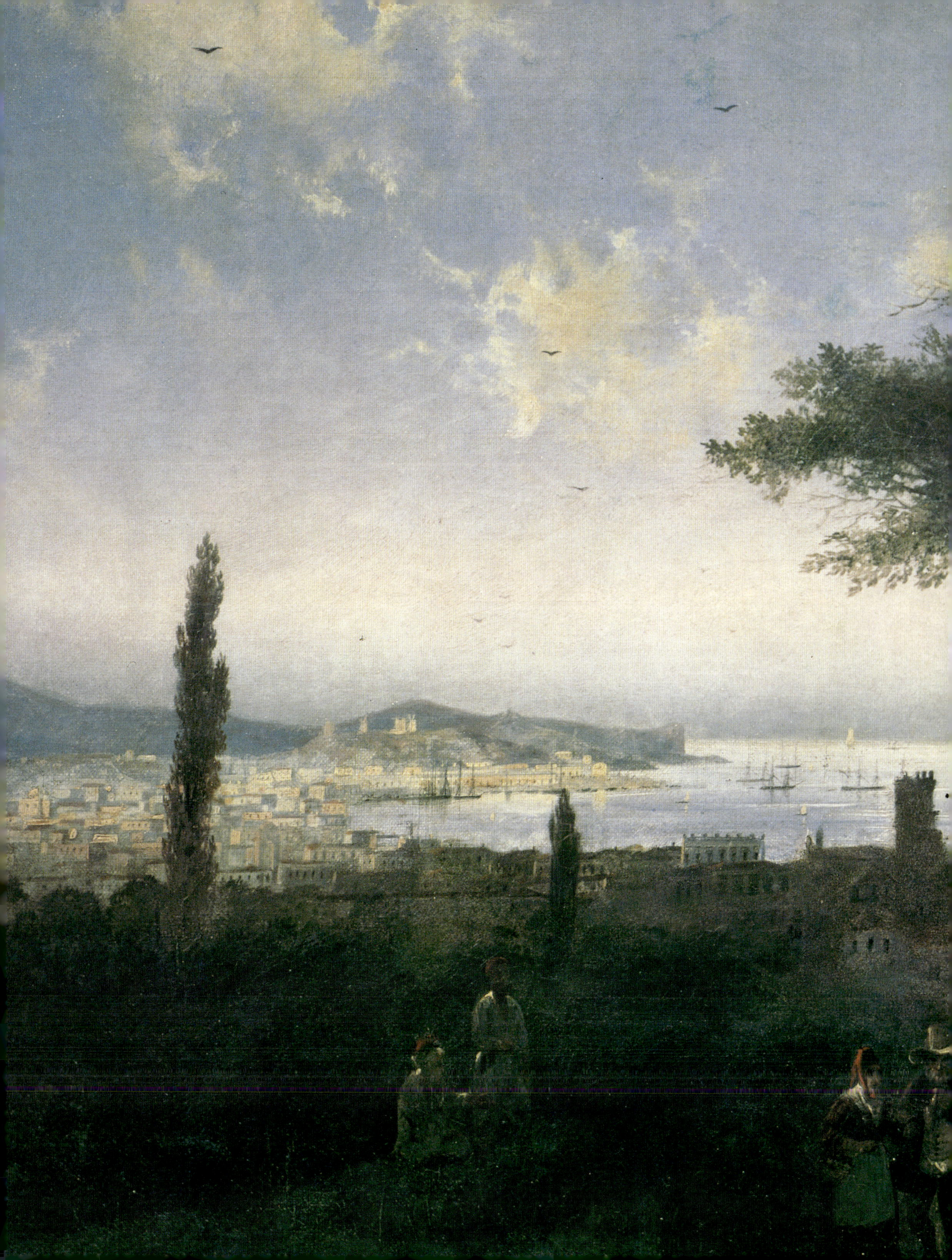

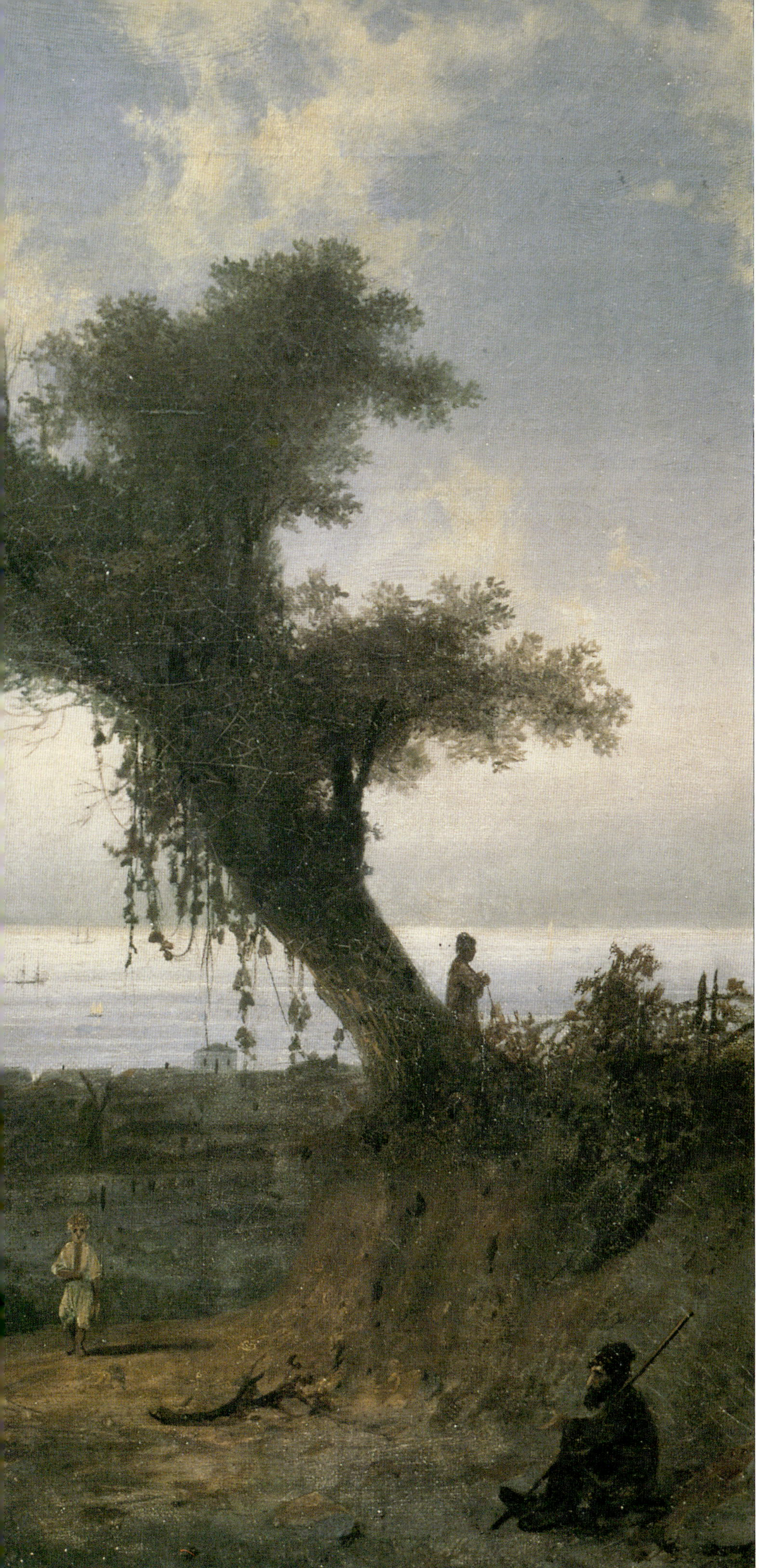

ugly imperial villas that looked like railway stations, offices and hotels in the imperial style. This museum of bad taste which claimed to rival international European puppet shows on the Riviera, is likely to remain the only monument of the "Russian Epoch" in the Crimea.

The fact that the Crimea was visited by several major Russian poets and that great writers came here to die from tuberculosis can hardly be considered an exposure to Russian culture.

But the fact that the land was taken away from those who loved it and knew how to till it, their place taken by those who could do nothing but destroy; the fact that the hard-working, law-abiding Tatars were forced to emigrate to Turkey, and in this national sanatorium were dying from tuberculosis in the thousands — this speaks volumes about the nature and character of the Russian cultural mission.

The Crimean Tatars were a Mongol tribe whose raw life force had been injected with strong cultural poisons, some of their punch already taken out by earlier Hellenized barbarians. This produced a wonderful efflorescence — economic, cultural, and intellectual — which totally destroyed tribal attitudes. In any Tatar, one can notice an inbred culture which, however, is infinitely fragile. The century and a half of imperial domination over the Crimea struck the ground from under their feet and, because of their Greek, Gothic, and Italian heritage, they cannot strike new roots.

Tatar art, architecture, carpet weaving, majolica, metal chasing — all that disappeared. Only textiles and embroidery remained. Tatar women continue, like silk-

□□ *Old Theodosia*. I.Aivazovsky. 1866. St.Petersburg, State Russian Museum.

worms, out of instinct, to spin out precious floral patterns. But that spring too is running dry.

The last sparks of Tatar folk art are kept alive by the group of dedicated people in Bakhchisarai at the Khan's palace, turned into a Museum of Tatar Art by the artist Bodaninsky, a Tatar by birth. Definitive collections of Tatar ornaments were put together by Chepurina in Eupatoria and Aleksandra Mikhailovna Petrova in Theodosia, but their works have not been published.

Russian artists regarded the Crimea as tourists would look at famed scenic spots. The tone was set by Pushkin, after whom poets and artists over the next century saw the Crimea as nothing else but a "fabulous land, a feast for the eyes."

Witness all the Russian poems and paintings of the nineteenth century. They celebrate the beauty of the southern shore, and there are as many exclamation marks in these poems as there are lean Yalta cypress trees in their paintings. Some of the visitors were no doubt talented people. But they had no link with the land, nor with the past of the Crimea, and this made them blind and deaf to the tragic history of the land they walked on.

Only one area of the Crimea, the least picturesque and attractive, and therefore less frequently visited, formed an exception. That area is Cimmeria. The last hotbeds of Mediterranean culture survived longer there than on the western shores, and the land still bears traces of the intense lifestyles of the Italian republics.

I have childhood memories of Piranesian visions of trees growing out of Sebastopol ruins — the aftermath of the siege. From my school years I remember Theodosia as a small town nestled in the shadow of vast Genoan towers which still bore their original names — Juliana, Clementina, Constanza — along the sweeping arc of the bay reminiscent of Apulea. The common folk still called Genoans *Zhenovestsy*, preserving the genuine Italian pronunciation *genovesi*. There were still people with Genoan names in the town. Some of my schoolfriends went to university in Genoa and not in Odessa or Khar'kov. There were still some old folk who remembered Garibaldi, who was a ship's mate on the Ligurian coast. The woman who came to our house to sell sausage was his aunt, and everybody called her, somewhat oddly, Frau Garibaldi. That small town was still linked by a thousand invisible threads to the old metropolis. The pavements in Italian Street were terraced, like those in Padua and Pisa; Italian speech was heard in the port, and some inns had Italian notices. The hills stretching outside the town were gaunt, without any sign of ruins, but with an ineffable historical sadness in the air.

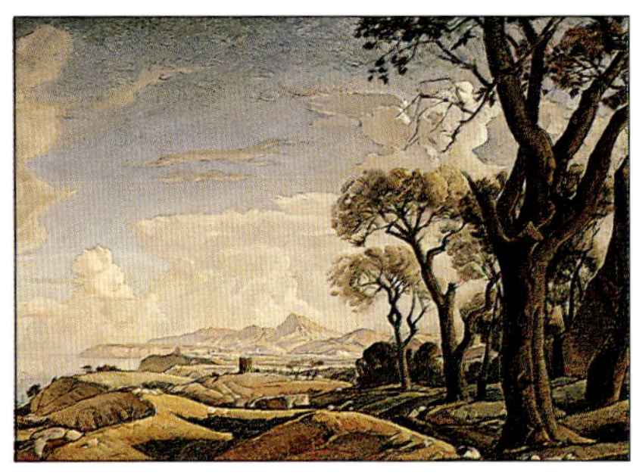

◻◻ *Landscape with trees.* K. Bogaevsky. 1855. Moscow, Tretyakov Gallery.

That scorched and unwelcoming land exposed to the alkali of all cultures and races, strewn with anonymous stones of buried foundations, found just enough strength to bring forth a distinct Cimmerian school of Russian landscape. The school features such names as Aivazovsky,[25] Kuindzhi[26] and Bogaevsky[27] and less well known names, such as Vesler, Petrov, Lagorio,[28] Shervashidze, and Latri, who were natives of Theodosia or its outskirts. These artists reflect the mix of races that fertilized the land of Cimmeria: Aivazovsky was an Armenian, Kuindzhi a Greek, Lagorio an Italian, Vesler a German, Shervashidze an Abkhazian, Bogaevsky of Polish-Russian blood, and Latri an Armenian-English-Greek. They all shared a romantic attitude to landscapes.

Aivazovsky played a major role in the fate of Russian Theodosia. A brilliant romantic of the sea who excelled in painting clouds and air — Aivazovsky's "brush" was admired at least as much as that of Brullov[29] — he contributed the glory of his name to the city, in which he was a coffee vendor as a boy. Aivazovsky should not be judged by his later works, in which he mechanically reproduced himself. It is not these copies to which he owes his glory. There was a time when he could convey the throbbing of the sea on which the sailships of the "arrogant" and "sly" Genoa approached the Piazzetta Dogale of his native city. His inborn perceptiveness to this glory lends a special color to his early works.

[25] Ivan Aivazovsky — 1817-1900, Russian seascape painter.

[26] Arkhip Kuindzhi — 1841-1910, Russian landscape painter.

[27] Konstantine Bogaevsky — 1872-1943, Russian landscape painter.

[28] Lev Lagorio — 1827-1905, Russian seascape and war painter, adherent of late romanticism.

[29] Karl Brullov — 1799-1852, famous Russian painter, author of a number of widely known historical pictures and portraits.

Kuindzhi, a shepherd's son brought by Aivazovsky to Shah Mamai to rub paints for him and who ran away from him to the Petersburg Academy after only one week, was also a romantic of the southern steppe and the clouds. Although the north lured him away from Cimmeria, the intensity of his colors bespeaks a southern soul that did not forget the gold, purple, and blue of Byzantine mosaics.

But perhaps the deepest insight into the spirit of Cimmeria can be found in the paintings of Bogaevsky, who gave a second lease on life to the historical landscape of Russia. No one had the same feeling for this harassed and worn-out land, no one had the same knack for reviving its dreams and mirages. Bogaevsky's art offers a key to the landscape of Cimmeria and to the soul of the Crimea, which was and remains a "land tormented by passionate fortune."

A visitor to the Crimea would look in vain for the works of these artists. In Theodosia he will find a gallery of the works that Aivazovsky did not manage to sell in his lifetime. Because he used to sell off anything worthwhile that came from under his brush, the gallery, containing such rejects, does not do justice to his work at its best. The Theodosian Museum has a few nature sketches by Bogaevsky that give no inkling of his creative, dreamlike landscapes. In the whole of Crimea, one cannot find a single touch of Kuindzhi's brush. To understand Cimmerian art, one must look for it in the galleries of Moscow and St. Petersburg. The same is true of archeological landmarks.

In the museums of Chersonese, Kerch, Theodosia, and Simferopol one comes across strange pieces of marble, inscriptions, and coins. All works that have an immediate appeal to the mind and heart have long been taken away to the Hermitage, to the section on antiquities of the Cimmerian Bosporus and Chersonese. The empire looted the treasures of the Crimea.

What, then, are the monuments in the Crimea? Ruins and landscapes. Every culture and every people have their own historical landscape.

I once had a chance to spend a few days in the Sierras[30] in Old Castile, in a remote mountain area where the pure Castile, that is, Visigoth type was preserved. Imagine my surprise when I saw all the elements of the Crimean Yaila[31] in the Sierro di Pancorbo separating the Old Castile Highland from the Ebro valley; the features of the local race and even some details of the costume reminded me of the Crimean Tatars in Highland Gothia.

No other country in Europe offers such a diversity of landscapes, differing in spirit and style, as those concentrated on the small patch of land that is Crimea. Even in Greece one does not find such a degree of compression. This is due to the racial and cultural richness of the Crimea.

The mounds and cone-shaped hills of the bleak coast of Cimmerian Bosporus; the salt lakes, eroded corridors, and ship-shaped rocks of Mount Opuk;[32] the yellow beaches of the bay of Theodosia that seem to be sprayed with ripe wheat; Theodosia's black Kremlin of Genoan fortifications; Koktebel with its Venetian ruins and Gothic hulking shapes of Kara Dag;[33] Meganom[34] with its classic clear Greek outline; Sudak with its romantic fortress; Novy Svet[35] with its juniper groves — winding and deep like the inside of a shell — this is just the coast of Cimmeria. Further on, the coast changes with every new turn and bay, now projecting watch towers into the sea, now hugging villages in its interior, now pink-and-grey and deserted, now fringed with greenery. The shoreline of Gothia reaches a steep rise on which the Chersonese ruins stand.

The litany of Crimean landscapes is interminable. On the shore they are strewn together like stanzas in a lyrical poem; on the northern slopes they tumble down with the mountain streams that run to the foot of the cave cities and fantastic lime cliffs of Bakhchisarai. The foothills and the steppe area of the Crimea are just as diverse as the mountainous area. But lack of space prevents me from even naming everything of interest in the Crimea.

Let archaeologists decipher letter after letter deposited on the old rocks over the ages and restore the complex and vivid mosaic of history. They will have to work long and hard to come up with a digested version of its history that laymen can understand. Today's — Russian — Crimea has nothing left of former cultures except the landscapes, but one can read its past in them. It is a glorious book of drawings by a great master. The southern coast is cheap Russian-made imitation. It is better unseen, not to break the harmony of perception. Those who prefer this had better not try to understand the real Crimea. ▮▮

[30] Sierras — a range of mountains in Spain.

[31] Yaila — a tableland in the Crimean mountain range.

[32] Mount Opuk — a minor mountain in the eastern Crimea.

[33] Kara Dag — a picturesque mountain in the environs of Koktebel.

[34] Meganom — a cape between Koktebel and Sudak.

[35] Novy Svet — Russian for "New World," a bay and a settlement close to Sudak.

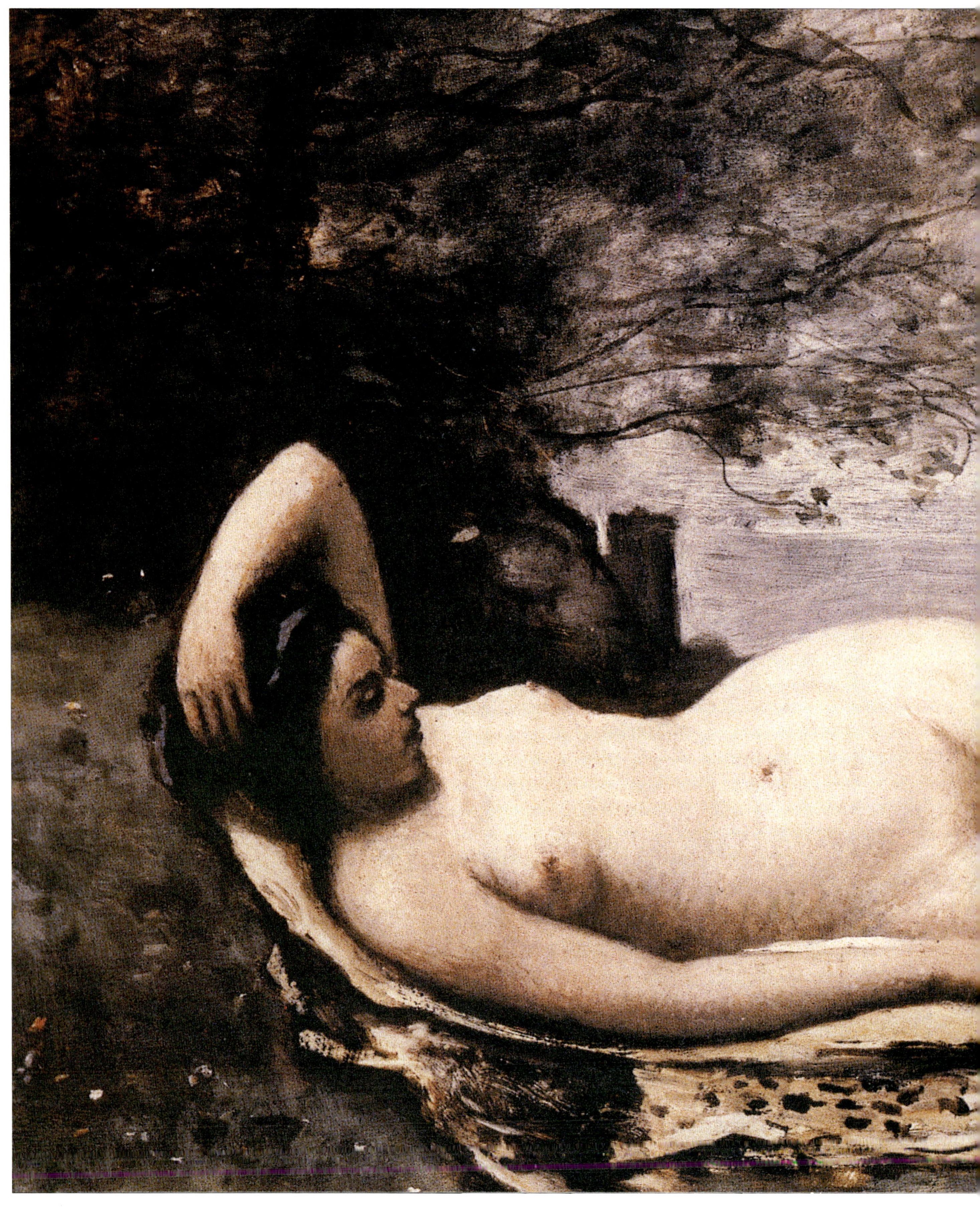

the art of travel / boris b. rodoman

If one hurriedly crosses a diverse landscape which promises numerous impressions, often the best use is not made of the majority of its sightseeing resources. It is the same as hastily gulping down a glass of fine cognac.

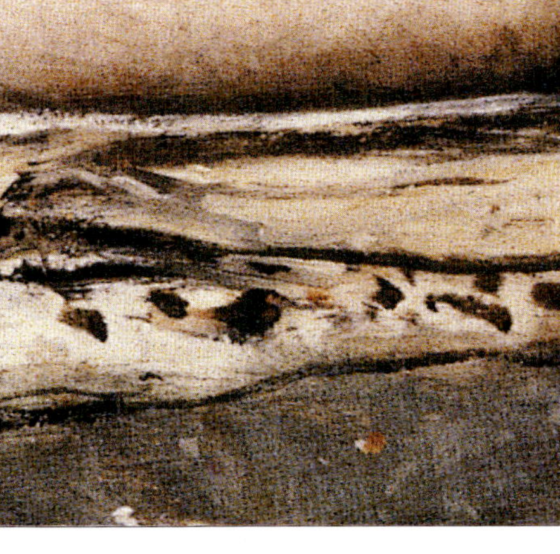

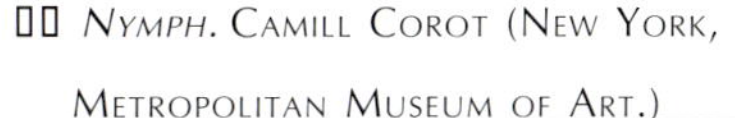

Nymph. Camill Corot (New York, Metropolitan Museum of Art.)

THE ART OF TRAVEL /
BORIS B. RODOMAN ▮▮

As is well known, the creative arts are often closely linked to travel. Painters, poets, writers, composers, and others are inspired by the diversity of the Earth, its nature and peoples. It would be hard to imagine a writer or artist whose creativity had not been influenced in some way by travel. Similarly, it would be difficult to believe that any creative artist, portraitist, or architect had not at least once tried his hand at a landscape painting.

But there is a lesser known connection between art and travel. As increasing numbers of tourists and travelers compass the Earth, so our planet itself has actually become the object of art. The ideas of a painter or architect, or natural elemental processes themselves, can transform a cultured landscape into one of beauty. Landscape architecture is now developing, though slowly. Earth, increasingly polluted and trampled by civilization, is waiting for artists who not only depict it, but improve it. Construction, land planning, melioration, and recultivation are incomplete without artful design aimed at the whole environment.

A landscape architect must be well-traveled if he is to become acquainted with existing examples of his chosen profession; his tourist experience thus enables him to evaluate objectively his own work. A beautiful landscape, whether a complex of buildings or a natural park, is designed not for inspectors or professionals considering the project according to a model or plan, but for ordinary people who will see, feel, and use the area from the inside as residents, passengers, pedestrians, or as workers, who pephaps will have the desire, the time, and the skill to look more closely into their landscape.

Such design is an art intended for tourists, meant to be seen by those who journey from place to place. Creating a new landscape purports the desire to influence a visitor's impressions. Landscape as the object of art is perceived not only visually, from a static viewing point. Movement, whether by walking or riding, also adds a special sentiment to the traveler's overall response. People lacking touring experience or the skills of independent travel, however, may fail to perceive, or may not notice the beauty of landscape and may thus be ambivalent towards the condition of the environment.

But suppose we do not go so far as to design new and marvelous landscapes.... What then? Imagine an open air "art gallery" where real, live sceneries are presented, the "exhibits" skillfully chosen on the basis of extensive touring experience and with the intention of stimulating the visitor's imaginative response to the environment. Is this art? In this case I believe that organizing trips and excursions can be treated as an original art.

MONTAGE OF LIFE, COMPOSITION OF IMPRESSIONS

What is creation? Painters, architects, writers, composers, and poets use materials, colors, sounds, and words that are familiar to us. They display them in a certain order, governed by rules, traditions and norms. Thus old elements come together as an original combination.

A similar process takes place during a tour. The leader, guide, or instructor is not able to move elements, but he does reposition the spectator. In the end, the same result is achieved as by the film maker. Thus, if choosing the subject and the montage of a film sequence is an art, then the choice and montage of life events by our tour organizer is all the more an art.

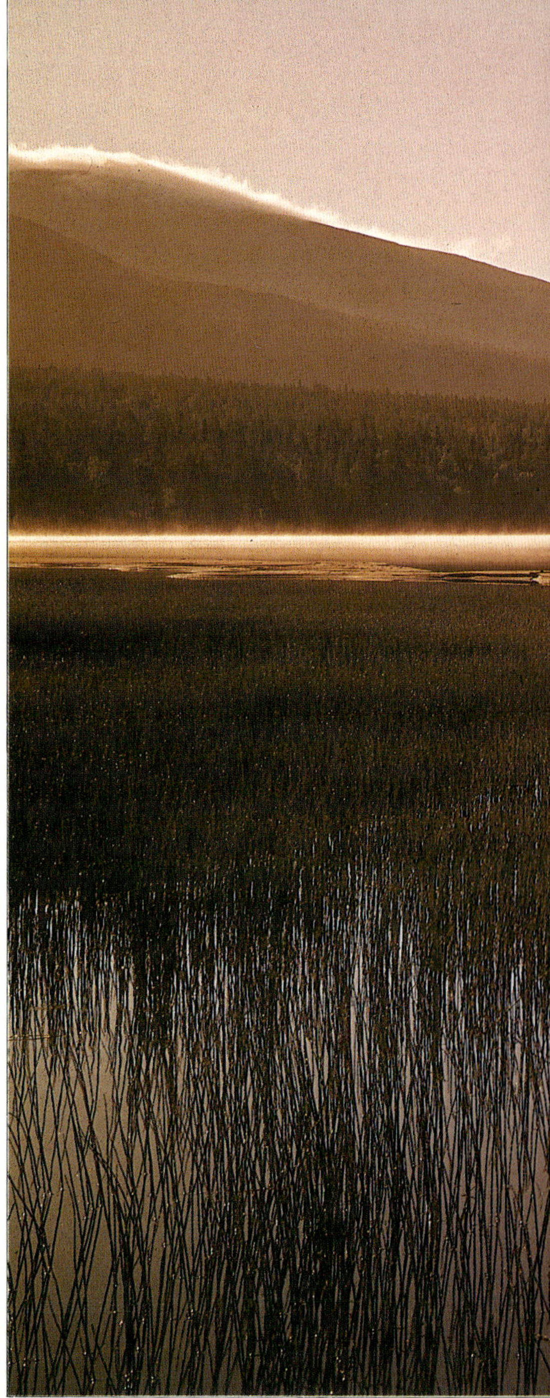

▯▯ *Coast of Lapland.* Vadim Gippenreiter.

Artists and specialists use their skills to display museum exhibits, to decorate shop windows or exhibitions, and to escort visitors around a picture gallery. In the same way, the arrangement of real landscape fragments before a tourist is a

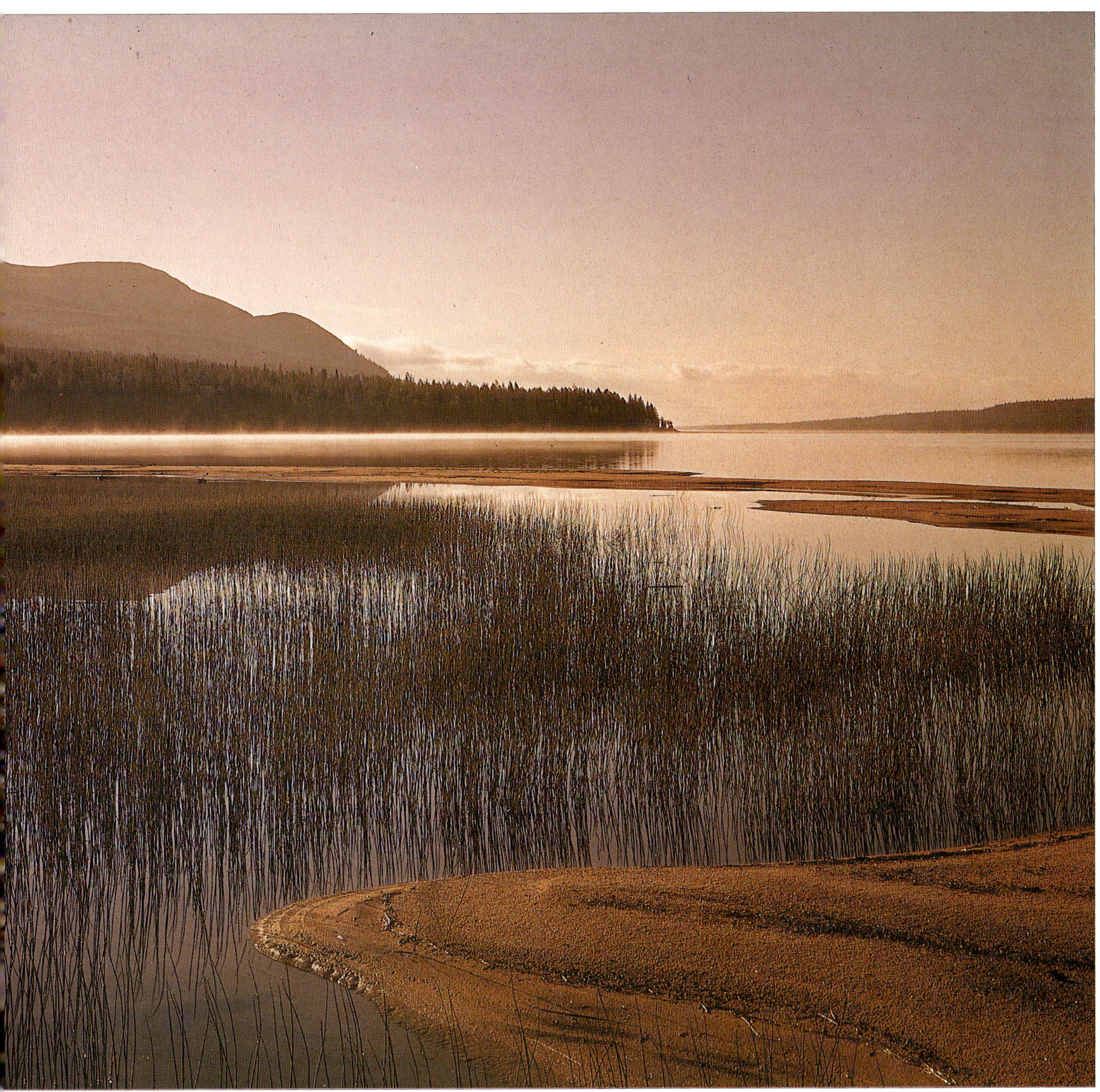

creative and artistic work.

Those following an independently chosen route feel themselves to be pioneers, discoverers of new lands. They consult books about the area, use maps and correct them, and often take notes; they repeat the bygone geographical exploration of "their" new territories. But when the same traveler leads new people along the route he has "discovered" and explored, then he resembles a painter. It was not he who created and decorated the woods and mountains, and it was not he who was the first to display them in painting and photography, but it was he, the leader of the trek, who created a unique composition of impressions in the imagination of his fellow travelers. He built and refined its images from sceneries and events viewed with an observant eye.

The guide who leads the group along

the route developed by others is a copyist-painter, a performer of a completed creation, a reproducer — although we often refer to a talented performer, a musician, a narrator, or an actor as an artist too. The creative abilities of a tour leader are revealed not only in the choice of the route, but also in the skillful choice of companions, as the perception of the locality greatly depends on them. To find a good group for an independent trip, to combine different human characteristics, to achieve "a harmony of souls" offering enjoyment and ease to everyone, is an art which demands not only theoretical knowledge, but the practical, intuitive use of the laws of collective psychology. Every tour leader must combine the parts of the painter and the film director in his own make-up.

Often the desire to visit and show to other people the places where one has been happy or to share locations of exceptional beauty can be strong. But the original feeling of happiness rarely returns completely. A successful journey is just like a unique work of art, which cannot be precisely copied. The "guiding art" can be compared to a theatrical improvisation, pavement or sidewalk paintings, or ancient Chinese butter sculpture. "Products" of this kind of art are of transitory value only, being short-lived and unique.

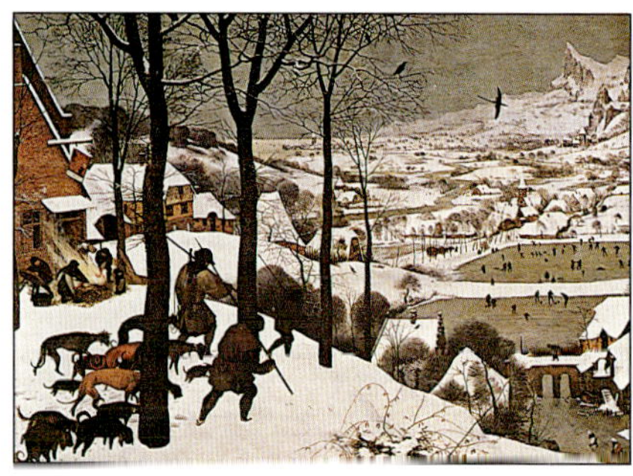

Hunters on the snow. Peter Breugel. Vienne, Kunsthistoriches Museum.

Desert of Khara-Kum. Vadim Gippenreiter.

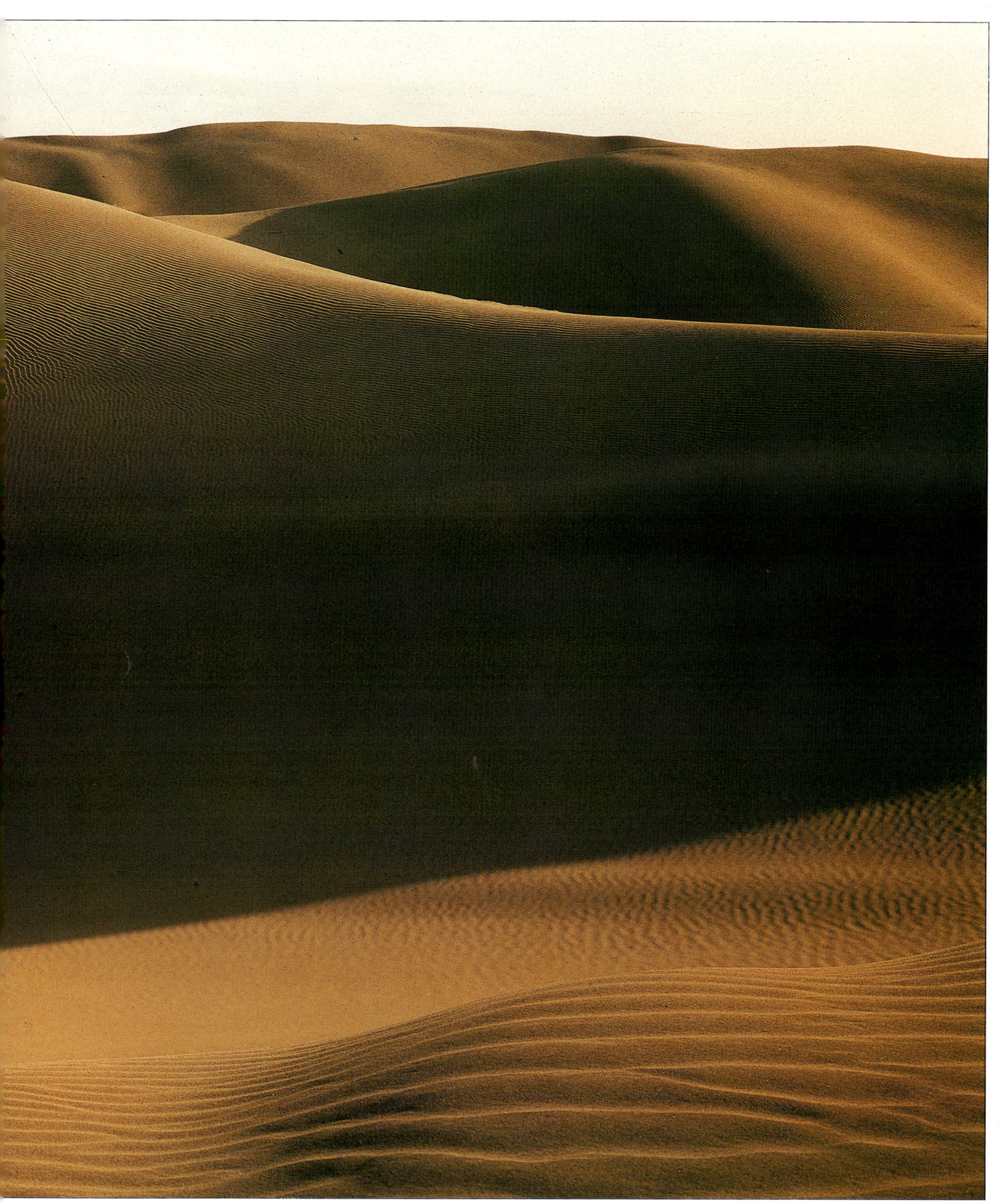

Films and color slides will vividly remind us of our travels, but they will rekindle but one-tenth of our initial feelings of awe or excitement, either for us or for outside spectators.

The works of "guiding art" are recorded, not on magnetic tapes or disks, but right on the surface of the Earth. The road, in its first and literal meaning, becomes the recording path. To offer a work of travel art to other people is to recommend a route, to find a path for hiking or sightseeing. Just like radio or television broadcasts, cinema, video, and records, these paths can be entertaining, educational or therapeutic. Finding a path is akin to the first cut of a new recording; moving along it is like a playback.

Tourism is also getting closer to theatrical art. City-dwellers wade across rivers, abandon the electric cooking range in favor of meals cooked over a campfire, or simply peel off unnecessary clothes at every opportunity they get. To a certain extent, they take one step back to mimic their prehistoric ancestors. This is not caused by a lack of bridges or by a rejection of the worldly convenience of the vacuum flask; nor is it necessarily a result of a natural desire to bathe in the sun and fresh air. This temporary liberation from civilization's urban comforts and conventions offers a wholesome change of roles, as well as a powerful means of recreation. Three stages of dramatization and perception activation can be distinguished in such *civilized* tourism. Imagine that during a trip through France you visit an ancient castle or a restaurant à la seventeenth century. First, you taste the typical dishes of those times. Second, you put on a costume of the era of Louis XIV. Third, you participate in a ball and dance a minuet wearing this costume.

Such role-playing allows travelers to get to know local customs and peculiarities. That is why historical and ethnographical exotica are part of an important trend in world tourism.

CONTRASTS AND RHYTHM, TYPICAL AND UNIQUE

Organizing trips is an art of synthesis. On the road not a single sense organ is bored. The environment impinges on the traveler with its appearance, sounds, and smells; it puts his body muscles to work. He becomes not merely a spectator but an actor, too. Many progressive artists of this century, first and foremost the avant-garde painters of the 1920s, dreamed of just such a synthetically active art, which would invite the consumer to cooperate with the artist. However, it is not only the variety of external effects — typical of any good-spirited episode of real life — which brings tourism and art together, but the numerous emotions of the traveler which are creatively programmed by the organizer and combined according to the laws of choice and composition, well known in art criticism.

Consider, for example, such notions as contrast, rhythm, typicality and uniqueness. These elements and characteristics are objectively contained in many natural landscapes, and often in those created by man. But these very features can be masterfully evoked and intensified by the trip's organizer.

The contrasts between ice fields and hot desert, mountains and sea, savagery and civilization fill the traveler with delight. When the kayak takes you along the raging torrent of a twisting river, its reaches, shallows, and bends follow high and low banks like poetic rhythms. Words with similar endings must be placed to-

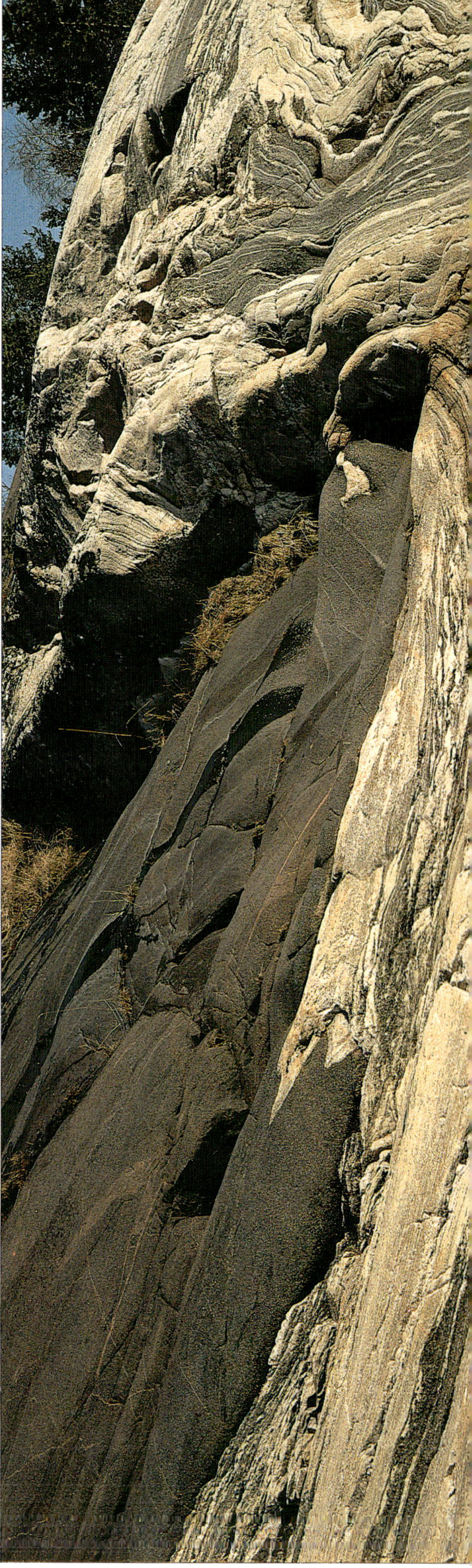

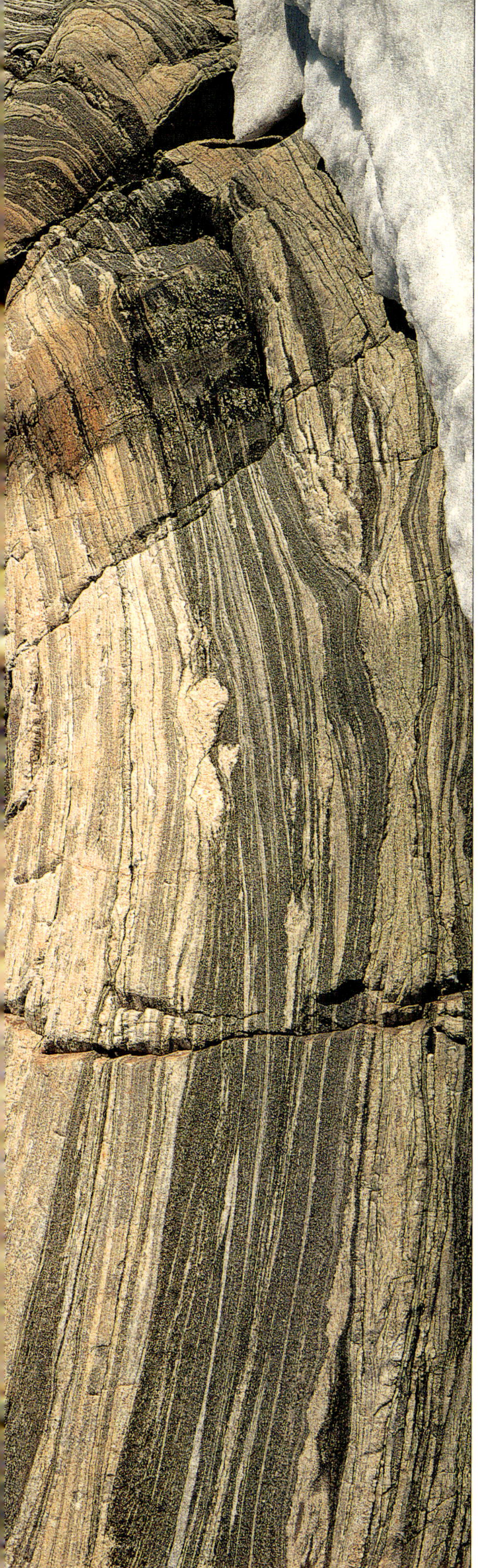

gether to be perceived as rhyming. Trip organizers have several ways of bringing the elements of an area closer in time and space, enabling the traveler to grasp alliteration and assonance, hyperbole and rhyme in the contrast and rhythm of the landscape. The contrasts of nature in the surroundings of Alma-Ata, the capital of Kazakhstan, are wonderful, but one must in one day move from sand hills to eternal snows to be able to feel these contrapositions. An unforgettable feeling can be experienced in the Khibin mountains on the Kola peninsula, when after several days of a difficult route tourists go out to the edge of the plateau and see, as if from a roof, the movement of the city far below, its buses and cars, and a train disappearing into the mouth of a tunnel.

A traveler approaches a hilly locality in discrete quanta; the undulating hills meet him with their rhythmic landscape. Similarly the driver on a straight highway first dives into a hollow, then climbs a pass, anticipating new scenery. If the road is both straight and even, new impressions come up very slowly and only in minor degrees. On seeing a long, straight, monotonous road ahead, the traveler pays scant attention to it. The consequences can be fatal for the driver. In some countries the road is skillfully bent, blended in with the landscape in an interesting way to provide the necessary psychological and aesthetic effect for travelers. Such roadways offer drivers variety and interest, thus limiting the common and dangerous problem of dozing at the wheel.

Fast transport can contribute to and intensify the traveler's perception of landscape contrasts. If helicopters and ski lifts were to connect the Caucasian mountain area with the Black Sea beaches, holiday-makers would have a good opportunity to experience and enjoy the contrast.

So, the feeling of contrast and rhythm can be varied by the choice of a suitable observation point, by the way the road is incorporated within the landscape, and by the speed of motion. The more monotonous the surroundings, the faster one wants to move along to somewhere more inviting. And if one hurriedly crosses a diverse landscape which promises numerous impressions, often the best use is not made of the majority of its sightseeing "resources." It is the same as hastily gulping down a glass of fine cognac.

From time immemorial, writers and playwrights have sought to focus the attention of their audience on unusual, wonderful, and often incredible heroes, events, and accidents. At the same time, however, realistic art is also indispensable for showing commonplace things and events. In travel, just as in art, the unique and the typical are related. On the one hand, the tourist sees the rarest, most inimitable objects of nature and culture; on the other hand, he also sees the most typical things that the country or town he visits has to offer. No one is able to travel the entire world and examine it in minute detail. But one can better imagine and comprehend all the main natural zones and the many countries if one visits a typical corner in each of them. This is made possible by the collection and display of portable objects — both unique and typical — in museums. Immobile treasures such as natural landscapes are maintained in nature reserves and national parks, whereas mobile, living creatures and plants are taken from their natural habi-

◧◨ *Structure of a stone.*

Vadim Gippenreiter.

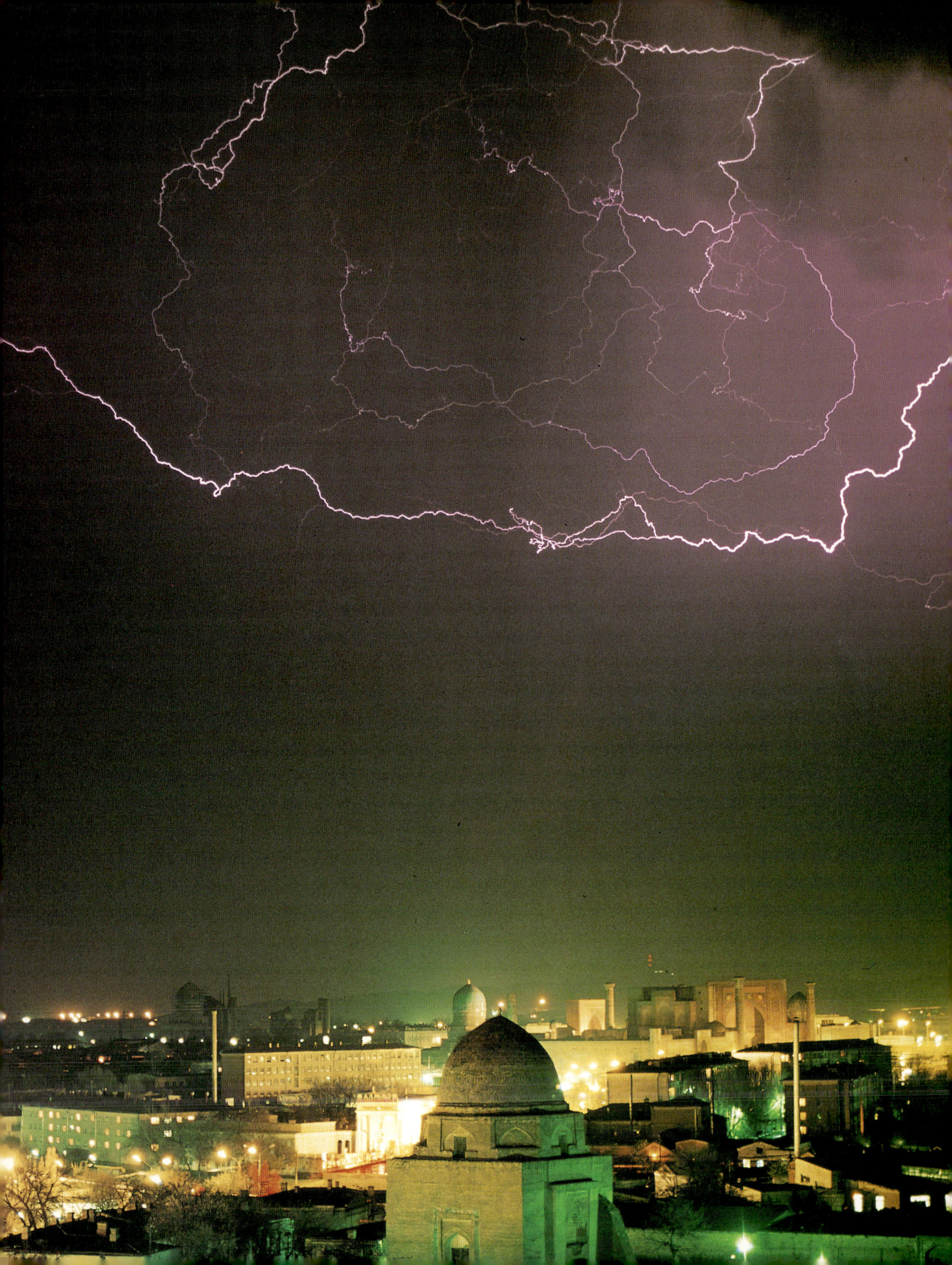

tats to be put into botanical gardens, zoos, and aquariums.

In the spiritual development of man, his interest in the unique and wonderful normally appears earlier than his interest in the typical and common. This is similar to his attitudes toward literature and art. Most likely, the typical is distinguished and perceived by a higher intellectual level; mankind progresses from surprise at the particular to the cognition of the general, from entertainment and play to study, from idle curiosity and observation to analysis and science. Cabinets full of curiosities and menageries have appeared as repositories of rarities, yet the main idea of modern museums and zoos is the systematized exposition of the typical.

CLIMAX INSTEAD OF THE GOAL

There must be a climactic moment during a journey — whether the journey is a long hike or a short walk — just as there is a personal favorite in any pop music concert or circus performance. In travel it is usually the most beautiful, interesting, inaccessible, or faraway place. Often it may seem to be the main goal of the trip, like a peak conquered by mountainclimbers. For a few minutes the climbers stay at the peak, but to savor these few brief moments they have climbed, usually for many hours, and prepared for many days. Delivering a group of languid tourists by helicopter, equipped with oxygen bottles, would not substitute for the climb, even if such an aircraft could get them there. But what appears as the goal and result to a detached outsider is often only a means and pretext to be drawn into an interesting activity.

Pitiful is the traveler or guide who treats a trip, a hike, or just a sight-seeing tour only as an accomplishment of a certain schedule: to visit three or four cities or museums, to cross, say, seven passes, and in between them to endure some inevitable riding, walking, or wading activity. A beginner often resembles the child, constantly asking, "Where are we going? Will we get there soon?" Whereas the more experienced traveler walks in order to feel the space changing around him. For inexperienced travelers the objects of sightseeing are divided by impersonal space, with monotonous, grey or green background. The train or bus is moving fast, but the passengers remain physically and intellectually immobile. The guide keeps silent, especially on the way back if the route is not a circular one; the travelers fail to look out of the windows, but sleep or talk; some try to read books or magazines, while the most interesting book, the one unfolding outside, all too often remains unread and misunderstood.

For myself, there is only one object of sightseeing: the whole of the continuous landscape. For me, the only goal is the all-around contact with the scenery, which is, if perceived as a whole, always unique, always new and changing to the one who walks along it for the first time. Redirect your attention from some feature and you will find something to compare it with, and you will see there parts of neighboring and far-off places. There is no end to the breathtaking play of the imagination over the whole vista. Travel is not a series of flea hops from one object to another, but a swim through a continuous sea of landscape. And within this landscape continuum are rarefactions and clots of impressions, hollows and peaks of feelings and sentiments, wave crests which should be stressed and sharpened.

The climax of the journey should be closer to its end than to its beginning. Awaiting the climax maintains the energy and attention of the travelers. Often when people get ready for a rendezvous or a holiday, similar feelings overwhelm them. After the climax there comes a recoil, but the ending of the trip also becomes a desired perspective. If the trip is distinctly divided into several parts, each of them can have its own mini-climax.

A skillful organizer will do his best to make each climax coincide with and enhance the preceding one. It is a good idea to halt at some spectacular place, when appetite and exhaustion have reached their peak, and justly reward the tiresome march, hard climb, or dangerous fording with a marvelous panorama. It is of greatest satisfaction when the relations between the traveling companions — their mutual understanding and sympathies — develop together with the impressions of the environment, reaching their climax at the highest point of the route, when both landscape and souls are open to each other.

Then the trip organizer may feel proud of the path chosen, just the same as he might feel about any other of his artistic achievements. ■■

◻◻ *Lightning over Samarkand, Middle Asia.*
Vadim Gippenreiter.

a review of *the condition of postmodernity* by david harvey

leonid v. smirnyagin

Many "Soviet" geographers will be unpleasantly surprised or even disgusted by postmodernity. ▌ "Soviet Geography," if you look at its traditions, is a prim, stand-offish, and stiff lady. ▌ These traditions demand clarity, black-and-white precision, and painstaking accumulation of knowledge for constructing the edifice of Science. The most honorable occupation for a scientist is "law-making," which explains everything.

One can say that no other work by David Harvey has had such overwhelming success as *The Condition of Postmodernity,* which came out in 1989. The book's success came as a surprise for the author himself. In November 1990, *Futures* magazine organized a special symposium on the book in the famous Tate Gallery in London.

As a guest of the Institute of British Geographers, invited to its annual meeting in Sheffield, I immediately became aware of the fact that Harvey's book was one of the main topics of professional discussion. Unfortunately, I missed the opportunity to buy it at the exhibition, and in the book shop it had been sold out. In London I went to buy it at *Dillons,* the largest book shop in the city. I went to the information desk and asked where the Geography section was, telling the clerk I wanted to buy Harvey's book. I was immediately cut short and informed that they did not have any copies left. Frankly speaking, it was the first time in my experience that a book on Geography was sold out in such a short time and, moreover, that a clerk, who was not a geographer, knew it by the name of the author. What are the reasons for the tremendous success of Harvey's new book? There are several. First, Harvey remained true to the broad approach which was characteristic of his first book, *Explanation in Geography.* Whereas *Explanation* dealt with the place of Geography in "science as a whole," now the subject was the place of Geography in "culture as a whole."

Today we can say that a scientist specializing in social sciences should stress not only passion in the perception of the world, but even partiality. In place of the argumentation of "pure" science for the appeal to logic, the search for universal regularities, and the belief in the power of Education and the ability of Science to put the world to rights, there has come a painful reflection—doubts about the rightness of a single "universal" view. The conflict of views is substituted by their coexistence, by attempts to achieve mutual enrichment. Science has lost some of its pomp; it is now immersed in culture and interacts with its other parts much more actively than before.

It is to these changes that Harvey's book *The Condition of Postmodernity* is devoted. Certainly, this is not the first book of its kind. Harvey published a paper on postmodernity about fifteen years after the phenomenon started to be discussed—first in architecture, then in culturology, philosophy, theory of science, and so on.

For professionals in different spheres of knowledge, Harvey's book was interesting primarily because he is a geographer, for he managed to set out vividly the specific role of Geography in solving the paradoxes of the development of modern culture and science. According to Harvey, a most strange tradition was formed in modern science as early as the last century; it was mostly concerned with Time, which it saw as live, flowing, and miraculous, whereas Space was—and still is—perceived as something given, solid, and trivial—a kind of passive container.

This disproportion was noted long before Harvey; even in Geography it was laid bare by the American, Edward Soja, in his book *Postmodern Geographies: The Reassertion of Space in Critical Social Theory,* which came out a year earlier than Harvey's book. However, it was Harvey who managed in an exceptionally masterful way to weave these problems into the general culturological context and who could strongly impress the educated public by the almost scandalous way in which he stated that this disproportion was deeply erroneous. Harvey asserted that the development of science had for one and a half centuries followed a false route, that it was blinkered by the time component, and that only one small part of science—Geography—had preserved the capacity to make insighted judgements about the spatial component, for that was its subject. Geographers came out as Old Testament prophets, custodians of the ancient harmony, capable of explaining things that escaped the attention of the others.

Most convincing in this context was Harvey's thesis that Geography does not simply illustrate phenomena whose nature is studied by other sciences, does not only add with its discourse some extra, curious brush strokes to the picture, painted on the whole by other sciences—but no, Geography achieves an insight into the essence of phenomena, and without its participation true knowledge is utterly impossible. Also enthusiastically accepted were theses which, in a different context, would seem distortion in the opposite direction. Time is poorer than Space, says Harvey. It is more trivial. It flows in one direction and does not leave us any choice, whereas Space is rich in dimensions and alternatives. Besides it appears to be more real, as it were, because it is directly perceived by our senses.

The title of Harvey's book implies that it is devoted to postmodernity—a new shift in the culture of European peoples. It is not easy to explain postmodernity briefly, the more so as there is no agreement among its numerous followers as to what it is. The easiest way of defining it is with the help of oppositions, which have become traditional for works in this sphere. Obviously, postmodernity spells out disappointment in the ability of science to find universal regularities, to enlighten the world, and to write out prescriptions for a happy, just life. It is flight into particulars, into the pluralism of questions. Instead of seeking general rules and norms or looking for a way of imparting these norms to those who have not learned them, postmodernity declares the admissibility of any norms and rules, the main purpose being to seek a way of ensuring their painless coexistence. The problem of modernity is discovering how one should act and live and how everyone is to be taught to do so. The problem of postmodernity is recognizing the way things are and finding how to make the coexistence of a wide range of variants possible. The main basis for the success of this coexistence is the postmodernist declaration that each variant has the right to exist alongside the others.

It would be a mistake, however, to think that Harvey's book is devoted to postmodernity proper and hence that it is an investigation in the field of culturology or, at least, Cultural Geography. True, the book is written in a postmodernistic manner—with broken rhythm, frequent switching of topics, an abundance of quotations, borrowings, clinching phrases, and references to painting, journalism, and literature. Still, for Harvey that is only a form of presenting his topic—partly entertaining, partly helping one to see the subject of investigation as it were from within. Harvey approaches postmodernity as a researcher, not a promoter, and the general tone of the book shows that the author does not overly sympathize with this phenomenon. Moreover, it is clear that it was not postmodernity in itself that got him interested, but postmodernity as an expression of much more momentous and essential processes, which it reflected in spite of itself.

Briefly, Harvey's reasoning runs as follows. More than two centuries ago there began in European culture a split into the scientific and the moral. Each of the parts developed with increasing independence, but still they were in a certain harmony with each other—at least in the "calm" epochs. When culture passed through crucial epochs, both trust in science and trust in morals declined, and against the background of their crisis there was a dramatic growth in aesthetics. The bare fact of a culture's increasing aestheticism can serve as a sign of a critical, crucial period. Art as an aesthetic kind of activity becomes the main medium for expressing new ideas and shifts in the character of world perception. That is mainly due to art's capacity for reflecting these shifts and setting them off most vivid—although they have not been clearly shaped—rather than to the ability of art to generate these shifts independently. It was the role of art as witness—and not generator—of cultural changes that interested Harvey, this time in the shape of postmodernity.

Harvey investigates the causes and effects of these changes by applying the Marxist method and relates them by using Marxist language. Here it is fit to explain how exactly Harvey understands Marxism. The Russian reader is sure to be impressed strongly by Harvey's conception of Marxism. On the one hand, Harvey's Marxist language abounds in phraseology, which has got up our noses, has become hackneyed through constant use in our textbooks and causes nothing but disgust as a set of cliches which many of our social scientists have used to cover up the pettiness of their thought. On the other hand, radical Marxists like Harvey distance themselves from the naive, straightforward treatments of Marxism in the spirit of the Second International, from reducing its social pathos to the class approach, from seeing the "class" as a clue to any scientific problems. Many of them treat Marxism in the spirit of "point of entry," as only one of many possible points of view.

It should be noted that this kind of structuralist Marxism has considerable authority in Western Geography, especially in theorizing. Having formed as a trend at the beginning of the 1970s, it came in very handy when Western Geography, almost at the same time, started drifting away from positivism, with its pompous deideologization, towards socially engaged hypotheses. It is curious to note how Clarke states, not without surprise, that in the Social Geography of the West, unlike most other social sciences, there was no "new right-wing" Thatcher-Reagantype of trend in the 1980s, but there were quite a few "old left-wingers," and so to dispute with the "new right-wingers" in Geography, Clarke had to make them up herself. In this light it becomes clear why the geographic public did not only "forgive Harvey his Marxism," but precisely for his Marxism looks up to him with closest attention.

Like a "true Marxist," Harvey seeks the causes for distortions in the dynamics of capitalist production, primarily in the phenomenon of the reaccumulation of capital. This phenomenon causes capitalism to be constantly on the lookout for new spheres of investment and to gain new territories by means of economic and political expansion. When the possibilities of extensive expansion are few, capitalism sets out to transform its time-space continuum and starts the so-called time-space "compression." Coming to the fore, then, is the process which the radicals call "annihilation of space with time"; introducing new means of transport and communication, capitalism tries to economize the time necessary for covering space, so space literally shrinks. And this shrinking is not gradual, but convulsive — following the introduction of new means of communication — and during the moments of sharp acceleration in this process there occurs something like successive collapses of space. During these collapses the society experiences a strong cultural shock which is manifested primarily in art, although it is not caused by art itself, but by the sharp, chaotic, and painful restructuring of social space.

The last shock of this kind came, according to Harvey, between the 1960s and the 1970s. Its external marker was the oil crisis of 1973, and its latent causes were the introduction of telecommunications, the successful development of aviation, success in space exploration and, behind it all, the main cause — another transformation of capitalism's territorial structure. The crisis devaluated a great number of localities, primarily the big industrial centers which had recently flourished, attracting lots of migrants. The whole demographic layout of developed countries came into motion, and none of its parts or centers could feel safe. Hence the acute sense of place which unites compatriots regardless of class, racial and other barriers in their fight for survival in the competition with other places.

Harvey especially stresses this paradox: the role of space diminishes, but the sense of place increases. This transformation becomes a real menace for those who are tied down to real estate, to fixed assets that cannot be moved from place to place, but it is a real feast for the rest of the capitalists, because the moveability of other kinds of capital grows dramatically, and their holders have a much wider choice for investment, can change places at an unheard of rate, making different places compete for their cooperation and thus gain extra profits.

Now, how does one go about choosing a place? Here Harvey turns back to culturological computations and tries to show that capitalism now has a new perception of place as well as space. He stresses that in today's rat-race "places" do not try, as they did until recently, to build skyscrapers and in every way imitate the universally acknowledged symbols of power, grandeur, riches. Instead they try to set off their originality, individuality, the presence of an inimitable cultural aura. Baltimore, where Harvey had lived for twenty years, served him as a wonderful testing ground for observations of this kind. He witnessed Baltimore's center turn from a conglomeration of slums into the now well-known complex "Harbor-place." Half of the architectural illustrations in the book are taken from Baltimore and it was Baltimore he spoke about in his famous report at the meeting of the Association of American Geographers which was held in 1988 in no other place than Baltimore itself.

His observations led Harvey to a thesis which tallies wonderfully with Western Geography and postmodernity, but for a Russian geographer sounds all but stunning: the creation of visual pictures of space, "images," is an essential part of social activity, and a geographical place is primarily a social product, not something passive, "objectively" given. This is what Harvey calls historical-geographical materialism.

A special place in Harvey's book is allotted to the discussion of post-Fordism. As it is, this idea has been discussed in radical Geography for many years, but Harvey logically weaves it into the general culturological reasoning, considering post-Fordism one of the initial causes for postmodernity. Modern capitalism obviously discards the pet methods of mass production with its economizing due to scope (Fordism) and switches to more flexible capital investments into the production of specific products in smaller batches but for specialized markets. Flexibility and flexible accumulation have become pet terms in Western Economic Geography, and the analysis of these phenomena in the practice of locating production forces is the main topic of their papers. Unfortunately, these ideas came as a revelation for our Economic Geography. In a word, Harvey's book is rich in ideas, which surely command close attention on the part of the Russian reader and primarily the geographer.

However, the "Soviet" geographer will not find this book

easy reading—mostly due to its postmodernistic form. It is suffused with irony and self-irony, which seems strange to the Russian reader brought up on gloomy "learned" papers and used to seeing in this "learned" manner a sign that the work is reliable, fundamental, and profound. Besides, Harvey uses postmodernistic form without professing postmodernity. He presents it as something unhealthy, brought forth by the intellectual and moral panic, which compels one to aestheticize reality beyond reasonable limits. Hence the contradiction between form and content, which beautifies the book in the eyes of people well acquainted with the cultural context and used to uninhibited thinking and reasoning, but for which the Russian reader may well seem ostentatious and hamper his understanding of the essence.

Most difficult for the Russian reader is the Western notion of a fashion in science. Strangely enough, fashion plays a significant role in Western Geography. Now the fashion is to write along the same lines as Harvey does—looking from within a thick cultural context, caring little about the inner logic, relying on the reader's ability to pick up the hints, to follow the reminiscences, to sustain attention in spite of frequent shifts of topic. At the meeting of British Geographers in Sheffield, which I mentioned earlier, their newly elected leader, Johnston, devoted about one third of his "inaugural speech" to medieval bells, which he knew fairly well, and only then he adroitly fitted it all into the geographic context. There is very little coercion in this style. Basically, it is a game, and the attitude to it is fitting and ironical. Still, an outsider—and this is what the Russian reader is—can through naivety take this fashion for a kind of scientific paradigm.

The reader should be cautioned against the naive perception of Eurocentrism which saturates Harvey's book. Almost everywhere he presents the shifts in the perception of Space by society as if they were global processes and not changes concerning only a small number of peoples within the sphere of the European culture. Speaking about postmodernity he does not stop to explain that it has nothing to do with the modern cultures of peoples beyond that sphere, counting billions upon billions. Passing off the adventures of the European culture as something universal or crucial for the history of humanity means lapsing into such an obvious "cultural imperialism" that it is hard to believe that Harvey was not aware of it — especially considering that he is a Marxist. Clearly, here we have another case of appealing to the intelligence of the readers, who do not have to be reminded that the context of the book is European. One can only regret that Harvey devoted the book on the history of "the sense of space" to Europe, and not to the geography of this sense on a global scale. Certainly, this may be an almost insurmountable task, but much in Harvey's book makes one believe that he could cope with it.

Finally the Russian reader should be warned about Harvey's original view of modernity. In Russian culture this term is understood differently. Worse, many features that Harvey attributes to postmodernity some Russian culturologists would attribute to modernity—an early twentieth-century tendency which many of us associate either with decadence or with the revolt against rationalistic traditions of the last century's enlightenment, or with both. Willy-nilly one gets suspicions that postmodernity is modernity gone to seed.Having arisen as something revolutionary, crushing down the old idols, modernity, having won a victory, calmed down, stiffened, was infiltrated by the ideals of the overthrown predecessors, and at this stage was swept by a new refreshing wave which was called, just to spite it, postmodernity.

Obviously, it would be fitting here to compare postmodernity and modernity with Kondratiev's big economic waves — only because postmodernity coincides with the beginning of Kondratiev's sixth wave. Too much about the signs of postmodernity look like signs of the beginning of Kondratiev's wave, especially the scaling down of space, which is so important for the geographer. The transition from space to place, general scaling down, and fragmentation can be likened easily to the rise of small business, typical to each one of Kondratiev's waves.

Far from the postmodernistic crowd, having preserved the immediacy of perception, the Russian reader is sure to have an urge to contradict his British colleague, and maybe more than once. The "annihilation of space with time" due to accelerated communication already seems doubtful. Does it not testify to the opposite? To the medieval man the world seemed huge because his life would not have been enough to get round it, but in actual fact his real world was tiny. To the modern man the world seems tiny, for he can fly round it within several hours or have a look at it from outer space, but his real world has become huge in comparison with the world that was accessible to the medieval man. It seems huge but was tiny, seems tiny but has become huge—this is the fate of geographical space as modeled by the time of man's life.

Harvey illustrates his "annihilation" with pictures readily

borrowed from Geography textbooks—the size of the globe diminishes as the means of communication develop. However, the trick does not lie in the fact that the map's diameter corresponds to the time needed to cross a hemisphere; one can see —now that a plane can make such a crossing within a few hours, this diameter is a hundred times smaller than five hundred years ago. Hence we draw the conclusion that "the world is shrinking." But if you choose a scale in accordance with the distance which a man can cover, say, within half a day, the picture changes. The modern world will be a hundred times bigger than the medieval; there will be enough room for detail. It will be richer—as it is in reality and not in a textbook or in the Alcatel ad which Harvey uses in his book. It looks as if Harvey here gives due to the tradition of distorting Science in favor of Time and against Space, which both he and Soja castigated.

In Russia, Harvey's works have not been translated for twenty years. It is most disappointing that *Social Justice and the City* was not translated. I like it much more than *The Limits to Capital,* which is very much like our home-grown political-economic samples of writing. But *Justice* would be very useful now that there is an acute lack of basic notions of justice in our ungainly squabble between republics, territories, and cities, in this economic war of everyone against everybody, in the mêlée of pseudoscientific economic autonomies. True, among Western geographers there are quite a few other brilliant authors, whose works every professional should know; suffice to mention Lefebre with his *La production de l'espace* or the American Yi-Fu Tuan. But if we had to choose one among them, it could be no other than Harvey's: it covers a broader range of topics, it is immersed in the general cultural context and, what is no less important, it is written in what is for us a familiar Marxian language. The latter quality would until recently have meant a death sentence for any attempt to translate such an author, for our censors, paradoxically, easily passed the books of openly bourgeois authors, but unrelentingly cut us off from the works of the Western radical Marxists. This is why for many years we were divorced from such most interesting journals as *Antipode* and *Herodot,* which were kept in the safes of special secret archives, if they got to this country at all. True, if the articles were reprinted in the bourgeois journals, they became accessible. The translation of Harvey's book will help us to correct this mistake.

Many "Soviet" geographers will be unpleasantly surprised or even disgusted by postmodernity. "Soviet Geography," if you look at its traditions, is a prim, stand-offish, and stiff lady. These traditions demand clarity, black-and-white precision, and painstaking accumulation of knowledge for constructing the edifice of Science. The most honorable occupation for a scientist is "law-making," which explains everything. Research here means looking for an unambiguous "yes-no" answer; it is aimed at generalization (simplification) of the investigated reality. Especially esteemed is branchy argumentation of each thesis (hypotheses here are treated rather scornfully). As can be seen, it is quite a modernistic paradigm, and working within this paradigm are the overwhelming majority of "Soviet" geographers. For many of them, papers written along the postmodernistic lines are at best a sample of stylistic slovenliness, displaying a lack of scientific self-discipline. At worst—hack-work due to the inability to find arguments, or simply malicious hooliganism, intentional ostentation of "living classics" aimed at becoming famous or at least notorious.

Postmodernity has been the subject of heated discussions for some time now among our culturologists, writers and painters. Recently there was a first symposium here devoted to it. Still running through the discussions, even now, are intolerance and ideological bias — features incompatible with postmodernity. Attempts to turn it into an ideology or into a sledge-hammer for crushing Socialist Realism—is that not antipostmodernity? What is the worth of the discussion between *Izvestia* and *Independent from Russia,* the widely read national papers, in the course of which the authors, protecting their exclusive right to interpret modernity, slung dirt at each other and at the on-lookers? Even the writer Andrei Bitov, almost declared a Russian classicist of postmodernity, was caught in the act of mixing up the antique Menandr with Borges' Pierre Menard — a sin inexcusable for a postmodernist.

In a sense, postmodernity is a cure for such pride, and if an expert of postmodernity is detected as having such pride, this means he is a false expert. True, it is hard to avoid outbursts of hot temper in the red-hot atmosphere of today's society, where calls for plurality—this alpha and omega of postmodernity—constantly trigger fierce fighting between contrasting opinions, and do not add to their coexistence.

It is obviously unrealistic to demand that everyone become a postmodernist and to brand all dissenters as obscurantists— this would not be postmodernist-like. One can only hope that it is these features of postmodernity—intentional lack of belligerence, complacency, realism—that will help the Russian readers at least to consider becoming postmodernist. ▮▮

a marxist geographer in postmodern time: an interview with david harvey

dmitry sidorov/oxford, august 1992

Dmitry Sidorov: You consider in your book two films, *Blade Runner* and *Wings of Desire*. They are good illustrations of the postmodern landscape. But two films alone cannot be considered proof of your point about a shift. On the other hand, presumably a few earlier films contained similar motifs of decay, ephemerality, change, and so on.

I WOULD ARGUE THAT THE HISTORY OF CAPITALISM WAS VERY SPATIAL. CHANGING DIMENSIONALITY OF SPACE AND TIME IS WHAT THE HISTORY OF CAPITALISM IS ABOUT.

David Harvey: Yes. One can add, for example, *American Graffiti* by Jameson as one of the first films of this genre — with a similar sense of nostalgia for the recent past. I have not a deep enough knowledge of films to represent a survey. What I did was to illustrate my argument with a couple of good examples.

Sidorov: Why are such common descriptors of urban living as *gentrification* and *yuppie* not considered in the book?

Harvey: These are general descriptive statements concerning changes in urban life. What I wanted to do was to get behind these simple descriptions.

Sidorov: Gillian Rose believes that "Harvey is using a simple base-superstructure model to account for cultural artifacts. He does this mainly through his entirely unproblematized use of the category of experience: we experience time and space differently according to their different formations under different regimes of accumulation, and changes in that experience under different regimes result straightforwardly in changes in our cultural representations. Unfortunately, this argument can only be made through a series of strategic absences."

Harvey: That is her model of base-superstructure, not mine. The problem is, people have a framework in which to interpret what you say. If somebody reads my book with an idea in his head that all Marxists use the simple model base-superstructure, it is difficult to change such a way of thinking. Suffice it to read my book carefully to see that I am talking about *processes*, not the model base-superstructure, of circulation of capital, which is affecting all aspects of our everyday life, the experience of space and time, for example. Everything is going on through money; money is the fundamental form of power. The world of cultural production is inevitably about money. When Rose talks about base-superstructure, it is on a presumption that there is an arena of activity which is not involved in money and capital flow. But films, paintings, and so on are commodities. Cultural production is part of the economy. A lot of what is done in contemporary cultural production is in a sense similar to the Benetton production of different color shirts.

Sidorov: But there are different cultures — mass culture and the elitist, high one.

Harvey: The point made by postmodernists is that the difference between them has disappeared. Yes, but how did this happen? And my point is: it happened through commodification.

Sidorov: You may be surprised, but postmodernism in literature, in the arts, is flourishing now in the former Soviet Union. The whole collapse of the system and the omni-penetrating commercialization of the arts are the first evident explanations.

Harvey: You had a real revolution, and a new experience of space and time probably has emerged.

Sidorov: Postmodernism may be considered both as a self-destructive tendency and as an attempt to find a way out. Rose writes, "Harvey can find little positive to say about postmodernism." Do you agree?

Harvey: And what do you think?

Sidorov: I think the postmodernism debate has at least raised a whole set of new questions. Challenges are at all events a useful tool.

Harvey: Yes. But what does it say that is new?

Sidorov: I think the attitude towards postmodernism should differ in each case. In the case of the Soviet Union, for example, the emergence of postmodernism has its own reasons and should be treated particularly. In this case it is a liberative reaction against the previous hyper-dogmatism.

Harvey: Postmodernism in its origins was a liberative movement, antiauthoritarian. A lot of questioning of authority was done by the Left movement. Marx was doing the same undermining of authority. My point is there is nothing particularly new in postmodernism in this respect. The problem is that postmodernists are questioning any authority without social concern as to what will replace it. They have no direction. But somebody still needs to govern. Those who occupy, or claim to occupy, a postmodern position cannot avoid modernist problems. They can talk about diminution of the authority of an author. Yet there is an interesting question; how do they exercise authority themselves? The intolerant response to my book of those who claim to be postmodern alone shows that they are quite authoritarian. In this sense one cannot avoid the modernist dilemma mentioned above, which was with us for the last hundred years. We are still in the modern world.

Sidorov: What are the signs that "the cultural hegemony of postmodernism is weakening in the West?"

Harvey: I don't know whether the *New York Times* is a good newspaper or not, but it is a popular and influential one. It recently carried the headline "Postmodernism is Dead." There are a lot of similar examples. The case of my book itself is sufficient proof. Five printings up to now, twenty thousand copies do not satisfy the demand. So evidently, supportive response to a book attacking postmodernism is itself a manifestation of the same kind. People who were very much involved in the debate frequently say now, "Wait a minute. Do we need to stop self-destruction in the cultural arena? Could we have gone too far with postmodernism?" Scott Lash, for example, in his critique has said the same. I've received a lot of letters since the publication which express concern about the state of affairs in this field and appreciation of my book. For example, the architect Rogers, the designer of the Lloyds Bank building in London and the Pompidou Center in Paris, has disagreed with my words about him as a postmodernist, but at the end of his letter to me, he mentioned that he had not read anything better about the whole postmodern discourse.

Sidorov: What is your attitude to the notion of post-industrial society, put forward by Daniel Bell?

Harvey: I don't like it. Generally speaking, I don't like the term *post*. I prefer to use in this context the term *flexible accumulation*. Secondly, the term *post* does not mean that we are not still under capitalism, under the processes of capitalist accumulation. The question is, "What is the relation between social changes, which exist in society and play an important role, and the process of capitalist accumulation?" I think that the notion of post-industrial society, which indicates we are all moving towards a service society, is problematic. Yes, there has been an increase in the service sphere, but in fact there has been a strong element of services in production for a long time. Of course, there was a shift in division of labor, that's right, and we should think how this division of labor has been changed. But this does not necessarily mean that we are in some post-industrial society.

Sidorov: What is the relation between the two terms *capital accumulation* and *the production of space*?

Harvey: Capital accumulation is always capital accumulation and then the production of space. The former is always about the production of space. You can't say there is, simultaneously, the latter. They are part of each other. All investments, buildings are the production of space. Within the Marxist tradition, I would add, there are actually not many people who are looking at the production of space. Even in Geography, where there are a lot of people trying to see how industry operates in space—but this is usually a very different way of looking at the production of space.

Sidorov: You have suggested that "we have been experiencing, these last two decades, an intense phase of time-space compression that has had a disorienting and disruptive impact upon political-economic practices, the balance of class power, as well as upon cultural and social life." I think it is a rather difficult task to estimate the comparative degree of insensitivity in such a delicate field as the experience of space and time. Any society encounters such compression. When you are speaking of "an intense phase of time-space compression" or changes in temporal-spatial perceptions, how can you prove the insensitivity of the process?

Harvey: I think there are two things. First, as Jameson, Berman, and others argued, the experience of space and time is implicit in the sense of modernity and postmodernity. Then, one should ask, "by what social processes are the experiences of time and space shaped?" We are creating certain ideas about space and time through the material organization of the economy. Where is the change of experience coming from? And then see changes in the cultural artifacts. I use the term *time-space compression* to capture what seems to me to be two central elements of capitalist economy. First, interest in time and speed-up. Secondly, interest in the collapse of spatial barriers. I would argue that the history of capitalism is very spatial. Changing dimensionality of space and time is what the history of capitalism is about. I think it is different from other forms of society in this regard.

Sidorov: I would argue that the greatest events which have significantly changed the human perceptions of space in this century were the launching of sputnik, the first satellite, and the first manned flights of cosmonauts. They occurred years before the economic crisis of the 1970s. You place your explanations on economic grounds.

Harvey: An important thing for me is not the launching of the first satellite, which has changed our understanding of space, but the creation of the world-wide system of satellite telecommunication networks. This became important for the world economy in the late 1970s and fundamental by the 1980s. This caused changes in people's everyday life, which were more important for the experience of space and time. Parisian fashions were sent immediately to Hong Kong and replicas of these same Paris fashions were produced within ten days. Another example was the direct transmissions from the Vietnam War. It was impossible before. As Engels said, the quantitative changes became qualitative. I do not want to say that what happened in these last decades was unique. Similar changes can be found, for example, in the Renaissance period. The recent process I estimate as a shift in the whole dimensionality of time and space, as a whole series of shifts, which followed the Renaissance onwards. This reminds us that we can find plenty of elements of what postmodernism is about for a much earlier period. The same is the case in the experience of space and time. So I do not want to say that a single revolution in this field has taken place, but rather a significant reconfiguration of the whole dimensionality.

I REGARD MYSELF PRIMARILY AS SOMEONE ENGAGED IN A MARXIST STYLE OF INQUIRY, RATHER THAN AS A GEOGRAPHER.

Sidorov: In the book you have mentioned different indicators of a widespread and profound shift in the structure of feeling, such as "the rediscovery of pragmatism in philosophy, the shift of ideas about the philosophy of science wrought by Kuhn and Feyerabend, Foucault's emphasis upon discontinuity and difference in history and his privileging of 'polymorphous correlations in place of simple or complex and chaos casualty,' new developments in mathematics emphasizing indeterminacy (catastrophe and chaos theories, fractal geometry), the reemergence of concern in ethics, politics, and anthropology for the validity and dignity of 'the other.'" Were there any similar and simultaneous shifts in contemporary human geography?

Harvey: Geographers have always been very skeptical of grand theories. The lack of grand theory in Geography is evident. Geography was much influenced by "borrowed from adjacent fields" theories like the writings of Foucault. I am trying to work out something that is independent, although in my early work I drew on approaches from adjacent fields. There are only a couple of people in Anglo-Saxon geography who tried to do something independent. I do not share positivist ideas, but people like Isard and Warntz were attempting to do this. And now Allan Wilson is doing something of this kind. So there are a few people who are concerned with grand geographical theories. Postmodernism believes itself to be a challenge to them. But in such a situation, with whom are postmodernists in Geography struggling?

Sidorov: The new experience of space and time since the crisis of the early 1970s may be considered as one of the reasons for the emergence of new theoretical geography (i.e., critical human geography).

Harvey: There are periods of various consideration of space. In the 1950s, when everything was stable — the United States was the center of power, the Soviet Union had its own region of dominance; the Berlin Wall, the Iron Curtain, various boundaries shaped space — it was treated as something unproblematic. During the last twenty years the sense of certainty and safety has shifted away. A new spatial problematic has emerged and as a result — new demands within geography. I think the fundamental changes taking place in the Soviet Union will pose a lot of new questions of space for us to grapple with.

Sidorov: Do you agree with such a distinction of approaches within the emerged theoretical human geography as Marxist, realist, structurationist, humanist, postmodernist?

Harvey: No, I disagree. They are only flags of different groups of geographers. For example, there is nothing contradictory by definition between Marxism and realism. On the other hand, realism is too complex and heterogeneous a group of scholars to be considered as one whole. There are two big philosophical figures, namely Rom Harre and Roy Bhaskar. They have very different views: Bhaskar is Marxist and Harre is not. There are, thus, two strains within realism. I don't think Bhaskar's strain is antagonistic to Marxism at all.

And my interpretation of how realism is used in geography by people like John Lovering and Andrew Sayer is more in Harre's tradition. Bhaskar and Harre differ on a lot of points. I have an affinity with the former and not with the latter. Andrew Sayer said that space is contingent in his article "The difference that space makes." This is absolutely different from my position. When I asked Bhaskar, he disagreed with Sayer's statement on the contingency of space. You would not find any concern with dialectics in Sayer's main book *Method in Social Science*, while Bhaskar is now writing a special long book on this topic. As you see, realists are not all the same, as is true of Marxists. There are a lot of things in Marxist works I can't agree with.

Sidorov: What is your estimation of the structurationist approach within theoretical human geography, which is supposed to resolve the tension between structure and agency and to construct a grand theory for the understanding of society?

Harvey: It seems to me that Giddens has said that human agency is about replication of structure. I would say the structurationist project in human geography was not successful. At least, attempts by Gregory, its most well-known protagonist, to put the approach into practice have failed.

Sidorov: And what about humanistic geography?

Harvey: There is a certain difference between the philosophical stands of the humanistic approach in social sciences and humanistic geography. I think that is due to the particulars of construction of the approach in geography. At the very beginning it was to be built as a reaction against positivism as well as Marxism in geography. This has changed the philosophical grounds of the approach in geography if they exist at all. Certainly, within it there are various interpretations; Ley's is something different from Buttimer's. The former seems to be not coherent philosophically, in some respects being a positivist approach, while the latter is rooted in a very religious tradition.

Sidorov: Do you think postmodern geography has emerged?

Harvey: Again, there is no homogeneous coalition. I share the description of so-called postmodern geography by Curry: "Postmodern geographers form only the loosest of coalitions. Some, like Michael Dear, explicitly claim to be 'postmodern.' Others, like Gunnar Olsson, Allan Pred, and Dagmar Reichert do work that is in clear sympathy with claims made both by Dear and by non-geographers like Lyotard and Derrida, who are typically seen as postmodern. Apart from those who have explicitly claimed to be postmodern, there are others, like Ed Soja, who have been somewhat more cautious while celebrating some features of postmodernism. There is also a group, including David Harvey and Julie Graham, who have been deeply critical of the entire enterprise. Finally, standing to one side are several others; David Ley has studied postmodern landscapes, without himself claiming to be a postmodernist, and Derek Gregory has approached the matter with some ambivalence."

I share as well Curry's opinion that, in general, postmodernists in geography have misunderstood the basic grounds of postmodern philosophical theory, still being modernists in their works, very traditional in the way of research. One should distinguish between claims and work.

. . . MY PROJECT IN GEOGRAPHY IS TO MOBILIZE GEOGRAPHICAL THINKING INTO MARXIST FOR A BETTER UNDERSTANDINGOF HOW THE WORLD WORKS.

Sidorov: The present wide interest in territorial diversity, in the research of localities within British human geography, are sometimes considered as an example of postmodern geographical research. Was the localities debate successful?

Harvey: This is a very old issue in geography. We used to have a regional problematic, regional geography, for a long time. The localities debate is a revitalizing of the topics discussed in the 1930s and the 1940s. So I don't think this discussion is particularly new.

Sidorov: I would disagree with you. A locality is not the same as a traditional region and the methods of their study are believed to differ at least because the scale is different. As I see it, the traditional region has disappeared from the Anglo-Saxon human geographical agenda.

Harvey: Actually, it takes on a very specific kind of term, but the general issue was in geography for a long time. The localities debate never got out of a very traditional way of discussion. My feeling is that geography has not learned much from the debate. It hasn't produced any significant theoretical results. The question which is not answered yet is, "how do you conduct research, how do you theorize localities?" It is interesting that the debate is a very British discourse. Nothing of this kind is in American geography or in European, and when it does occur it is in terms of the "new regional geography."

Sidorov: You started your career in England, then moved to

America and now have come back. You are familiar with both regional wings of Anglo-Saxon geography. What are the main differences between them?

Harvey: Actually, working at the Department of Geography and Environmental Engineering at Johns Hopkins University, I had very little contact with geographers. For most of my years in America I was in contact with sociologists, anthropologists, urban planners, people like that. My critical tools, developed at this time, derive from these circles.

I think that critical human geography in Great Britain is engaged with questions of politics going on inside of the Labor Party. Thus, it is homogeneous in its development. Look at the localities debate. Everybody is fixed on the same kind of questions here, while critical geography in America is much more decentralized, diversified. Very often it has a strong relation with community movements. At the level of human geography as a whole, the two geographies are more or less the same. Although, again, in Britain there are rather a few influential people determining the whole debate, while in America the way of consideration of the same problem is different in each university.

Sidorov: It seems that theoretical books like Sack's *Human Territoriality,* which tries to explain the forms of the spatial organization of social life, are not satisfying you. Is it because they do not deal with the key questions, with the engine of social changes?

Harvey: Yes. He describes certain configurations without any attempt to understand what forces are producing changes in society, space, and time. The key question is "Why?"

Sidorov: Why in your books are there few maps, if any?

Harvey: Most of my books do not have maps. The problem is that maps do not show dynamics. If you are interested in processes of change, then what maps do is that they simply freeze. Of course, maps are very useful, but for me they are too static a means.

Sidorov: The book contains many rather simple two-dimensional tables. Does this simplicity bother you?

Harvey: Well, you are quite right. I have simplified the way of representation of some information. It was done to draw attention to some question. But what I did to the end with the tables was to try to think of them as dialectical oppositions, and they became much more complex.

Sidorov: The whole book is in general about oscillations in social life between dialectical extremes. Do the ideas of cyclical development of the Kondratiev type appeal to you?

Harvey: I do not deny that cyclical development exists, but the interesting question for me is the explanation of their nature. By what process are cycles produced? Otherwise one may think they are natural. This does not enrich our knowledge.

Sidorov: Your only book published in the former USSR was written as long ago as about a quarter of a century. I refer to *Explanation in Geography*. How do you estimate it today?

Harvey: I learned a lot from writing it. I was trying to find a way to create a theoretical framework for the subject matter of geography. In the 1960s such a framework looked to be able to emerge from positivism, scientific inquiry, systems analysis, and so on. I have found since that they do not work. I don't regret this; we learn from our mistakes. The method which is set out in *Explanation in Geography* is still valuable in a study of, say, journeys to work, or to a shop, but if you are interested in the historical geography of capitalism you can't use the same techniques. The problem with positivism is not that it is wrong, but that the techniques adopted restrict the number of questions which may be asked.

Sidorov: If I am right, your project now is not just to borrow the Marxist theory to use in geography, but to change the theory itself from the beginning, to implement space and spatial dimension into it. How do you see your main aim in geography?

Harvey: The fundamental notion in Marxist method is materialism. If you use the method, you should ask basic questions of material processes. I can't avoid questions like materiality of space and spatial organization, materiality of time, how different dimensions of social life are given material forms, and what this material form does in relationship to how we act and society changes.

There is always a fundamental dilemma within Marxism, which has not been solved: how do we view Nature? Is it a material base? In such a case, you can come to some version of geographical determinism. If you take labor as a material base, then you will come to different conclusions.

I have not so much a project within geography. In the end the most important question for me is how the world works. I regard myself primarily as someone engaged in a Marxist style of inquiry, rather than as a geographer. So my project in geography is to mobilize geographical thinking into Marxist for a better understanding of how the world works. ■

andrei v. bokov

(b.1943) — an architect, author of articles on the theory of architecture and the two manuscripts *Categories of a Cultural Landscape* (1985) and *Architecture and Worldview* (1992). Lives in Moscow.

david harvey

(b.1935) — a geographer and culturologist; author of many books and articles. Main publications: *Explanation in Geography* (1969), *Social Justice and the City* (1973), *The Limits of Capital* (1982), and *The Condition of Postmodernity* (1989). Lives in Oxford, UK.

sergei v. rogatchev

(b. 1959) — a geographer, an expert in the geography of the Arab World and Russia. Author of articles on educational and regional geography. Lecturer at Moscow State University. Lives in Moscow.

leonid v. smirnyagin

(b.1935) — a geographer-Americanist and professional traveler. Main publication: *Regions of the USA: A Portrait of Contemporary America*. Other publications in the field of social and political geography of Russia. Lecturer at Moscow State University. Lives in Moscow.

pavel a. florensky

(1882-1937) — a Russian theologist, philosopher and physicist; an Orthodox priest from 1911. Author of the book *The Pillar and the Confirmation of the Truth* and of many articles devoted to icon-painting and the theory of art. In 1937, died in a Stalinist concentration camp on the Solovetskie Isles in the White Sea.

boris b. rodoman

(b. 1932) — a geographer-theoretician, regionalist and professional traveler; author of the Polarized Biosphere Concept and the Cartoid Theory. Author of publications on geography and traveling. Lives in Moscow.

victor n. sholpo

(b.1932) — a geologist; author of articles and books on geotectonics and theory of geology. Main publication: *The Structure of Earth Space: Chaos or Order?* Senior researcher in Institute of Earth Physics. Lives in Moscow.

max voloshin

(1877-1932) — a Russian poet, amateur artist, and literary critic. A significant figure in early twentieth-century Russian culture. Spent second part of his life in Koktebel', Crimea.

▯▯ (Back cover) *Horizon,* Katya Kovaleva.